I've Got the Blues

I've Got the Blues

A No BS Guide to the Use, Abuse, and Potential Dangers of Legal and Illegal Mind-Altering Drugs

Donald Chapin, M.D.

Published by NeoVision Press
An Imprint of NeoVision Publishing

For information about permission to reproduce selections from this book, write to Permissions,
NeoVision Publishing
8130 La Mesa Blvd., #133
La Mesa, CA 91942

Visit the author's web site at DonaldChapin.com

ISBN 978-1-935976-14-1 (ISBN-10   1935976141)
Library of Congress Control Number: 2010933862
Library of Congress subject headings:
Psychotropic drugs
Drug abuse
Substance abuse and addiction
Drugs of abuse
Psychopharmacology
Antidepressants
Pharmaceutical chemistry
Mental illness—Classification—Political aspects
Mental illness—Diagnosis—Political aspects
Drugs—Social History
Psychiatry

Contents

Dedication

On a professional level, this book is dedicated to all of my former patients who had serious troubles with drug use and/or psychiatric problems.

On a personal level, I dedicate it to my father, Frank, and his brother, Lewis, who taught me from the time I was a little boy the virtue and importance of tolerance, patience, and kindness by their own example.

Disclaimer

The information, ideas, and opinions expressed in this book are not intended to be a substitute for consultation and treatment by a qualified physician or other health-care professional for anyone with physical or mental-health problems. Nothing in this book should be misconstrued as professional medical, psychological, or psychiatric advice for anyone reading it.

The drugs described in this book can have a variety of effects on different people, sometimes resulting in adverse or even fatal reactions. The author and publisher disclaim any responsibility for untoward effects resulting directly or indirectly from information contained in this book.

A great deal of information is presented in this book and every attempt has been made to be accurate. However neither the author nor the publisher represent that all of the information is correct or up to date. If you find what you believe to be factual mistakes, as opposed to ideas or opinions you may disagree with, please contact the author so that he can make corrections in upcoming editions.

Warning

Do not ever discontinue taking prescription drugs without the approval of your doctor, psychiatrist, or other health-care provider. Sudden discontinuation of some drugs can cause serious adverse reactions and in extreme cases even death.

Author's Note

Although I have cautioned against starting many of the drugs I discuss in this book without knowing what you might be getting into, no drugs prescribed by your health-care provider should be discontinued except based on his or her advice. I am not giving professional medical or psychiatric advice to anyone reading this book.

Let me explain this further. Even if you decide to get off of some drug, especially one that has been prescribed, you need to be very careful. Do not do it based on anything you read in this book. I am not your doctor and don't know anything about you. No one can legitimately say that he or she stopped some prescription drug because I advised it.

I only give advice to patients if I have taken a complete history, performed a thorough physical exam, and run any tests that may be required to analyze their problems. If I reach a definitive diagnosis, I will inform them of that. Then I will explain what all of the potential treatments might be. If they are unsure what to do at that point and ask for my advice, that is the only time I will offer it.

No one reading this book has that kind of doctor-patient relationship with me. You are not my patients and I am not giving any of you advice about your particular problem, whatever it may be. I am only expressing my opinions about a variety of topics in this book. I don't want you to blindly accept anything that I say. If a doctor has started you on a psychoactive drug and you think you might want to try to get off of it, then you need to discuss that with your health-care provider. If you don't like his or her advice, then you should look for someone else. Unfortunately I cannot be your doctor and certainly not help you withdraw from drugs if that's what you think you should do.

I'm sorry that I have to get so involved in legal disclaimers. But here are the facts. I have been sued for medical malpractice and have served as an expert witness in medical malpractice cases and trials. Although the three cases against me were eventually dismissed, none of them was an enjoyable experience. I know how the system works, especially in the United States. Let me repeat myself—I am not giving anyone professional medical or psychiatric advice in this book. I am only expressing my opinions about a variety of topics.

Acknowledgements

Below you will find a list of many of the most important teachers I have had over the last thirty years or so who gave me information that helped in some way to make this book possible. Although I have learned something important from each of them through their books, I list them only in alphabetical order. I have never met any of them. A few who were most influential regarding the content of this book are mentioned in it. Others played different roles in my learning process that gave me critical knowledge and information. Regarding more technical issues, some taught me what I needed to know about book and website design as well as creating videos.

A few of these people introduced me to ins and outs of the world of music which I knew nothing about several years ago. I discovered about a year ago that I had a decent singing voice. That gave me the idea of using music to promote my books. That may seem strange because I have never had any formal voice training or singing lessons and can't read or write music or play any instruments. Nevertheless some of you probably found this book after hearing me sing a song or seeing a video on the Internet. I have written several songs myself such as *I've Got the Blues*. A few others that you may hear in the near future are derivative works originally composed by musicians some of whom have made their music available under creative commons law. I will give them proper attribution for their work on music videos and my web site so that they get credit for what they have done.

Great thanks to everyone below as well as people I may have forgotten to put in the list for all your help in one way or another.

Marcia Angell
Moses Avalon
Aaron Beck
David Blatner
Bobby Borg
Peter Breggin
David Burns

Katie Byron
Deepok Chopra
Garrick Chow
Anne-Marie Conception
Kenneth Cooper
Wayne Dyer
Hale Dwoskin
Bart Ehrman
Albert Ellis
Nigel French
Paul Gahlinger
Joseph Glenmullen
Avram Goldstein
Irving Kirsch
Lester Levinson
Roger Love
Kevin MacLoed
Deke McClelland
Stephen Mitchell
Joanna Moncrief
Donald Passman
Chad Perkins
Todd Perkins
Daniel Perrine
Candace Pert
Dan Poynter
Aaron Shepard
Thomas Szasz
The Great Courses
Paul Trani
Andrew Weil
Lynda Weinman
Robert Whitaker
Ken Wilber
James Williamson
Lee Wilson

Preface

Why should you read a book about legal and illegal psychoactive drugs written by me? Am I a recovering addict who has used a lot of them in the past? No. In fact, with a couple of exceptions I mention in this book, I have never used any of them. The reason you should listen to me is that I have treated thousands of patients over my various medical careers, many of whom were using and often addicted to the drugs I am talking about. I have seen firsthand the consequences of such drug use. The information I give you here is based on vast experience combined with a great deal of research and knowledge gained over many years.

Some of you curious people out there might be motivated to read many books and articles on psychoactive drugs. But even if you did, very few would have more than a small fraction of the knowledge that I do in this area. Much of the information in books and on the Internet is incomplete, inaccurate, and sometimes just primarily propaganda by people, groups, or organizations interested in pushing their own biased opinion on you, the reader, looking for answers to difficult questions.

Maybe you have had a problem with drugs in the past or currently do. Or maybe you have friends with such problems who you would like to help if you knew what to say to them. Perhaps you are parents concerned that your children may start using drugs when they are older and just want to get as much accurate information as you can before you have to face that possible situation or hopefully prevent it from happening in the first place. Or maybe you are parents, relatives, or friends of a teenager or an adult already addicted to drugs. What can you do?

The answer is the same for all of you who fall into any of those categories. You can read this book and then give it to the person with the drug problem. It won't magically change what is going on, but it will hopefully give many teenagers and adults the kind of information they need to possibly transform their lives for the better. If you want to find out why I am someone you should pay attention to, read the first chapter of this book. You will know a lot more about me after you have done that.

This book contains a number of true stories, many of which came from a few years of my life when I worked as a jail doctor. All of the names have been changed to protect the privacy of my former patients and various people I worked with. If your name or the name of anyone you know appears in the text, it is purely coincidental. Although all of the stories are real, some details and facts have been altered to preserve each person's privacy as much as possible and yet still relate the truth of what happened.

This book covers a lot of topics, some of which are quite controversial. My position on each of these is expressed directly and clearly. Although you may hold a contrary opinion, you will at least know what mine is based on. I have no illusions about changing people's opinions. However, I would like to make you aware that many of your beliefs are based on indoctrination and propaganda that has been force fed to you by the government, corporations, religious institutions, and the media all of your lives. What we perceive to be the undeniable truth about something often proves to be a deceptive lie when critically examined.

Our society is plagued with hypocrisy, and I will point out a number of examples as I go through this book. Politicians, of course, are major offenders, and some of the laws they create are grounded in hypocrisy. The end result is much of the human suffering that I witnessed in providing medical care to people in jail. The way we deal with legal and illegal drugs in this country exemplifies the terribly destructive effect hypocrisy can have on many people's lives. You may agree or disagree with some of my conclusions and suggestions, but hopefully you will at least give serious thought to the controversial subjects dealt with in this book.

Here is a question many people may have. What does this book have to offer that you can't get from other books at a library, in bookstores, or reading a few articles on the Internet? What is it that makes this book different from other books on this subject? There haven't been many over the last 20 years that I would call good. And not one of them was written by someone who has treated hundreds if not thousands of people with psychoactive drug problems. The few good ones are recommended on my website.

One of the first books was written by Dr. Andrew Weil called *From Chocolate to Morphine* almost 30 years ago (with a revision in 2004). It's a good book with a lot of information. Another successful book was written by four psychologists, again with plenty of good information. But when have they ever evaluated or treated people with acute or chronic drug problems other than talking to them during or after their recovery phase? They discuss the molecular biology of the various drugs, but where did they get that knowledge? I don't know any psychologists who know much about that stuff.

Another excellent book was written by a chemist who delved into molecular biology and did a lot of great research on the history of psychoactive drugs. But is he knowledgeable about real-world drug use and abuse? One of the most qualified authors wrote a comprehensive book about illegal drugs of abuse a few years ago. Extensively researched, it was written by an ER doctor who has obviously treated many people who were acutely intoxicated on various drugs (I know because I used to be an ER doc). But has he ever dealt with the chronic problems of drug abuse and addiction?

I have done all of these things and spent some of my years dealing with the dark side of life. Have many of you doctors have ever developed cordial relationships with people accused of rape and murder? (If some of you find that statement offensive, please remember that these were my patients, not my friends.) Those experiences increased my understanding of human psychology. I am not talking to you from my cozy little office where I interview people with past drug problems.

I have also seen the other end of the spectrum (and everything in between) when I took care of some rich and famous people as a plastic surgeon. How many of you surgeons out there have operated on a billionaire business woman from Hong Kong, Fortune 500 CEOs, or people of royalty in their countries who could have chosen any other plastic surgeon in the world to be their doctor? I have and they referred many other patients to me because they were happy with their results and the medical care I gave them.

I am coming to you from the real world—the one you live in if you are having drug problems (and even if you aren't). That's what makes me different from many authors who have written about psychoactive drugs and addiction. I do understand your life problems and have had plenty of my own. Another thing that makes this book unique besides my unusual background and experience is that I deal with all psychoactive drugs, legal and illegal, including antidepressants. I haven't seen any other books that took on that kind of scope and also kept it simple enough to be read and understood by the average person.

Many of the authors of books on this subject that I think are good and recommend take a neutral or noncommittal position on the drugs they talk about. Some even provide information about how to most safely use many illegal drugs. If I think a drug is dangerous, I explain why in some detail and advise you directly to stay away from it. This is quite different from many books I've read by some drug warriors who just say that all illegal drugs are equally dangerous. It is that kind of disinformation that has led many people, especially teenagers, to ignore their warnings and sometimes start using drugs that really are dangerous, as I explain many times in this book.

As far as what psychoactive drugs do and how they work, many authors just parrot back what they have read elsewhere. Those without adequate knowledge of pharmacology and chemistry are not in a position to challenge many of these theories—and that's just what they are. I do exactly that at many points in this book. If I think that the prevailing accepted theories are wrong, I tell you so and explain exactly why I say that.

What I am trying to do in this book is give readers what is called in medicine an informed consent regarding the decision to use any drugs that directly affect the brain. To give you a medical example, let's say that a patient comes to me for a facelift consultation. After a brief introduction and quick evaluation, I tell her that she is a good candidate and can expect a nice result. She has confidence in me and agrees to schedule the surgery as soon as possible. Because I have failed to explain the details of the procedure as well as the risks and potential complications, she is completely unaware of a lot of important information I should be providing. Until she has all of that information, she can't really make a properly formed and intelligent decision about whether to have the operation. I can't tell you how many patients came to me after having surgery with other doctors saying that they would never have seriously considered going through the operation if they had known that the poor outcome they got was even a slight possibility.

People taking prescription psychoactive drugs often have the same complaints when they experience serious side effects or become addicted when their doctors never mentioned the possibility of these problems at the time he first recommended the medication to them. My goal in this book is to give you exactly that information before your doctor or anyone else suggests the use of any mind-altering drugs. You will also know what kinds of questions to ask about various drugs when a doctor suggests that one or more of them might benefit you. In other words, you will be able to get enough information to make an intelligent decision with a good understanding of not only possible benefits but risks involved as well. Those who have read this book considering using illegal drugs will also be more reluctant to accept them casually based on the recommendations of friends or others.

I don't have any agenda to push in this book other than getting as close to the truth about psychoactive drugs as I can and as far away from the propaganda that has become widespread and pervasive over the last fifty years. If you want to continue to believe the mythology of the pharmaceutical companies, drug warriors, and many psychoactive drug proponents, then don't read this book. If you would like to know more about me and are curious to know how I went from being a respected and successful plastic surgeon to becoming a jail doctor, then keep reading.

1

From Surgeon to Jailhouse Doc

My history is kind of a long story, but I'll try to shorten it as much as I can. I originally went to medical school to satisfy a rescue fantasy that I had from childhood. As a child, even as early as the seventh grade, I often fantasized whenever I heard a siren that I would one day be on the receiving end of an ambulance. In tenth grade, I started doing research for a biology class at the National Library of Medicine in Bethesda, Maryland, that was only a few miles from my house. Having access to medical textbooks for the first time, I often sat for hours looking through surgery books, especially plastic surgery books dealing with facial trauma. I fantasized that someday I would be able to fix people with such problems.

After going through medical school and finishing in the top ten percent of my class, I decided to become a surgeon. Medical school was grueling, but the general surgery residency that followed made it seem easy in comparison. It was six long years of blood and guts intermixed with pain and suffering—my emotional pain is what I'm talking about, although a lot of my patients had their fair share as well. The big difference was that their pain was primarily physical, while mine was almost completely emotional.

Anyway, after six years of a lot of psychological trauma, I decided that I didn't want to live the difficult life of a general surgeon and opted to do another two-year residency in plastic surgery. Although I didn't know much about it, I figured that that specialty had to be considerably less stressful, without life and death problems hanging over my head all the time. Although the training was not exactly easy, it wasn't even close to being the stress factory that general surgery was. Once I caught on to the basics, my performance as a plastic surgery resident was quite good, in contrast to the constant up and down turmoil of my prior training. During those six years, I had seriously thought about quitting almost once a month, at least during the first several years before I finally made a commitment to finish no matter what. (The complete story is in my upcoming book *Boy to Man: The Making of a Surgeon*.)

Having completed my general surgery residency in San Diego and liking the city and climate, I wanted to move back there from Michigan after I finished my plastic surgery residency. Many people warned me that it would be extremely difficult to start a practice because the city was already oversaturated with plastic surgeons. Nevertheless, I went back, lived in San Diego, and spent a year working in Los Angeles emergency rooms as an ER doc. I was finally offered a job at one of the most prestigious hospitals on the West Coast, much to the surprise of those who made dire predictions about any possible future for me in San Diego.

In fact, it worked out quite well. Within a year or so, I had developed an excellent reputation as a staff surgeon at Scripps Clinic and Research Foundation in La Jolla and as a member of the clinical faculty at UCSD Medical Center, where I helped train plastic surgery residents. Despite my success, during the fifth year, I decided that I needed to take a break for at least a year and told everyone that I was going on a one-year sabbatical leave to write a book. Most people thought that my idea was crazy, but I didn't care. I felt compelled to do it.

FutureLife Saga

The following six months were spent researching a self-help book that I planned to write with visions of becoming a best-selling author coming out of nowhere. As you may have guessed by the fact that I later ended up working as a jail doctor, things didn't turn out exactly as I had hoped. Originally, everything did start out well, as I succeeded in researching, writing, and editing the book within less than a year.

The problem was that I knew nothing about the publishing business even though I had, according to some friends and relatives, written quite a good book. I took a brief course on self-publishing at the Learning Annex, where the class teacher appeared to be very knowledgeable about the entire business. I discussed my book with him, and he suggested that I come to his office and talk about printing and publishing it with his help and guidance. Knowing little about agents or other options, I decided to take his advice.

What followed ended up being one of the most unpleasant events in my life. It turned out that he was an incredibly skilled con man who had lined up many clients like me from the courses he taught. One of the reasons so many people came to him for help was that he did know a great deal about the publishing industry (at least in comparison to us aspiring writers). In retrospect, everyone remembered how he had repeatedly emphasized in his classes that you had to be extremely leery of people involved in self-publishing because many of them were only out to rip you off.

And that's just what he did. He collected a lot of money from about thirty men and women to publish their books and then just disappeared one day. As a group, we tried to pursue him legally, but were never able to track him down and recover any money. I later saw it as a useful life lesson, but it was emotionally painful at the time.

Although this had considerably delayed my plans, I found an honest man who helped me go through the steps I needed to follow for self-publishing. Out of that came a completed self-help book called *FutureLife*. With almost no attempt at marketing, I began to sell it through bookstores in San Diego and did book-signing sessions at some of the stores. At that point, I realized how complicated the process of marketing and distribution was and thought about looking for an agent.

One of my former patients who loved the book suggested that I see a high-powered agent he knew of in San Diego. Because the agent was incredibly successful, I was warned that it would take a few months to get any response after sending my book to her. Several days after mailing it, I got a call from a woman who ran the agent's office. She had read the whole book and was sure that Barbara would love it. Her boss was in New York but would return the next day. The following evening, I came home to find this message from Barbara on my answering machine: "Donald, you have written a very, very, very, important book. Please call me in the morning."

When we met the next day, she said that she would like to represent me and had already taken the liberty of calling a major publisher who wanted to see the book immediately on an exclusive basis. Her clincher was this: "This book will make you rich. I would estimate you will make about three million dollars." That sounded good to me. Within a week, we were in New York meeting with a number of people at William Morrow, then (the late 1980s) one of the top publishing houses in the U.S.

Those at the meeting were the senior editor, the company president, the CEO of all Hearst Publications, the director of marketing, and several other people. We spent two hours talking about the book in a love fest. They made many comments like this: "You are an excellent writer" and "You have written a very empowering book." They also said that they were highly impressed with my public presence and ability to communicate.

Toward the end, the CEO suddenly mentioned the only thing in the way of making a deal right then and there; Barbara was asking for an awful lot of money for a first author. I was stunned and simply smiled because I had no idea what to say. Barbara had left me completely in the dark, telling me nothing about the discussions she was having with them. I placed my complete trust in her, much as many patients did with me as a doctor. Her attitude was always one of complete confidence. On the way to the meeting, she told me about all the high-powered people who would be there. She said, "They never do this for anyone, not even well-established, successful authors. They want this book."

As we headed for the elevator after the meeting, accompanied by the president and senior editor, they shook my hand and said, "We know we will be working together." Barbara then told me to go back to my hotel and let her take care of things. I trusted her and asked no questions. In this book, I will warn you about the perils of being a passive patient and just blindly accepting prescriptions or advice that doctors give you. I made the same mistake here.

Later that evening, Barbara called and said we would be going to an interview at Doubleday the next morning. I was flabbergasted because I thought we had an exclusive deal with William Morrow. She explained that she was just putting pressure on them to meet her offer. Again, I stupidly didn't ask what the offer was or what even constituted a good offer.

Perhaps the thing that kept me confident was something Barbara had said before the first meeting. If I had been a previously published author and already proven that I could do well on talk-shows, the people at William Morrow said that they would not have hesitated to pay a million-dollar advance for this book. But I had no idea what they were actually offering. Just as many patients are conditioned to always trust their doctors or other health-care providers, I continued to place my blind trust in her. After all, I had no experience in these kinds of negotiations.

We met with a senior editor at Doubleday the next day. She liked the book but was certainly not as enthusiastic as everyone had been the prior day. We had another meeting with the senior editor and president of Warner Books the following day. They also loved the book and seemed quite impressed with my communication skills. The only thing that they expressed concern about was the best way to market it. They asked my opinion, but I had no idea. I thought that was their area of expertise. Although they were very enthusiastic, the meeting was a letdown compared to the first one at William Morrow.

Barbara told me to fly back to San Diego; she would call me when she got things worked out. When I heard nothing for a week, I called her office. She got on the phone and I asked, "Barbara, what is going on?"

Her answer was, "I'm so depressed." That was not what I wanted to hear. The other offers had come in lower than William Morrow, so she rejected them. William Morrow, in turn, was angry that she had taken the book to other publishers and withdrew their offer.

I said, "But, Barbara, they loved this book. Let's go back to them."

"I can't do that," she said. "They would know I was begging. I have a reputation to preserve."

Long story short, my hot best seller had suddenly turned into yesterday's newspaper. As you might well understand, these two demoralizing experiences resulted in my developing a serious phobia for the entire publishing industry for years to come.

Let me interject here that I never felt any anger or animosity toward Barbara. I have not used her real name because I have no desire to impugn her reputation in any way. She has been a successful literary agent for a long time and helped a lot of authors become best sellers. Maybe she did exactly what any other good agent would have and things just didn't work out as she planned. Perhaps I should have played a much more active role in the whole process. For whatever reason, *FutureLife* didn't end up on any best-seller list.

Nevertheless that may have turned out to be a great stroke of luck for me, even though it seemed devastating at the time. My life ended up going in a totally different direction than it would have otherwise. This book will hopefully help a lot of people if it reaches a wide enough audience. I have the same hope for my upcoming books. They might never have come into being without the experience I gained as a result of having my life unexpectedly pushed in a radically different direction.

Although I did continue to write after that initial failure, I could never bring myself to go through the whole process of trying to sell a book again. I became like a lady in New Zealand named Keri Hulme who wrote a novel called *The Bone People*. She sent a manuscript to a few publishers who completely rejected it, saying that no one would be interested in reading it. Feeling humiliated and dejected, she had the manuscript laminated in plastic and used it as a doormat for the next fifteen years. At a party one day, she mentioned the book to an editor who asked to see it. It was eventually published in 1985 and turned into a worldwide best seller.

I have been throwing manuscripts on the floor of a closet for nearly twenty years and figured it's finally time to grab the bull by the tail and face the publishing industry once again. So get ready, my friends; here I come, and hopefully this time I'm ready to go.

Becoming Jailhouse Doc

But wait a second; how did I end up working in jails? Duh, this is a hard one. I knew I would run out of money if I didn't start working again. Obviously, I could have gone back to practicing plastic surgery, so why didn't I? Because I wanted to continue writing and only work part time. You can't realistically have any kind of surgery practice on a part-time basis. The malpractice premiums, office overhead, and other things make that impractical. Scripps Clinic would not have allowed me to return on a part-time basis. One of the few specialties in medicine that lets you control your schedule and work part time is emergency medicine. So that those of you working regular jobs understand what I mean, compared to my previous work schedules, part time for me could be 40 or 50 hours a week. I had done it before, so I decided to go back to it.

I made contact with a doctor who ran the emergency rooms for several local hospitals. When I met with him to discuss my options, he mentioned that he had just made a contract with the Sheriff's Office to provide medical care in the jails. The Sheriff needed to hire outside contractors because the full-time county physicians and nurses were understaffed and not able to deal with the huge population of inmates at all the jails in the county. Dr. McKinney, a well-respected emergency physician, had a large pool of doctors and nurses already working for him in his emergency rooms that he could draw on to work in the jails for roughly the same or better pay. But he was always looking for new people to work for him.

McKinney said that I was over qualified for the jail work, which would be more like urgent care and general practice. But when I received the details of his malpractice coverage in the ERs, I was somewhat alarmed about the low coverage limits. Then I asked about the jail work. "What's the malpractice coverage like in the jails?"

"We have a hold harmless agreement with the county for all our physicians and nurses who work as independent contractors in the jails," he said.

A little puzzled, I asked, "What exactly does that mean?"

"Our staff is given the same malpractice coverage as the full-time county medical staff."

Still unclear what he meant, I asked, "What is the level of coverage?" I had the security of an excellent five-million-dollar umbrella policy during my previous practice, which could be used for a single physician incident, if necessary.

"Well, there's no specific amount," he said. "I guess the upper limit on the policy would be the county's ability to tax."

That sounded like a pretty damned high limit to me, so I expressed my interest in checking out the jail scene as soon as possible. I figured this job would create less potential liability than emergency medicine and not be as demanding.

I thought I had abandoned my rescue fantasy when I became a plastic surgeon and left behind the life and death world of general surgery and emergency medicine. But in a way, I was still rescuing people emotionally as a plastic surgeon by restoring a more youthful appearance that many desperately wanted to achieve or correcting deformities caused by accidents, nature, or cancer.

Although I originally thought that being a jail doctor would be a low-stress job, it didn't turn out that way. I returned to taking care of people with complex medical problems and had to become a real doctor once again, dealing with the whole gamut of medical practice. But I was faced with something even more difficult this time. Treating illness and disease involves restoring balance to a body that has become imbalanced. But my patients in jail had far more serious problems. Many of them not only had bodies that were out of balance, but their minds and spirit were broken as well. Trying to rescue these people was a task too daunting for me, but I did the best I could.

Not only were many of my patients mentally ill, but a substantial proportion of the people I treated in jail were there on drug-related charges. A number of those with mental illness were self-medicating with alcohol or illicit drugs, but most of the abusers were just trying to deal with the stress of life. Of the many inmates abusing alcohol, some had developed serious alcohol-related disease. Although I had some prior familiarity with drug use and abuse and experience taking care of alcohol-related medical problems, my knowledge in this area increased exponentially during my years as a jail doctor.

Fast Forward

Let's fast forward to 2011. I was startled to find out several years ago that that the original copies of my first book *FutureLife* had been selling online for many years as a collector's item on Amazon, eBay, and other sites. They often sold for three, four, or even five times the original cost of $20. As I followed this with amazement, at times you couldn't get a used copy of the original book for less than about $70. Those in better condition sold for $90 or more. Because the number of used books in decent condition was limited and kept decreasing, the demand and pricing eventually tapered off. However I realized that if I had simply left it on the market and gone through many printings, it could have slowly gained recognition and popularity by word of mouth. As Barbara had initially predicted, I may have made a lot of money, and hopefully a lot of people would have been helped by the book. But that didn't happen.

Because I had put this process off so long, I wasn't sure where to start again almost 23 years after *FutureLife* was published. Should I republish an updated version of that book, or should I start out with one of several other books I have written. I decided that I hadn't really let go of my rescue fantasy as I thought I had. Although I have no great illusions about being able to save people in the sense of radically transforming their lives, I still want to do as much as I can to help as many people as possible. I would especially like to help them steer clear of the problems I have experienced in my life as well as those of many of the patients I have treated in my long career.

My experience has taught me that mind-altering drugs of all kinds cause a major impediment to health and happiness for many people who use them, including a lot of upstanding citizens who have never been in jail. Whether we are talking about illegal street drugs or those prescribed by physicians, when they are psychoactive, they can often cause major problems. People are faced with an onslaught of not only information but also much disinformation from a variety of sources. My goal is to give them a different perspective with useful and practical information that will actually help them to make better choices in the way they live their lives, hopefully with a lot less stress than they are currently experiencing. Now let's look at some basic information about addiction and psychoactive drugs in general.

2

Addiction and Psychoactive Drug Basics

Before talking about drugs to which you can become addicted, let's examine what addiction is. Of course, in today's America, we use this word loosely and apply it to almost everything. People are warned about potential addiction to love, sex, shopping, and so on. If you want to read more about that kind of stuff, go to the self-help section of any bookstore. You will find an endless selection of books to choose from. (By the way, the real problem for those people is psychological addiction to pleasure, which I will talk about at some length in an upcoming book.)

Here I'm only going to discuss what most medical doctors and scientists view as real addiction—to drugs. A simple definition for addiction would be the compulsive use of a drug or other substance, generally believed or known to be potentially harmful. Many people add to that the persistent use of a drug despite repeated adverse consequences to the user.

There are basically two kinds of addiction that can overlap each other. The most common is psychological addiction. You use a drug because you think you must have it in order to achieve a result you want (relief from pain or anxiety, falling asleep, etc.). The second, and much less common, type of addiction is physiological. This often manifests as tolerance for the drug that requires you to use higher and higher doses in order to achieve a particular effect. When the drug is not consumed, you may develop noticeable symptoms of withdrawal.

Tolerance is usually believed to be metabolic in origin (I'll have more to say about that later in the book). The more you use the drug on a regular basis, the higher the dose required to give you the same effect. One person may be obviously drunk with a blood alcohol level of .08, whereas someone with a high tolerance may not seem to be impaired at the same level.

However, there is also something called behavioral tolerance. You learn to control your behavior to disguise your level of intoxication. For example, I have a friend who drinks a lot. When I call him, he is sometimes obviously inebriated. But when his cell phone rings, he answers with a completely different tone of voice, sounding as if he is completely sober. After he hangs up the cell phone, he comes back to me with his real voice.

Why do people use drugs and get addicted to them? Most scientists say that people use psychoactive drugs because they release chemicals that create pleasure. Conventional wisdom says that the primary fundamental human drive is self-survival. After that, it is seeking pleasure and avoiding pain. Many drugs create instant pleasure and often relieve pain (physical or psychological). From my perspective, there are deeper motivations that I will discuss later.

The problem is that the initial pleasurable effect is often followed by a rebound unpleasant effect. What goes up must come down. For example, cocaine or methamphetamine will create a surge of dopamine and other neurotransmitters in the brain but then often be followed by a temporary depletion of the chemicals, leading to a feeling of depression or energy wipeout. The quickest way to relieve that is with more of the drug. As the cycle repeats itself, addiction can develop.

Dosage and quality are the keys to safety with all drugs. Overdose manifests differently with each group of drugs. Most of the drugs I am going to talk about fall into one of two categories; they either stimulate the central nervous system (CNS) or they depress it. Heroin, opium, and other narcotics are CNS depressants (like alcohol and other sedative hypnotic drugs). In low doses, they can make you high (euphoric), but in high doses, you become sedated. In severe overdose, you lose consciousness and or even stop breathing because of depression of the respiratory center in your brain. The heart can only keep beating a few minutes if you stop breathing; then you are dead.

Cocaine, methamphetamines, and ecstasy are CNS stimulants. In small doses, they create a sense of euphoria. Higher doses can make you quite agitated, and overdose can lead to acute psychosis. In that state, you might engage in destructive or even suicidal or homicidal acts.

Neurotransmitters

Let's look at what the brain's neurotransmitters do. Nerve fibers conduct electrical impulses. The impulse may then stimulate another nerve cell, a muscle, or a gland. However, there is a gap between the end of the nerve fiber and the next cell. In order to cause a muscle to contract, a gland to secrete, or another nerve cell to fire off an electrical impulse, a neurotransmitter is released into the space between the nerve fiber and the next cell.

Chemicals that speed up transmission in the central nervous system are our built-in uppers. The most common one is noradrenalin (norepi-nephrine) followed by dopamine. The most common ones that slow things down are serotonin and GABA (gamma-amino-butyric acid). The body has many other neurotransmitters, probably a lot more than a hundred.

The release of stimulant neurotransmitters makes you feel awake, alert, and sometimes happy or even euphoric. The release of serotonin makes you feel calm and relaxed. The moods and states of mind you experience at different times are believed by many scientists to be a function of what these various neurotransmitters are doing. According to that theory, people might be able to learn to stimulate the release of certain neurotransmitters by processes such as deep meditation. On occasion, I have been able to have rather unusual experiences during self-induced deep trance states (including wild hallucinations). With no drugs in my system, this effect would seem to be coming from my own neurotransmitters, if you believe in that theory. By the way, I don't because it seems far too simplistic to me. (You will hear more about that later in the book.)

The human body makes many chemicals in the brain as well as some glands that can profoundly affect our moods and thoughts. Many psycho-active drugs work by interacting with specific receptor sites on nerve cells. Once the drug attaches to the site, it may either cause a nerve cell to fire an impulse or prevent it from firing. For example, morphine and other narcot-ics attach to opiate receptors in certain parts of the brain.

Why would the brain have receptors for a drug that comes from a poppy plant? Because we make our own kind of morphine. Endorphins are molecules very similar to morphine, which may cause a person to feel euphoric or get relief from pain. People who experience severe physical trauma sometimes have little or no pain. This may occur because their brain is flooded with endorphins before the paramedics arrive and can give them any morphine (although there are other neurological explanations as well).

So if we make our own drugs, why do we need those that have been refined from plants or synthesized? The fact is that few people, including me, have figured out how to create the effect they want at the time they want it in any predictable way. Consequently many who are not happy with their current mental state have a drink, grab a pill, smoke a joint, or snort a line to get the feeling they want—right now.

By far the most addictive drug used by humans is nicotine. Ninety percent of all users become both psychologically and physiologically addicted. That is why it is so hard to stop smoking and a good reason not to start. Most other recreational drugs have rates of addiction in the 10–15% range (alcohol, cocaine, heroin, and methamphetamine), although these numbers are really just ballpark guesses. Some experts have developed elaborate systems of rating the addiction potential of all these drugs from zero to one hundred. The only thing consistent about them is that nicotine is always at the top. Marijuana may be somewhat less addictive than the previous drugs mentioned, and hallucinogens, like LSD, rarely, if ever, create physiologic addiction. (Flashbacks may occur months or years later but are not a manifestation of addiction.) Physiologic withdrawal symptoms may occur within hours or days after stopping some drugs.

Animal Experimentation with Psychoactive Drugs
A lot of the information about drug addiction comes from experimentation with animals. The level of addictiveness of a particular drug is usually based on how hard the animal will work to get it. If it presses a lever and gets an effective dose of a given drug, it will wait a while before doing it again, presumably allowing the drug effect to wear off. But if the person conducting the experiment changes the rules and requires maybe 10, 50, or 100 lever presses to get a single dose, something different happens. The animal will now have to work much harder to get each drug dose.

Using this experimental model, researchers have nominated cocaine as the most addictive drug of all. We're talking about i.v. cocaine here because the animals are not smoking pipes with crack rocks in them. For example, a monkey put through such an experiment will not eat, drink, or do anything else until it is completely exhausted. It will eventually die of starvation, dehydration, or overdose.

If the dose is constantly altered instead of the number of lever presses required, they will go back to self-titration. In other words, if the dose goes up, the animal presses the lever less frequently. If it goes down, it will press more frequently. All of this sounds very interesting, except for the harm done to the animals, but I really have another problem with it. (By the way, I love rats, monkeys, cats, dogs, snakes, lizards, and all animals.) I have no idea how to extrapolate this information to the drug use of my fellow human beings using mind-altering drugs. Nor does it tell me anything I might be able to do to help them with their problem. That's all I'm really interested in personally.

Some of the most interesting animal experiments come from trying to figure out the so-called reward pathway in the brain. (I think this may be what scientists are referring to when they talk about the brain's pleasure center.) It is called the mesolimbic dopaminergic pathway that goes from neurons originating in the ventral tegmental area (VTA) running forward in the brain to the nucleus accumbens (NAc) and frontal cortex. When the neurons in the VTA are electrically stimulated in experimental animals, they deliver dopamine to the dopamine receptors in the NAc and frontal cortex.

For those of you whose neuroanatomy is a little shaky, just feel the back of your head above the neck with one hand and your forehead with the other. That's where this reward pathway is located. More specifically, the VTA is in front of (anterior to) the cerebellum, just over the spinal cord and brainstem. The NAc is about halfway from there to the forehead, a little above and anterior to the pituitary gland. The frontal cortex is just under the forehead bone.

The reason this is called the reward pathway is because animals will press a lever to get electrical neuronal stimulation in the VTA in the same way they do to get food, water, or psychoactive drugs. It sounds fascinating but what does that really have to do with you or me getting high on alcohol, cocaine, marijuana, bennies, benzos, ecstasy, Vicodin, or sniffing glue? I don't have a clue. If you do, let me know. I'll put it in my next edition. We'll get back to neuropharmacology toward the end of this book.

What Isn't Addiction?

I said at the beginning of this chapter that I was only going to deal with what most medical doctors view as addictions—to psychoactive drugs. But I feel compelled to mention some of the other things that are often called addictions, such as exercise. Can you really get addicted to exercise, and if so, what would be the mechanism to explain it? An article in a medical journal about twenty years ago described a young man in Finland who was a long-distance runner. A work-up for a few dizzy spells revealed that he had significant narrowing and dysfunction of the valve pumping blood from the left ventricle into the aorta (aortic stenosis). His doctors advised him to give up running as it would be unsafe for him to continue. Nevertheless he continued and during his training for an upcoming marathon at the age of 22, he dropped dead.

Some people tried to interpret this young man's dilemma as an addiction to running. They surmised that he was getting such a rush of his own brain endorphins that he had become addicted to the so-called "runners high." I found this quite interesting because I used to be a runner myself. For a few years during my late 30s, I ran eight miles every other day at a pretty good pace, although I was not training for any competitive races. I just did it because I wanted to. Actually there was probably more to it than that. I liked being thin and healthy but had a problem—I loved to eat, and often these included really bad foods filled with sugar and cholesterol. I saw running as a way to compensate for that. Oh, my God, did I become addicted to running to compensate for my food addiction? I don't think so.

Several months before I turned 40, I took a vacation trip to Vancouver which quickly became one of my favorite cities in the world. My hotel turned out to be near Stanley Park, which lies on a small peninsula surrounded by Vancouver Bay. I went out for a run one sunny day and planned to just do one go-round which would be about five miles. As I came back to my starting place, I was not the least bit tired and had really enjoyed all the scenery on the run. I decided to do it again and then a third time after that. After running the longest distance I ever had, I went back to my hotel to take a shower, feeling quite refreshed.

Now here's a question it would be reasonable to ask. Did I experience a runner's high that day that might be in any way, shape, or form comparable to taking narcotics? The answer is no. Nor had I ever experienced such a thing previously while running that would be comparable to a drug-induced high. I must admit that I had limited experience, only taking narcotics for pain after injuries, not to get high. So I ran because I liked to stay healthy and fit. When I got back home, I had scheduled a complete cardiac workup to make sure that my heart was in good shape now that I was going to be soon hitting 40. The cardiologist who did all the testing said that he was amazed by my performance, especially on the exercise treadmill test. He had evaluated many players from the San Diego Padres and Chargers and said that my aerobic conditioning was better than some of the professional athletes in their 20s.

So what does this have to do with the Finnish guy I mentioned a few paragraphs ago? Now that I have established that I know something not only about addiction but running as well, I can give you my opinion. Was that guy really addicted to running and a subsequent rush from his endogenous endorphins flooding his brain? No, he was suffering from something much less complicated—stupidity. If your doctors tell you that the valve controlling blood flow to your entire body is screwed up and won't allow you to safely engage in vigorous exercise, then what should you do? If you have decent insurance and/or are rich, you just get a new valve put in and will then be good to go. Although I don't know anything about the Finnish health-care system, I assume that this guy's operation would only have been approved if his problem became serious enough to interfere with normal activities. That may not seem fair, but that's the way things work in a world run by corporations and governments.

I already mentioned love, sex, and shopping addiction. Should I also bring up Russian roulette? Yes, there was actually a famous writer who claimed that he became addicted to Russian roulette—with a real gun loaded with real bullets. Graham Green played this "game" repeatedly as a teenager and in his early 20s. He explained in his autobiographical book, *A Sort of Life*, that these games never represented suicidal gestures. He was simply doing it because he was bored with his life (You might have guessed that from the book title). As a good friend of mine and a great ER doctor likes to say about some of the patients he treats, "You can't cure stupid."

Now that may sound a little flippant to some of you. Am I just an arrogant doctor who doesn't have sympathy or empathy for my patients and other people? Can't I try to put myself in their shoes and show some compassion? Yes, as a matter of fact, I can, as you will find if you read a lot more about me and my personal life in upcoming books. Furthermore can I empathize with those dealing with the blues or even full-blown depression? The answer is yes.

Some psychiatrists and psychologists reviewing my life history and emotional reactions to events in my life might well conclude that I was suffering from low-grade depression most of it. Maybe I was, but all I can say knowing what I do now is that I'm grateful that I never tried to deal with my problems by taking drugs, except alcohol, which doesn't resolve those problems either. Been there, know that. The good news is that I've been happy and enjoying my life for many years, so maybe you should consider listening to what I have to say. And, yes, I do care and sympathize with all of you and what you are going through in your lives.

Are You Ready to Know?

That is to say, are you ready to deal with how you are using mind-altering drugs and whether that is helping to make your life better or maybe actually making it worse? A lot of people are not ready to confront their use of psychoactive drugs. They may think that the drugs they are taking are great (such as antidepressants or benzos) but at the same time be worried about friends or family members using drugs that they believe to be problematic or maybe even dangerous (such as marijuana or cocaine).

To hopefully help make a point about the problem many people have in recognizing their own self-destructive behavior, I would like to briefly describe a movie that I saw many years ago about teen prostitution in a former Soviet country. Some of the girls had special rules about what they would do. Namely they would only have anal sex with men so that they could remain virgins. They had heard stories about wealthy men coming from the West who would pay a lot of money for a young virgin. They were saving themselves for that special person. Trying to explain to them that their strategy was seriously flawed would not likely work. These girls wouldn't want to be told that they were dramatically increasing their chances of contracting HIV or hepatitis by having anal rather than vaginal sex, regardless of whether the men wore condoms. Many of the girls described were even willing to forego that protection, despite the increased risk, in exchange for more money. They were bound and determined to wait for Mr. Right before they had vaginal intercourse. (The movie director said that his characters accurately reflected what was really going on in his country at that time.)

One of the most memorable scenes concerned a boy who was having sex with men. The storyline revolved around a man whose son had left their small town to look for work in a nearby city. After several months of hearing nothing, the father went to look for his son and found that he had been working as male prostitute. A week into his investigation, he discovered that his son had been killed. He tried to track down someone who had known him and ended up with one of his son's friends who was also working as a hustler. The father didn't tell him why he had come and the boy just assumed that he was looking for sex. After talking to the man briefly, he told him that a blow-job would be $20 and invited him into a small bathroom. The man went in with him, handed him $50 as he started crying, hugged the boy, told him that he loved him, and then walked out. When the kid later recounted the story to a friend, he said, "Can you believe how many sick bastards there are out there?"

That boy was not ready to hear that there might actually be someone in the world who cared about him, rather than just wanting to use him for sex. If someone were forced to read this book who had just checked into a rehab center against his will, he would likewise not be receptive to what I have to say. If he has been getting high on butt rockets (meth suppositories) and smoking ice for the last six months, he would most likely react negatively to my statement (coming in Chapter 6) that meth is bad shit. He might say, "This guy's insane. Meth is fantastic shit. I can't wait till I can get out of here."

A lot of you upstanding citizens may react to that statement by thinking that illegal drug abusers are stupid but that this issue has nothing to do with you. Many adults will also fail to see any connection between what they are doing and the self-destructive behavior of the teenagers in the movie I just described. But lots of adults engaged in self-destructive behavior are just as blind to it as many kids. Quite a few are not even aware of the adverse effects psychoactive drugs may be having on them, not unlike younger people. They are not ready to take a hard look at how what they are doing may be hurting their brains, bodies, and overall health.

Let's take a successful litigation lawyer started on antidepressants a year ago by his internist who he believes is one of the best doctors in L.A. His physician told him that his marriage problems and excessive drinking were a result of depression. He had a biochemical imbalance in his brain and probably needed to be on antidepressants for the rest of his life. Even though his life has gotten much worse and he has developed problems he never used to have, is he ready to hear the truth from me?

And what would that truth be? Perhaps it might be that this doctor may know very little about depression or antidepressants and what they actually do. Not many patients want to hear that about their doctors, especially if they have a decent relationship with them. But maybe that is exactly what this successful but unhappy lawyer needs to hear to get him on the right path. Is he ready for that? Is he ready to know the truth that he may find disturbing? Many people are not ready to hear the truth, especially after they have been exposed to extensive propaganda from the pharmaceutical industry, usually coming through the media and their doctors who often don't really know the truth themselves about psychoactive drugs.

One of my favorite Zen sayings is this: When the student is ready, the teacher arrives. As someone who has been helped by a number of teachers in my life, I hope I can become a teacher to as many people as possible who are willing to keep an open mind and listen to what I have to say in this book. Many people will not be ready, but perhaps some will. Hopefully I can help them make their lives easier and more enjoyable. If you think you might be one of those people, then keep reading.

3

Caffeine

Most people recognize that alcohol and narcotics are drugs, but let's look at one that many people do not even think of as a drug—caffeine. If you start your day with caffeine, then you start your day with a drug. This is not only true for adults but children as well. Caffeine is a central-nervous-system (CNS) stimulant, just like nicotine, amphetamines, and cocaine. For many people, it is not just a harmless little substance in their coffee.

Technically speaking, it is the world's most popular psychoactive drug, with alcohol and tobacco taking second and third place. At least 90% of Americans consume caffeine every day in one form or another. Coffee is a major source and the vast majority of people know that it contains caffeine, even though most consider it to be an innocuous drug; it remains legal pretty much everywhere. When you consider the much more potent effects of alcohol on the brain, it deserves the prize for the favorite psychoactive drug of the human race as far as I'm concerned.

The use of caffeine for a stimulant effect is not something that was just discovered by students pulling all nighters studying or truck drivers trying to stay awake in the 20th century. Although coffee didn't make it to Europe and become popular until the 17th century, many Africans were chewing on kola beans for a pick-me-up several thousand years ago (much as South American natives were doing with cocoa leaves for the same purpose).

Caffeine is in chocolate flavored cereal, chocolate donuts, and chocolate milk. At school, kids will get higher doses when eating chocolate candy bars and drinking sodas or iced tea. Caffeine is also in many over-the-counter medicines, diet pills, and prescription medications.

The four major sources are coffee beans, tealeaves, cocoa beans, and cola nuts. You might wonder why this substance is made by the plants that contain it. For many of them, it serves as a natural pesticide killing insects that might otherwise be able to feed on and possibly destroy the plants. The most common products in which caffeine is found naturally are coffee, tea, chocolate, and cola drinks. Caffeine is also added to non-cola soft drinks and many other products.

Depending on how it is brewed and the quality of the beans, a six-ounce cup of coffee contains 80–150 mg of caffeine (cheaper beans usually have more caffeine). The same amount of brewed tea has 20–40 mg. A 12-ounce glass of iced tea has about 70 mg. A chocolate candy bar can contain 50 mg of caffeine or more, and a 12-ounce soda contains in the range of 35–55 mg. So-called energy drinks can have as much as or more than coffee per serving.

Pharmacology and Chemistry
Caffeine is the best known of a trio of drugs called xanthines. They have a similar double-ring structure (one of those interesting hydrogen, oxygen, nitrogen, carbon things). All are stimulants with the most potent being theophylline and the mildest being theobromine. You've used the former if you've ever inhaled Primatene for breathing problems and the latter if you've ever eaten chocolate, which also contains caffeine. Small amounts of theophylline are found in tea, but caffeine is the main constituent and only slightly less potent.

They all produce their stimulant effect in the brain by blocking adenosine receptor sites. Adenosine is a neurotransmitter that mediates a depressant effect by virtue of the fact many of them are on the GABA neurons. The GABA neurons inhibit the release of dopamine in the reward pathway. By blocking its action, a stimulant effect is created. In the lungs, theophylline dilates the bronchioles making it useful in asthma, chronic bronchitis, hay fever, and other conditions. It is also used as well as caffeine in newborns with primary apnea.

Now let's take a little closer look at adenosine and what its function is in the brain and the rest of the body. I'm sure you have heard of ATP, which is the primary energy molecule in the body. The A stands for adenosine as in adenosine triphosphate. When the brain is cranking away and using up energy, it creates a lot of adenosine. This then interacts with the adenosine receptors on the GABA neurons in order to slow things down.

Remember that the brain and the rest of the body are always seeking a state of equilibrium. What caffeine does is actually prevent adenosine from doing its job by binding to its receptors and thereby continuing the activity that it was supposed to suppress. So there you have it. Just like most other psychoactive drugs, caffeine disrupts the normal action in the brain. When the brain wants to rest, it gets pumped up. So caffeine is like most mind-altering drugs. It creates a biochemical imbalance by stimulating a brain that would rather be taking a break. This is certainly a mild effect when compared to much more potent stimulants like cocaine and methamphetamine, but it's there.

At the same time, caffeine is doing something else significant by decreasing the amount of blood flow to the brain. Studies have shown that blood flow to the grey matter containing mostly nerve cells is decreased by 25% with 250 mg of caffeine (2–3 cups of coffee). How much significance that may have clinically, I have no idea. But it's just something else to consider with what many believe to be a totally harmless drug.

Some try to deny that caffeine is addictive because they like to keep it in the class of a risk-free drug. But since it induces both tolerance and physical dependence in many people, it seems somewhat illogical to say it's not addictive. Many people dependent on it feel sluggish, unable to think clearly, have a headache, and even feel depressed when they are unable to get their morning coffee. All of these symptoms are quickly relieved by some caffeine.

Unlike moderate users of cocaine and alcohol, caffeine users have more in common with those addicted to narcotics and nicotine. They need a fix to get rid of withdrawal symptoms every day. In one study of more than 150 randomly selected users, more than half said that they wanted to stop using caffeine but had been unable to do so because of unpleasant side effects of withdrawal such as headaches. That seems to fit with the standard psychiatric definition of drug dependence.

Given that 90% of adults and maybe a similar proportion of children are using caffeine, it would be hard not to assume that a major portion of the population of many countries are addicted to this drug. The reason this is tolerated is probably that there don't appear to be any serious long-term problems from caffeine use in standard doses. Also people do not engage in disruptive behavior as they do under the influence of other psychoactive drugs. Nor does it seem to cause any brain damage or injury to other organs. So if you're not concerned about any of the issues I've raised, enjoy your coffee and tea, even if you are addicted.

But remember this. The major effect is a feeling of increased energy and ability to concentrate. I hate to give you bad news, but many studies have shown that caffeine does not improve performance in any way when compared to placebo in normal people. The only exception comes in people whose concentration and performance are already degraded because they are tired, bored, or sleep deprived. So you may end up getting addicted to a drug that really doesn't do anything more than give you a placebo effect. (If you want to know a lot more about that subject, you'll find it in chapter 13.)

Effects
The half-life in a healthy adult is about 5 hours (the time it takes half of the drug to be metabolized). However, this is quite variable since people have been shown in many studies to have dramatically different sensitivity to caffeine. In some people it may be metabolized in a few hours while in others it may be in the bloodstream for 8–10 hours or more, explaining why some people complain that too much morning coffee keeps them from falling to sleep at night. The quick metabolizers are the ones most likely to end up being the heavy users while the slow ones turn out to be the most sensitive to its effects.

I have heard people in coffee shops who just finished a cup of coffee in ten minutes or so complain that they still don't have the energy they need and quickly order another cup. Taking drugs orally is not the same as smoking a cigarette or maybe some crack. You don't get the same rapid effect from oral medicines. If you do, it is usually a placebo effect, although liquid solutions will obviously be absorbed more quickly than pills. I should point out that some drugs in carbonated beverages can be absorbed by the stomach fairly rapidly, such as the alcohol in champagne. The carbonation increases the absorption rate. Drugs in liquid form are absorbed more rapidly than pills because those take time to break down in the stomach.

The relatively long half-life also means that caffeine may still be in your system when you try to go to sleep several hours later if you drink it after dinner. If you are looking for something to give you a quick energy blast, no legal safe drugs are going to do that. If you are addicted to caffeine, all it will do is make you feel less fatigued than you did shortly after you got up in the morning. Many people need to take it in the morning just to feel normal (kind of like the first cigarette after waking up for those addicted to nicotine). It won't pump you up and help you face a bad day as you may be hoping it will. If you're getting ready for a big business presentation, but feel down in the dumps, some amphetamine an hour before your performance would certainly be much more effective than caffeine—but I wouldn't recommend it.

Withdrawal
Withdrawal symptoms for those with tolerance and addiction can develop within 12–24 hours and may include headache, joint pains, abdominal discomfort, drowsiness, insomnia, and difficulty concentrating. Depending on the person and prior use, they may last for a day or sometimes five days or more. Those who keep using caffeine in high doses can develop problems with anxiety, irritability, insomnia, headaches, and increased stomach acid production sometimes causing upper abdominal symptoms. Caffeine-induced anxiety disorder may mimic other psychiatric conditions such as obsessive-compulsive disorder, panic attacks, or more serious disorders. If the caffeine problem isn't appreciated, misdiagnosis and harmful medication may be initiated instead of simply stopping the caffeine intake.

Anecdotes and Suggestions
Because I like to drink a lot of diet soda, I have consumed only decaffeinated soft drinks for many years. My caffeine consumption would have been huge otherwise in previous years until I started cutting down on my intake. I have never been much of a coffee drinker but decided to experiment with it about ten years ago. I wanted to find out what the big attraction was and see what kind of effect it had on me.

First I started with two, then three, then four cups of regular coffee a day over a period of a few weeks. I didn't really get a noticeable buzz from even four cups and my heart rate only went up a little. However, after about six weeks, I started to develop gastrointestinal problems that I had never experienced before. The symptoms were abdominal bloating, intermittent crampy pain, constipation, and occasional diarrhea. At first, I didn't think at all about the coffee, even though that was the only thing that had changed in my life recently.

If I had a patient with these symptoms, I would make a diagnosis of irritable bowel syndrome. This is a chronic problem many people have off and on for years, with no good treatment available. Whenever I want to find a solution to a problem for which traditional medicine doesn't have a good answer, I pull out some of my books on alternative medicine.

In this case, I found something in one of Dr. Andrew Weil's books that got my attention. He described a female attorney in her early 40s who came to him with a history of irritable bowel syndrome for 20 years. None of her many doctors over the years had been able to help her. Dr. Weil took a careful history and discovered that her symptoms had started in college when she began drinking coffee. Despite the fact that she only had one or two cups each morning, he suspected that the caffeine might be causing her problem.

When she stopped it, she had headaches and irritability for a few days. He told her that this indicated she had a physical addiction to caffeine, despite using a relatively low dose. Within two weeks, all of her gastrointestinal symptoms had disappeared, and they never came back.

After I read that, I stopped drinking regular coffee and my symptoms also went away. I have to admit that I just related a totally unscientific, anecdotal story. But I found it interesting that my problem came and went with the introduction and discontinuation of caffeine. Whether other doctors besides Weil have noted this connection, I don't know. Caffeine is well known to cause gastric symptoms in some people because it seems to increase acid production. But if you're having strange GI problems that your doctor can't solve, why not try getting off caffeine for a while, especially if you are addicted to it? If it doesn't help, at least it might have and you can always go back to your previous habit.

Caffeine in Kids

Here is a question for you. Why do soda makers put caffeine in their drinks when they are perfectly able to make the same drinks without it? They will probably say it's because consumers want it. Perhaps they do, but maybe they just are not aware of the problems it can cause.

Officials in the tobacco industry suffered a big setback when a whistle blower exposed the fact that they had purposely spiked their cigarettes with higher doses of nicotine and other additives. Why did they do it? Because they wanted to increase the chances that any given user would became addicted so that they could sell more cigarettes.

Since I have no evidence for it, I won't ascribe similar motives to the soda industry; but the fact is that the more caffeine addicts we have, the more sodas they will sell. People will become addicted to low doses, develop tolerance, and need to consume more and more soda drinks in order to avoid withdrawal symptoms. This has another serious side effect, both in adults and children, with non-diet drinks that have sugar in them. Because of their caffeine addiction, many children and adults consume much more sugar than they would otherwise and consequently often gain weight. Could this have anything to do with the fact that so many American children and adults are overweight? What do you think?

The real victims of the caffeine craze are not so much adults but children. The younger they are, the worse the problem is. Let's look at a mother who takes her six-year-old boy to a coffee shop with her one morning. He gets a soda (50 mg), a chocolate muffin (50 mg), and drinks some of her mocha frappuccino. The boy has now consumed 200 mg of caffeine. Assuming he weighs 35 pounds, an equivalent dose for his mother would be 600–800 mg. If she is not addicted and tolerant, a dose like that would get her completely wired and probably somewhat irritable for the next few hours. Well guess what likely happens to her boy?

People frequently attribute behavioral problems in children to a sugar rush, but I think a lot of the time the real problem may be a caffeine overdose. Maybe adding caffeine to products for children under 12 should be regulated in some way (if that's possible). At the very least, parents should be educated about this potential problem.

Maybe you didn't realize this before, but some of your child's psychological problems and perhaps even medical problems may be related to caffeine addiction. Caffeine is everywhere. It would be nice if we could minimize children's exposure to this drug and make adults more aware of its potential detrimental effects. Of course, this problem is nothing when compared to the widespread use of psychiatric drugs in children, which I will discuss later in this book.

4
Nicotine

Now let's look at a more serious drug—nicotine. As the third most popular psychoactive drug of the human race, it is found almost everywhere. Although caffeine is not regulated and available to everyone, tobacco is only legally available to adults in most developed countries. Nicotine, our most addictive psychoactive drug, is found in tobacco, which causes about 430,000 deaths a year in the U.S. alone (cardiovascular disease, lung cancer, and emphysema account for most of these). A few hundred years ago, such health issues were not a significant problem in Europe, Asia, and Colonial America. How did we get into our current situation?

History of Tobacco
Most people are familiar with the history of the early explorers in the Americas starting with Columbus. The natives were often slaughtered by the conquering European explorers but most of those who died did so as a result of contracting diseases such as smallpox. Having never been previously exposed to them, they had no immunity. In some large areas of Central America, as much as 90% of the native population disappeared over the first hundred years of colonization. But in the end, you could say that they got their revenge over the next five hundred years by introducing the Europeans to tobacco.

The Europeans were not the only people to become addicted as tobacco eventually made its way to every remote place in the world. But what got people hooked was not the tobacco itself, but its most potent alkaloid chemical ingredient, nicotine. It got its name from a man called Jean Nicot, a French cabinet minister, who in the mid 1500s was given a plant in Lisbon that had recently been brought from Florida. He gave the plant to Catherine de Medici, who basically ruled France during that time on behalf of her young sons. She began using powdered tobacco snuff and popularized it throughout her court. Seeing a great opportunity, Nicot started importing large shipments to Paris where tobacco was called nicotiana after him. That eventually became the name of the 50 species of tobacco plants

Despite its popularity in Paris, opposition to tobacco quickly grew. James VI of Scotland, son of Mary Queen of Scotts, who later became James I of England succeeding Queen Elizabeth I, was a great enemy of tobacco use throughout his reign. (Sorry for the detail, but I love British history.) Religious opposition was also strong in France from the Jesuits. Opposition was much greater in some countries where smokers were punished with dismemberment or even death. Despite the initial opposition, tobacco use became rampant throughout England and Europe in the 17th and 18th centuries, not to mention America and many other countries.

A lot of you might assume that people around the world have been smoking cigarettes for hundreds of years, but that is actually a 20th century phenomenon. Before that, people were getting nicotine delivered to their brains in the form of snuff, chewing tobacco, pipes, and cigars. Few of the smokers were inhaling because the tobacco was far too irritating to the airways in the lungs.

Several things began to change all that in the late 1800s with two discoveries. One was a new way of curing tobacco that made the smoke much less irritating to the air passages. The other was the invention of the safety match and the discovery of a way to mass produce them as well as cigarettes. Advertising and marketing then played a major role in popularizing cigarettes during the first half of the 20th century. By the 1930s and 40s, movie stars were smoking throughout many movies. During much of World War II, cigarettes were included with every soldier's rations.

Express Drug Delivery
Because most people these days are getting nicotine from smoking cigarettes, let's look at why smoking is the fastest way to get a drug to your brain. First consider a little basic anatomy of the circulatory system. The blood is returned to the heart from all over the body via small veins that empty into larger ones until they get to the superior and inferior vena cava. These then drain all of their blood into the right atrium of the heart. The blood is pumped into the right ventricle and then out to the lungs where it receives oxygen in the capillaries of the thousands of tiny alveolar air sacs. The oxygenated blood returns to the left atrium and is then pumped out by the left ventricle to the brain and the rest of the body.

Here is an interesting fact not many people know. First of all, arteries carry red blood and veins carry blue blood. Everyone knows that. Blood turns red when the oxygen attaches to the hemoglobin molecule. But here's the catch. The vessel coming out of the right ventricle pushing blue blood into the lungs for oxygenation is called the pulmonary artery. The vessels bringing the red blood into the left side of the heart are called the pulmonary veins. Now you can impress your friends with that little bit of anatomy trivia. Just ask them if all arteries carry red blood.

What does this have to do with drugs? A lot more than oxygen is passed into the blood in the lungs—such as cocaine, methamphetamine, nicotine or any other drug that can be inhaled in the form of smoke. This drug is then pumped out of left ventricle into the brain through the carotid arteries. This is the most efficient way to get drugs into the brain, which is saturated with the drug almost immediately after each inhalation. You can deliver more and more drug by simply taking deeper and more rapid inhalations. This is how cigarette smokers are able to regulate the nicotine spikes in their brains.

This delivery system offers another advantage besides a rapid effect. It also provides a built-in protective mechanism from taking too much drug. If the drug turns out to be a lot more potent than you expected, you can stop after your first hit or at least control drug levels by waiting longer between puffs and inhaling less deeply. Such built in controls are not available to anyone injecting drugs or taking them orally. By the time you suddenly get the feeling you may have taken an overdose, the next thing you know, you may be comatose, have brain damage, or be dead.

Some of you may be wondering why intravenous injection wouldn't be just as fast and effective as smoking. Well let's go back to the anatomy. If you inject a drug into your arm, it is going to be thoroughly mixed with all the blood coming in from the rest of the body before it ever gets to the left side of the heart. Then when it is pumped out of the left ventricle into the aorta, a lot of it will be dispersed to other parts of the body as well as the brain. In other words, it will have been significantly diluted. It will act quickly, but not as fast as a smoked drug. Also if you take too much, it will keep circulating and more drug will be pumped into your brain over some period of time. This is something you can't do anything about if you have taken too much, except to call 911 and get medical help right away.

Mechanism of Action

Now let's explore what nicotine actually does. Like the less potent caffeine and the much more potent cocaine and methamphetamine, nicotine is a stimulant. Although the mechanism of action of depressant drugs is generally believed to be through action on the GABA inhibitory synapse, there is much more variability with the stimulants. Nicotine is called a cholinergic drug because it binds to acetylcholine receptors. In contrast, cocaine, methamphetamine, and herbal ephedra are called catecholamines, which act primarily by affecting dopamine and noradrenalin. As I mentioned in the last chapter, caffeine acts by binding to adenosine synapses as do the other xanthine drugs in coffee, tea, and cocoa.

For those who may be interested in what nicotine is actually doing to create its feel good high effect, I've got some bad news. We don't really know. The fact that it attaches to acetylcholine receptors certainly doesn't explain its hedonic effect. Somehow it seems to act on the mesolimbic reward pathway causing release of dopamine, in much the same way as the stimulants do (more on this later). Regardless of how it works, most people would agree that its behavioral effects are subtle, much like those of caffeine in normal doses. It certainly doesn't cause the behavioral impairment seen with many of the other psychoactive drugs. That's why we let people addicted to nicotine drive cars and fly airplanes.

However, don't underestimate its power. It is a poison in high doses. Of course, that's true of everything. Too much oxygen can kill you. The reason its effects are limited is that little of the nicotine is getting into the body, especially with smoking where most of the nicotine is burned up by the heat. But people smoking pipes and inhaling in ritual religious ceremonies, for example, can get quite stoned, not just have a little buzz. In fact, the total nicotine content of one cigar is enough to make anyone quite ill and could even been fatal for some if it were extracted and then ingested or injected intravenously.

Although it is considered a stimulant, people have varying responses to it. Even the same person can experience either a stimulant or depressive effect at different times of the day. The nicotine may make someone feel more alert at times and provide a relaxing or tension-relieving effect at others. This is similar to the various reactions to alcohol even though it is classified as a depressant. Someone may feel euphoric at lower doses and relaxed at higher doses. Whether the varying effects with nicotine are dose related as they usually seem to be with alcohol, I don't know.

Although many people claim that they smoke just for the aroma, oral gratification, or visual experience, double-blind studies have shown that not to be true. When comparing nicotine-free (or low nicotine) with high-nicotine cigarettes, it becomes clear that most are smoking for the drug effect. The effects reported are variable and range from pleasure and re-laxation to increased mental alertness and concentration. In any case, it's the nicotine effect that most people are after.

Health Risks

Although smoking is the fastest way to get a mind-altering drug into your brain, it does have some undesirable side effects over and above whatever the drug effect is. When you inhale combustible material that is burning, the side effects can be serious or fatal as in smoke inhalation from fires, a problem I have treated many times in burn patients. Although there is less danger with tobacco, marijuana, or coca leaves being smoked for drug ingestion, long-term negative effects can create health problems. Inhaling various irritants and certainly carcinogens in smoke can take its toll over time. Lung cancer and emphysema caused by smoking have nothing to do with nicotine, even though it has plenty of negative effects in other parts of the body. Those diseases are caused by the combustion products in the smoke often referred to as "tar."

During the first half of the 20th century, no one realized that cigarettes posed any significant risk to people who smoked them. What got scientists thinking about the possibility was the rapid rise in lung cancer cases in men between 1920 and 1950. That disease was relatively rare in 1900. Although some scientists thought this might be the result of industrial pol-lution, others started to get suspicious when carcinogens were discovered in cigarette smoke. The epidemiologists then got to work studying men's smoking patterns to see if there was a correlation with lung cancer.

This finding was impressive enough to cause a voluntary change in the behavior of British physicians who gave up smoking in droves worried that it might pose a significant health risk to them. Over time, their lung cancer rates dropped dramatically, supporting the theory that cigarette smoking caused lung cancer. Although this theory was disputed for many years by the tobacco companies and others, some governments began to step in and issue warnings to its citizens.

The danger of tobacco was first publicized in the U.S. when the Surgeon General, Luther Terry, announced in 1963 that tobacco was dangerous to your health. (I remember his name because he lived several blocks from my house when I was a kid, and I was his paperboy for a while.) Education has slowly worked over the last 40 years. The percentage of American adults who smoke has gone from 42% then to about 21% now.

Although the heath risk best known and probably most dramatic is lung cancer, the number of smokers who die from cardiovascular disease is greater. And here I'm talking about the cardiovascular deaths that are accelerated by smoking. In general, smokers have more atherosclerosis, more heart attacks, more strokes (both those caused by plaques blocking arteries and weakened arteries that burst), and more serious high blood pressure than nonsmokers. The number of cardiovascular-related deaths in smokers may be about the same as those dying from lung cancer.

Whether the vascular damage is caused by nicotine or other components in the smoke is not clear. It is pretty certain that an increased level of carbon monoxide in smokers is playing some role in the damage to the heart and blood vessels. However the spasm and narrowing in small vessels leading to oxygen deprivation in the tissues they supply is most certainly related to stimulation of acetylcholine receptors by nicotine. This plays a big role in decreasing blood supply to the skin.

As a plastic surgeon, I can guarantee you that smoking accelerates the skin's aging process. Your skin will lose its elasticity sooner and take on a less healthy appearance. In other words, you will look really cool smoking those Marlboros or Virginia Slims, but you may end up looking older a lot sooner than you would have otherwise. Because of the problem with decreased blood flow, I always refused to do a facelift on anyone who wouldn't quit smoking for at least several weeks before and after the operation. Smokers have much higher incidence of complications, especially skin necrosis due to inadequate blood supply.

As far as the overall adverse effects on health go, smoking just a pack a day increases a person's risk of death from any cause to twice that of a nonsmoker in any given year. Long-term smoking of a pack a day will increase the likelihood of death from bronchitis, emphysema, or lung cancer by tenfold. Two packs a day will increase the risk twentyfold and it just gets worse from there. If you're an adult and want to smoke and are not hurting others in the process, that's your business. I just want to make sure you know the facts first, especially if you're healthy now.

A study done in Britain many years ago showed that a teenager who smokes more than one cigarette has a very low chance (15%) of remaining a nonsmoker. As I will say about other drugs in this book such as cocaine, one hit may be all it takes to get you on a path you will later wish you had never started on. A slogan like "just say no to drugs" may sound simplistic or even stupid to you, but once you have some real knowledge about what drugs do and the long-term problems they may create for you, it's not so stupid after all. I'll have to make an exception for alcohol, since I've used that drug off and on during my life and don't want to be a hypocrite.

If you are thinking about starting a family, then you've got a whole new set of worries. The potential problems caused by smoking during pregnancy are somewhat controversial, but after that it's clear. Children whose parents smoke have a much higher incidence of breathing disorders, including asthma, and substantially more respiratory infections. If you are young and know for sure that you want to have a family, don't ever start smoking for that reason alone.

Addiction

Only two of the Nicotiana species are used in commercial tobacco production, N. tabacum and N. rustica. The nicotine content varies widely in various parts of the plants from 0.6% to 18% with almost two thirds of it found in the leaves. The addiction is due to the nicotine content. If that drug was in thyme and bay leaves, people would be smoking those too instead of just using them for food flavoring. How addictive is nicotine? Mark Twain said it well: "To cease smoking is the easiest thing I ever did. I ought to know because I've done it a thousand times."

Just compare it to other psychoactive drugs. Most people who drink alcohol have a couple of drinks and then stop. Some only drink a few times a week or occasionally. The same can be said of most cocaine, meth, and marijuana users. But most consumers of tobacco products do it every day and usually many times during the day. Physical dependence occurs quickly and is manifested by a rapid withdrawal syndrome on stopping which usually consists of headache, nausea, increased appetite, and sometimes diarrhea. In some studies, former smokers reported experiencing tobacco cravings for up to 5 or even 10 years after quitting.

This is why I think that smoking is not a great habit to get involved with. First of all, most people who are addicted report that the most enjoyable cigarette is the first one they have in the morning. Although they may have spent the previous day gradually increasing their nicotine blood level with intermittent spikes after each cigarette, the whole process stops when they go to sleep for the night. Nicotine gets metabolized within a few hours so by the time they get up, many smokers are already starting to have withdrawal symptoms. These are quickly relieved by smoking. In other words, they're not really getting a hit that makes them high. It just takes away their withdrawal symptoms so they don't have to start off the day feeling like crap.

As I mentioned in the previous section, nicotine's mechanism of action is far from being well understood. Although many people report a calming effect from smoking, this may simply come from a reduction in craving or relieving withdrawal symptoms rather than any actual anti-anxiety effect of nicotine. A side effect that does occur in many smokers is appetite reduction for unclear reasons. However there is a boomerang effect causing many people to gain substantial amounts of weight if they quit smoking.

At least with alcohol, narcotics, and many other drugs, you actually get high when you take them, even if you're a chronic user with a high tolerance. I don't know whether chronic smokers really get high since I've never been one, but if you must be addicted to something, smoking doesn't seem like a great choice to me. Oscar Wilde, a big smoker, seemed to express the same sentiment in this statement: "A cigarette is the perfect type of perfect pleasure. It is exquisite, and it leaves one unsatisfied. What more can one want?" Easy to start, hard to stop, and not that much pleasure in between. No thanks.

Hookah Craze

Just to be complete, I want to discuss something that has been around for a long time but in recent years has become fashionable, especially to younger people and girls. Water pipes have probably been in use in parts of the Arab world for almost 500 years. There are several versions. One is the bong which most of my fellow baby boomers are familiar with often used to smoke marijuana. You light the leaves and suck on the other end to pull the smoke through water which cools it and makes it somewhat less irritating to many people. With the water pipe, you do the same thing with tobacco as the drug source.

The hookah pipe is just a variation of the water pipe. Instead of igniting the tobacco with a flame, you heat it with charcoal placed above it. The so-called shisha is a combination of a sugar such as honey or molasses mixed with tobacco. Flavorings such as cherry are often added, possibly to make it more appealing to women. It has become chic for younger women especially and sounds very innocent. But what are we really talking about here? Many people no longer consider cigarettes to be cool, but a lot of younger people and especially girls are attracted to this hookah craze. I just want people to realize that it's merely another nicotine drug delivery system (unless you use a tobacco-free source for the smoke such as dried fruit).

Personal Experience with Cigarettes

Let me end this chapter with a few stories from my life that deal with tobacco use and specifically cigarettes. On a personal level, I quit smoking myself when I was eight. I smoked with friends a few times in the privacy of the woods near my house in Rockville, MD, at the time, but my brother told on me one day. My father washed my mouth out with soap and told me never to touch another cigarette. I never did. Actually that's not completely true. I occasionally puffed on a cigarette or cigar with friends who smoked years later, but never inhaled and certainly didn't ever get addicted. I wasn't such a good boy that I never tried to inhale. I just always choked and couldn't do it. By the way, my father was a Camel smoker (no filters, of course) for all of his adult life.

On another personal note, let me explain where I'm coming from. I've always been a laid back, live and let live kind of guy. You may get the idea from reading this chapter that I am trying to discourage people from smoking or give it up if they can. You would be exactly correct in thinking that. The same would be true of most of the drugs I talk about in this book. Remember that most of the damage caused by smoking is reversible, including the risk of developing lung cancer. Your health will benefit if you stop no matter how long you have been smoking, assuming you don't wait until you have inoperable lung cancer or terminal emphysema.

However I am not a rabid antismoker by any means. If people are smoking around me outdoors, it doesn't bother me at all. I can even get along OK in a smoke-filled room for a while if that's the situation I find myself in for some reason. I have had friends and family members who were heavy smokers and never lectured any of them. When children are being exposed to a smoke-filled environment, that bothers me most, but I still don't generally intrude unless someone asks for my help or advice. That is to say that I don't like to engage in direct confrontation if it's avoidable. The only time this really hit close to home was with my sister.

She got married in the 1970s to a nice guy who was a smoker. When they decided to have children in the 1980s, I hoped that maybe he would decide to stop smoking during her pregnancy, but he didn't. In fact he never did, until recently. Anyway when the children were young, I used my mother to do the dirty work. She was a rabid antismoker anyway, so all I had to do was tell her I was concerned about my sister's kids.

One Christmas at their house when the children were about two and four, my sister's husband went out to smoke a cigarette before dinner. When he came back in the house, my mother said, "You shouldn't be smoking those goddamned cigarettes around the children."

His response was, "That's none of your business."

"Well, it is my business because they are my grandchildren." My sister, brother, and I just sat there sheepishly trying to stay out of the line of fire. We had many holidays like that. Those were the good old days. I must point out that my sister was just following in my mother's footsteps by marrying a smoker. But when Mom did that in the 1930s, nobody knew there was any problem with smoking. Once the truth came out later, she may have regretted that she had raised all of her children in a smoke-filled environment. That said, let me tell a few more true stories about the habit that has caused and continues to cause a lot of problems for people all over the world.

Smokers I Have Known

During the summer after my third year of college, I got a research job working for the head of pathology at the George Washington University Hospital. It was a stroke of luck that my mother had made possible earlier that year. I was worried that my grades might not be good enough to get me accepted at a good medical school, or maybe any medical school. If I performed well and got a good recommendation from Dr. Perry, that would definitely help me, especially at G.W. The project involved creating latex skeletons of the coronary arteries using the hearts of patients who died in the hospital.

A few days after starting the job, I spent my first rather grotesque morning with Dr. Chan watching him do several autopsies in the morgue. He was a pathology resident put in charge of helping me and supervising my research project. Talk about being thrown right into the fire; I had never even seen a dead body before. The first one had been moved by the assistant in the morgue onto a large rectangular steel table where it was lying when I came into the room. Dr. Chan put on gloves and asked me to do the same. He started dictating a general physical description of the body into a microphone as we both stood over the chest. I was nauseated, but I doubt that it never even occurred to him that this was the first time I had seen and touched a dead body.

He picked up a large scalpel off the table next to the body and made an incision from the neck to the abdomen. He went back over it until he was down to the breastbone. Then the assistant handed him a buzz saw and he cut through the entire sternum. He separated the ribs with an instrument and then took some blood samples directly from the heart with a giant needle and syringe. This was a long way from the frogs I had dissected in the first year of college biology. He pointed out the heart, lungs, and great vessels and then had me stick my hand in and feel them. Intellectually, perhaps I should have been fascinated by this experience, but I was actually horrified. Trying not to let him know how gruesome this was for me, I attempted to show no reaction.

The patient had died less than an hour before and still had a normal body temperature. When he asked me to feel this man's warm heart, I almost vomited. This was a man in his 50s with lung cancer. Part of one of his lungs was gone and he had little nodules scattered around his other lung, which Dr. Chan said were metastatic lesions from the original tumor.

As he leaned over the body, a pack of cigarettes fell out of his shirt pocket onto the heart. He picked it up and put it on another table. I wondered how he could smoke after doing these autopsies all the time, but I didn't say anything. (The Surgeon General's original report on smoking had come out three years before in 1964.)

Chief of Surgery

Several years after my summer with Dr Chan, I was a third-year medical student at G.W. (Yes, my good letter of recommendation from Dr. Perry definitely helped.) The most enigmatic surgeon on the faculty was the chief of surgery, Dr. Paul Atkins. He did thoracic and cardiac surgery and had trained under Dr. Brian Blades, a pioneer in thoracic surgery and former chief of surgery at G.W. Dr. Atkins had worked his way up through the ranks of the Department of Surgery as one of Dr. Blades' former residents into the position of chief of surgery.

Dr. Atkins was handsome and usually friendly, but his mood swings were the talk of the hospital. After being outgoing and pleasant for several weeks, he would then sometimes walk around the hospital for days in a somber state paying no attention to those walking by him in the halls. His morose periods usually came after one of his patient's deaths following cardiac surgery. He frequently seemed to take such events as a massive personal defeat and would often require weeks to recover.

We were warned as medical students about his idiosyncrasies when we came on the surgical rotation at G.W. As I mentioned previously, the Surgeon General had issued his warning about the connection between cigarette smoking and lung cancer six years previously, and this relationship was emphasized in our clinical training in 1970. A smoking history was considered a routine part of any patient history and physical exam; yet we were told when we started our surgery rotation at G.W. never to mention the smoking history of any patient, especially one with heart or lung disease, when presenting cases to Dr. Atkins. We all considered this very odd since he operated on many people with lung cancer until we found out that he had been a chain smoker for years.

There is a sad ending to the Dr. Atkins story that occurred about ten years later. Having had a cough for several months, Dr. Atkins finally got a chest X-ray one day. He looked at it and then took it to the chief of radiology. He asked him what he thought and the radiologist said, "Well, it's just as obvious to you as it is to me. This patient has an inoperable lung cancer."

Dr. Atkins replied, "Yeah, that's my X-ray." His health followed a rapid downhill course and he died about six months later. To add to the irony, Dr. Blades was also a chronic smoker and had died of lung cancer several years before that.

Jason's Lesson

Let me end this chapter with a question and a little story about one of my former patients. Is nicotine really much more addictive than alcohol, marijuana, cocaine, methamphetamine, and heroin? I'll let Jason answer that for you.

During my plastic surgery residency, I treated a patient named Jason, a man in his early thirties with Buerger's disease (thromboangitis obliterans). Because people with this disease have extreme sensitivity to the effects of nicotine, small blood vessels in their hands and feet go into spasm when they smoke cigarettes. Over time, this progressively cuts off the circulation to the fingers and toes which can develop gangrene. If the patient stops smoking, the problem goes away.

Before going in to see Jason for my preop evaluation, I read his chart and noted that he had undergone amputation of most of his fingers and toes. He was now being admitted to amputate his gangrenous right thumb. When I walked in the room to introduce myself, I was dumbfounded. He was sitting on the edge of the bed puffing on a cigarette that he was holding between his black dead thumb and the stub of his index finger. After seeing that, no one needed to try to convince me how powerful the addiction to tobacco could be.

If some of you still are not convinced, let's try this. Whatever your drug problem may be, I am going to establish a program to help you quit. Here's the deal. I will have you undergo random drug testing several times a month. If there is a trace of the offending drug in your blood or urine, I will amputate the tip of your little finger. The next time, I'll take off the middle part. How many of you heavy meth, cocaine, and narcotics users think that I would get your entire little finger before you decided to stop using? Not many, if any. But Jason lost all his fingers and toes because he couldn't give up cigarettes. Put that in your pipe and smoke it.

5

Cocaine

When I was practicing plastic surgery, a patient who came for evaluation of a nasal deformity related a story to me. She had been operated on by a plastic surgeon in Los Angeles approximately a year before. During her return visit to him six months after surgery, he continued to tell her as he had done previously that her postoperative deformity would go away with more time. Before and shortly after the operation, this patient had developed a good rapport with one of the doctor's scrub nurses who had assisted him on her operation. One day when the patient called for a new appointment nine months after surgery, she asked to speak to this nurse. A receptionist told her that she had left and was now working for another plastic surgeon in the San Diego area.

Instead of making another appointment with the doctor in L.A., she contacted the nurse at her new office and was curious to know why she had left. The patient explained that she was still unhappy with her result and wanted to know how she should handle the situation. The nurse then said, point blank, "Don't ever go back to him. He is a cocaine addict. That's why I left. He really messed up your operation because he was high when he did it."

After the patient told me this story, I contacted several of my colleagues who knew all about this doctor. They described him as a good-looking, charming guy who was a decent surgeon but did have a serious drug problem. He had taken a month off from his practice twice in the last several years to go into rehab, but it obviously didn't work for him. Normally if the other surgeon was competent, I would have advised this woman to go back to him and get her revision surgery for little or no cost. In this case, I couldn't do that. She had to pay me for another operation to fix the first one.

History and Pharmacology

Because many drugs occur naturally in plants, their psychoactive effects can be obtained directly from the plant. Or the primary active ingredient in a plant can be extracted from it by creating a refined but still natural drug. Often plants need to be manipulated in some way to create an effect. The South American Indians have been drying coca leaves and mixing them with ashes to enhance their stimulant effect for thousands of years. They put the leaves in their mouth for a half hour in order to relieve fatigue, getting a stimulant effect within a few minutes. They also get numbness in the check because cocaine is a local anesthetic as well as a stimulant.

The dose of drugs in plants is often quite low, making them much safer than the refined drugs made from them. To isolate a plant's active ingredient can be complicated and require sophisticated laboratory equipment. But sometimes it can be simple, as in the case of cocaine. Coca leaves are soaked in a solvent to extract the cocaine. This process is often carried out in primitive labs in the jungle, which explains why street cocaine often contains many impurities.

Cocaine is found naturally in the leaves of the coca plant that is indigenous to the Andes Mountains in South America. Coca leaves usually have about 0.5% cocaine. Street cocaine may be 15% when dealers have cut (diluted) it to increase profits using sugars and local anesthetics, but it is often closer to 60% and can be made completely pure (100% cocaine). It is currently the second most commonly used illegal psychoactive drug in the U.S. after marijuana.

The process of extracting the plant's main alkaloid was developed in the late 1850s in Europe. Its use was first popularized by adding coca leaves to wine, which was marketed as a cure for depression and fatigue. The refined form of the drug became popular in the 1880s after it was first isolated as pure cocaine and added to many tonics that were touted to treat a variety of ailments. Its use as a local anesthetic was a big help in medicine, especially eye surgery. (I used it many times in nasal surgery because it is an excellent local anesthetic and also causes vasoconstriction which dramatically decreases bleeding in areas with a great blood supply.)

When Coca Cola was first invented in the 1880s, its primary active ingredients were caffeine from African cola beans and cocaine from South American coca leaves. During the so-called "gay nineties," there were no homosexuals in the U.S. (they didn't come into being until the 1960s in

San Francisco), but there were a lot of happy people who could literally go to the local drug store and get high. When someone needed a pick-me-up, he went to the soda fountain. You might think he said, "Give me a Coca Cola." The phrase many people actually used when they wanted a Coke was, "Give me a shot in the arm."

By the end of the 19th century, cocaine was portrayed as the "in" drug. In the book *The 7% Solution*, Sherlock Holmes is described as injecting the drug almost every day. Widely used to treat morphine addiction, it came to the attention of a young Austrian neurologist named Sigmund Freud. He began testing the drug in a scientific fashion—on himself. He found that the drug gave him energy, improved his nerves, and enhanced muscle tone. During his first few uses, he noticed that the drug made him feel more sexually charged around his fiancée and conveyed this to her in a love letter.

He began giving cocaine to his patients. He believed that the drug simply made you more normal. Patients who were depressed were given cocaine and if the depression continued, he increased the dose with each visit. He drew a lot of attention to what he called "this magical substance" and published a paper describing its tremendous benefits. At that time, he had been using cocaine morning, noon, and night for many months.

Other doctors were not convinced and began to do their own studies. Dr. Erlenmeyer published a notable study regarding the use of cocaine to treat morphine addiction. He found that it did no good at all and predicted that cocaine would become the new great scourge after alcohol and morphine.

With his reputation seriously challenged, Freud moved to Paris and abandoned cocaine after using it for about three years. He rehabilitated his name with his work on *The Interpretation of Dreams* and ultimately went on to become the father of psychoanalysis. After I learned about his experience in college, I felt that if cocaine was able to lure him into its web, I probably wouldn't stand a chance with it—so I never even wanted to try it.

Opium was also widely available in the late 1800s and prescribed by doctors for a variety of diseases and health problems. After twenty years of this happy-go-lucky life many Americans were leading, the government decided to put an end to it at the beginning of the 20th Century. They made the Coca Cola Company take the cocaine out of their drink. The Congress passed the Pure Food and Drug Act of 1906 requiring all makers of patent medicines, many of which contained cocaine, heroin, or morphine, to list their contents on the label. The drugs were later strictly controlled under the Harrison Narcotics Act of 1914.

Cocaine Use and Effects
Most people who use cocaine these days snort it. Used this way, the stimulant effect comes on fast (a few minutes), is intense, but is very short lived. Shooting it gives faster and more intense effects (within 15–30 seconds), but this goes away even more quickly. Smoking gives a faster rush than i.v. cocaine (almost immediate), but it's gone in a flash. Cocaine can be taken orally, but few people do that. Although the effect is not nearly as intense, it is a much safer way to use the drug if the dose is properly controlled.

Depending on how it's taken, the pleasure of a hit can range from a few minutes to a half hour or so; then the user may be faced with a problem of neurotransmitter depletion, which may sometimes occur only after repeated sessions. It's kind of like running as fast as you can for as long as you can until you suddenly collapse. You have completely exhausted your energy supplies. Of course, a body that has depleted its energy can't just jump up and keep running. It has to rest and restore itself. But when their brain needs to rest from its drug marathon, many people just snort some more cocaine because they can't stand to feel like crap. This is another reason I have never had any desire to use cocaine. You get high for a few minutes but may be on a serious downer for hours after that. Who needs that?

Smoking Cocaine
Cocaine hydrochloride, the molecular form found in powder cocaine, is water soluble and can be eaten, snorted, or injected intravenously. The reason it can't be smoked successfully is that the high temperature of combustion destroys the drug. It needs to be converted into a form that can withstand the heat—freebase cocaine.

This is made by heating cocaine hydrochloride in water containing a base, usually sodium bicarbonate. After the base has "freed" the cocaine from the HCl, a solvent such as ether is then mixed in. Once separated into two layers, the top layer is removed with an eyedropper and the rest left in a dish to evaporate into cocaine crystals. The resulting alkaloid is now heat resistant and smokable as well as being fat soluble giving it quick access to the brain.

Some of you may see the little problem here. If you don't let the solution completely evaporate, then when you light up the drug, the ether will catch fire. Explosions and facial burns can really ruin the whole experience. I am sure that many of you baby boomers like me remember the late Richard Pryor's mishap. Freebasing was a big rage in the late 70s but became less popular after Pryor's experience was publicized.

In order to avoid these dangers, a simpler technique was developed. You skip the first step of extracting pure cocaine and just mix the powder with baking soda and water. The mixture is then boiled or heated in a microwave and then cooled. The chunky brick that forms has the texture of soap and can be cut into "rocks" and smoked. By the way, it is called crack because when it is being formed during the cooling process, it makes a crackling sound. It also does this as it is smoked. It first appeared in 1985 and its use was epidemic within a year.

Crackdown on Crack

Although I wanted to stay away from controversial issues in this book, I just can't when it comes to crack. Many of my patients in the jails were there because they used it. Most people using cocaine prefer the powder form, as did my patient described at the beginning of the next chapter and the doctor I spoke about at the start of this one. The reason crack became popular was that it was a cheap way to get a cocaine high. A gram of cocaine that sells for $90 can be converted into crack and then cut into 30 "rocks" that cost as little as $3–5 a piece (more for bigger chunks obviously).

However, look at the penalties for different kinds of possession in the U.S. for almost 25 years. Powder cocaine, the rich person's drug of choice, carried far less severe penalties, gram for gram, than crack cocaine, the poor person's drug. Congress enacted sentencing provisions in 1986, making possession of 500 grams of powder cocaine carry the same mandatory-minimum five-year prison sentence as possession of 5 grams of crack (the 1/100 rule).

From a pharmacological point of view, this is absurd; there is vastly more cocaine in 500 grams of powder than in 5 grams of crack. But from a racist point of view, the policy does make sense. Crack is predominantly a poor black person's drug. Seven years after the law was enacted, federal prison sentences were 41% longer for blacks than whites. The primary reason for this was the disparate punishment for possession of crack versus powder cocaine. At that time, blacks made up 12% of the population, 13% of all monthly drug users, 35% of those arrested, 55% of those convicted, and 74% of those sentenced for drug possession.

Although a few politcians have expressed concern about this law over many years, nothing was done about it. After 24 long years, the congress finally corrected this absurd law in July 2010—a little too late for the thousands of people whose lives have been ruined by it (some of my former patients included).

Although I have no desire to use cocaine in any form, if I were forced to choose between crack and certain psychiatric drugs, I would take the crack. Perhaps being forced to take psychoactive drugs will be a form of punishment in some future society—or is it now for many people who are incarcerated? OK, that's it for controversy. I promise I won't do it anymore. Not really.

Mixing drugs

If you mix a variety of alcoholic beverages at a party (beer, wine, cocktails), you are more likely to have a hangover the next day. With cocaine and other drugs, it gets a lot worse. First of all let's look at cocaine and alcohol. When they are consumed at the same time, the liver forms a new drug called cocaethylene. This produces a longer and more intense high than cocaine by itself and also increases the prospect of addiction and withdrawal problems over time.

Although overdose or a fatal outcome is possible with even a very small dose of cocaine in some people, there are ways to increase this likelihood. One is to mix cocaine with heroin or some other narcotic or depressant. The use of stimulants and depressants together can make for a bad combination. Someone using too much cocaine will start to realize it and back off if he gets too wired. But if he is also doing downers, this will mask the effect of the cocaine, and vice versa. This could result in a heroin or cocaine overdose when both are being consumed at the same time.

A case in point would be the famous comedian John Belushi who died in 1982 at the age of 33. His girlfriend, who went to prison for involuntary manslaughter, had injected him with heroin and cocaine some 20 times during the course of that fatal day. Supposedly Chris Farley, another SNL comedian who came along later, also met his demise using both cocaine and heroin together.

Here is another famous case where relatively little drug may have been used. After being drafted by the Boston Celtics in 1986, Len Bias got together with a friend and decided to celebrate. They went to a college dorm room with a six-pack of beer and a bottle of cognac. Two other friends who joined them had brought some cocaine with them. Although he had reportedly never used cocaine, Bias took a few snorts. (Some have said they were free-basing but I doubt that.) The party went on for some time, and he may have had more cocaine, in addition to alcohol.

At some point, he started having a seizure, which stopped after several minutes. His friends initially panicked but then decided that he would be OK. Unfortunately, he started seizing again as they helplessly watched. He again stopped but then had another seizure. After the third seizure, his friends called 911. When the paramedics arrived, Bias was in full cardiac arrest; they performed CPR on him for two hours before they finally gave up.

Although I don't know what the autopsy showed, several things could have happened. He may have snorted a number of times from a highly concentrated preparation of almost pure cocaine, causing an overdose. Alternatively, he may have had an acute allergic reaction to the cocaine. Or there could have been contaminants in the mixture that caused the seizures and perhaps an abnormal heart rhythm. Yet another possibility is that he might have had a massive heart attack from coronary vasospasm.

But here's an important question: Why didn't his friends call 911 when he first started seizing? I would guess that their primary concern was that they would be arrested for using an illegal substance. As a result of that fear, they waited far too long to call for help. Bias might well still be alive today if they had called 911 immediately after he first started seizing.

This kind of scenario happens frequently. Sometimes people who have an overdose or other adverse reaction are just left to die by their fellow users who are afraid to call for help. As far as I'm concerned, anyone who reports such an emergency should be free from prosecution for drug possession or use. No one in that kind of situation should be afraid to call for help. This is another issue that the president and congress might want to look at now that they finally did something about the 1/100 rule.

Just Say No Thanks

As a powerful stimulant, cocaine will give you a tachycardia. High doses will make you hypertensive and may create abnormal heart-rhythm disturbances. However, the body has a great capacity to metabolize this drug quickly, making overdose a rare occurrence. Most cases of alleged cocaine overdose you have heard about, like River Phoenix, actually involved multiple drugs. The fact is that many reported cocaine overdose victims are also using other drugs such as meth, heroin, and/or alcohol at the same time. I must mention here that there is no specific antidote to cocaine overdose (or other stimulants), so I would much rather be faced in the emergency room with someone who has OD'd on narcotics. An injection of a drug like Narcan reverses the drug effects almost immediately.

Cocaine use is an expensive habit and leads to many of the psychological problems that I talk about in the next chapter with addiction to methamphetamines. Although I had access to pharmaceutical-grade cocaine for many years, I never seriously considered trying it. And that wasn't because I had some strong religious or moral reasons for staying away from it. If street cocaine was all I had access to, there is no way I would have ever considered using it. The best way to avoid getting addicted to cocaine is to never even try it. One hit may be all it takes to start you down a road that you do not ever want to be on.

6

Amphetamines/Methamphetamines

One night when I was doing sick call in the jail, the deputies brought up a young man from the intake area, shortly after booking him. Because he had complained to the nurse of severe shoulder pain, she wanted me to see him. A white male in his mid 20s, he appeared to be quite manic. "What's the problem, Michael?" I asked.

"Those cops really fucked up my arm when they put the handcuffs on."

"Let me check it," I said. There was a lot of pain on passive movement of the right shoulder but no evidence of dislocation. "I think it's just a soft tissue injury, but I'll put you in a sling and check you again in two days."

"What about the fucking pain, dude?"

"I'll give you some Motrin."

"That won't do shit."

"Well, I'm not going to give you anything stronger since I have a feeling you're high on something right now."

"Yeah," he said. "But I won't be tomorrow. Please, man!"

"No, I can't. Sorry."

When I saw him two days later, he was much more reserved. "How's the shoulder?" I asked.

"It's a lot better. I guess you were right."

There was less pain on active and passive motion. "You'll be OK in a few days," I said. Speaking in a low voice so the deputies couldn't hear me, I asked, "What were you high on when you came in?" I tried to maintain whatever privacy I could, especially when talking about illicit drugs.

"Speed and cocaine," he said, matter of factly, in a normal tone of voice. He didn't seem to care if the deputies overheard the conversation.

"Must be an expensive habit if you use very much."

"Yeah, but I make a lot," he said.

"Doing what?"

"I run a telemarketing company and have a bunch of people working for me."

"Is that a good business?"

"Fuck, yeah. I make twenty grand a month."

"Sounds pretty good to me," I said. "I'm going to take the sling off. Come back in a couple of days if you're not back to normal."

"No problem, doc. I'll be out tomorrow. I have a good lawyer."

Here was a drug user who was making a lot of money despite his habit. Most of my patients were on the opposite end of the money spectrum and needed to steal or sell genital services to pay for their drugs.

History and Chemistry

The origin of the synthetic drug amphetamine is the ephedra bush that has been growing in desert regions of Asia and North America for thousands of years. It was probably used at least two thousand years ago in China as a tea for the treatment of asthma and other respiratory problems. Much more recently in the mid 1800s, the Mormons began to use it as a stimulating drink because their religious beliefs did not allow them to drink tea or coffee.

Isolated from Ephedra in the late 1800s, ephedrine became a standard treatment for asthma by the 1930s. When scientists found that it was chemically similar to epinephrine (also called adrenaline) excreted by the adrenal glands, further research led to the discovery of a synthetic drug called amphetamine. It was first sold as a nasal inhaler for asthma in the early 1930s. A few years later, pills became available and people quickly discovered that this drug not only boosted energy but also counteracted fatigue, hunger, and the need for sleep.

I will divert momentarily to explain a little chemistry. Amphetamine comes in two molecular forms that are mirror images of each other but have different chemical effects. Transposing from anatomy, they have been named left and right handed (or levo and dextro from Latin for left and right). Levoamphetamine can constrict vessels in the nose and relieve nasal congestion but doesn't get into the brain. On the other hand, dextroamphetamine, originally called Dexedrine, has potent effects on the brain. A modified stronger drug called methamphetamine was quickly developed.

As I mentioned in the chapter on nicotine, soldiers' rations in WWII almost always contained cigarettes. But they also included another much more psychoactive substance—amphetamines. Although these drugs were widely distributed to most Allied and Axis soldiers, some have estimated that use by American soldiers throughout the war may have averaged as much as one pill per soldier per day. Japanese and German soldiers may have used even more.

It was not just the soldiers, sailors, and pilots using these drugs. Winston Churchill had some rough times during the First World War as First Lord of the Admiralty when he was blamed for the sinking of three British warships in one day as well as the long and disastrous campaign in Gallipoli. He was reputed by many to have alcohol circulating through his veins much of his adult life and this may have helped him in WWI. However he apparently found another helper to get him through the long nights as Prime Minister during WWII—the same amphetamines his soldiers were using. Hitler was supposedly doing a lot more than taking pills to keep him going. He became severely addicted to methamphetamine during the last few years of the war and reportedly had his doctors inject him several times a day. These two men seemingly had something else in common besides being mortal enemies and two of the greatest orators of the 20th century.

During the Korean War, soldiers moved beyond using speed for endurance, energy, and to fight sleep deprivation. American soldiers began to use it to get high and developed the so-called "speedball," an injection of heroin and amphetamines together. In the next decade, this same process continued in Vietnam where the soldiers consumed millions of doses of amphetamines as well as a whole lot of heroin and other drugs. Supposedly more of them were taken out of theater because of drug problems than war wounds.

Soldiers weren't the only people having problems with life in the 1950s and 60s when amphetamines accounted for 20% of all prescriptions in the U.S. Billions of pills were sold and a lot of them used for recreation, not just weight loss, athletic training, or staying awake. The Feds tried to regain control in the late 60s by getting amphetamines off the streets and making it more difficult for doctors to prescribe them. This led to the development and proliferation of clandestine laboratories, especially on the West Coast, which remains a huge problem today.

No new innovation occurred until the mid 1980s when a base version of dextromethamphetamine appeared in Asia. This allowed people to smoke pipes containing pellets that have a similar appearance to crack cocaine but are clearer, looking something like shattered glass (thus leading to the nicknames of ice, crystal, and glass.) Compared to regular cocaine or crack, the duration of action is much longer and could last ten hours or more. Smoking ice is kind of like taking LSD. You're not likely to get much accomplished that day. Unlike crack, it is of interest to note that the smokable forms of meth can be dissolved in water and injected intravenously.

Big Lies and Truth

Methamphetamine is a potent CNS stimulant that releases dopamine, nor-adrenalin, and serotonin in the brain and other areas of the body. What makes it different from cocaine, which has a similar effect on the brain, is that it lasts much longer. Depending on drug dosage, tolerance of the user, and how it is taken, meth may be active for anywhere from four to possibly twenty-four hours. Its effects can be variable from person to person and somewhat unpredictable.

Because of widespread abuse of the amphetamine class of drugs in the 1960s, it was classified as a Schedule II drug by the DEA when the drug enforcement act went into effect in 1970. In this case, the category is appropriate as opposed to that of marijuana, which has always been a Schedule I drug (no medical use and highly addictive). Prescription amphetamines have limited approved medical use (obesity, narcolepsy, ADD), and a high potential for abuse and addiction, which is the definition of a drug in the Schedule II category. If the first drug czar appointed in the 1930s, Henry Anslinger, had been talking about meth and other amphetamines instead of marijuana when he said the drug induced violent behavior, was highly addictive, and could lead to insanity, he would not have been distorting the truth quite so drastically.

However, because he and subsequent politicians have persisted in telling many lies about marijuana, almost two thirds of American high school students do not even consider meth to be a drug. They try some weed and the deception is exposed. Then they assume that those in positions of authority are lying about other drugs in the same way, leading many to believe that meth can't really hurt you. As a result, about 25% of meth users are under 18. It is definitely a young and primarily white person's drug (less than 20% of users are over 30, and very few are over 40).

The truth is that it can hurt you or even kill you. Thousands of young people are treated in ERs every year all over the U.S. for serious problems resulting from meth use (as well as many other drugs). In some city hospitals, the ER doctors might be tempted to approach young patients differently from the older ones. Instead of asking the patient what his chief complaint and medical history are, it might be more efficient to make the first question to anyone under 25, "What drugs do you take, and what are you high on now?"

High school kids start using it for what they consider legitimate reasons. Athletes use it to boost performance. Girls use it to lose weight. Boys and girls use it at rave parties to help keep their energy up so they can dance for hours. It is cheaper to buy than cocaine and lasts much longer. Because it is much cheaper, some have dubbed it redneck cocaine.

The initial effect depends on how it is used. Usually meth is taken orally or injected. Smoking it or i.v. injection will produce an intense rush within seconds. Snorting it will produce a euphoric effect, but not the rush, within 3–5 minutes. Oral ingestion will produce a high within 15–20 minutes that can last for many hours. Supposedly the effects are similar to cocaine but last a lot longer. (I can't personally verify that since I've never taken either one.)

Acute effects of the drug include euphoria, alertness, decreased appetite, and increased physical activity. Higher doses lead to paranoia, athetosis (jerky movements), anxiety, aggression, incessant talking, insomnia, irritability, and confusion. Very high doses can produce acute hypertension, heart attacks (from coronary vasospasm even in young people), strokes, convulsions, and dangerous hyperthermia.

As kids dance and party the night away for hours on end, some become severely dehydrated and develop malignant hyperthermia, sometimes with a core body temperature as high as 108 degrees (F). They present to the emergency room with heat stroke, if they don't die before that. Meth is bad shit.

Prolonged usage can produce a mental state similar to schizophrenia, with extreme anger and paranoia, repetitive behavior patterns, hallucinations, and delusions (like insects crawling on your skin). Suicidal and homicidal thoughts may lead to a fatal outcome for the user or someone else.

Once someone becomes addicted to meth, they will experience pronounced withdrawal symptoms, which may include palpitations, sweating, hyperventilation, drug craving, depression, insomnia, and extreme irritability. They can get over these effects in a few days, but hard-core addicts often remain depressed for months or years; they feel that life can't possibly be pleasurable without meth and may continue to crave it for several years before they can finally adapt to life without it. It is a hard addiction to treat and recover from. Give me liberty or give me meth. You can never really be a free person if you are addicted to meth (or any other drug for that matter).

Controlling the production of meth is almost impossible. Clandestine labs have been set up in almost every imaginable place. You can even fit everything you need into a suitcase and have a portable lab to take any-where. The primary ingredient is ephedrine, which has become more dif-ficult to obtain in the U.S., but is still easy to get in Mexico where many meth labs are also in operation. American meth makers often buy cold medicines containing pseudoephedrine and then break that down chemi-cally to produce ephedrine. A few hundred dollars spent on the main in-gredients and necessary chemicals can yield a supply of meth worth many thousands of dollars.

Meth production is highly dangerous. These guys are not chemists; they may have learned how to make the stuff from a dealer who's only done it once or twice himself. Or they may be doing it for the first time us-ing a recipe they got off the Internet. Explosions and fires in meth labs kill many innocent people, including firefighters and police officers.

Meth Mouth and Meth Face

Since most people want to look good, here's one final warning. Many teenagers, and especially girls, are not happy with their appearance. If you would like to ensure that you will never look good, then become a chronic meth user for a few years. Dentists are well aware of meth-mouth problems. As a plastic surgeon, I want you to know that your face will take a big hit as well if you get trapped in this addiction. As an example, one of my patients in jail was a prostitute in her early 20s. Good looking at the age of 18, she now had rotten gums, many missing teeth, and looked like she was in her 40s. The accelerated aging process can be dramatic in some people. You may feel good when you're high for a few years, but you won't be happy with the end result. Don't use meth. That's my advice.

7

Marijuana

Sometimes the drugs my patients used when I worked in the jails were the least dangerous kind, and yet their arrest for possession led to the most severe of consequences. One such person was Enrique, a 35-year-old Hispanic male, arrested for possession of marijuana. The nurse sent him up from the intake area because he was having heart palpitations. I had arrived 15 minutes early for sick call. This allowed me plenty of time to do a thorough evaluation and EKG, both of which were normal.

That evening, there were problems in several of the housing units, which delayed sick call for at least a half hour. Although I expected that the inmates on the sick-call list would be arriving any time, I continued to talk to Enrique, as I found his story interesting. With plenty of time to spare, I got a brief summary of his life story.

His criminal career started when he was 18. He found a car with the keys in it one evening and decided to take it for a joy ride. He got into an accident in which someone was injured. After three years in prison, he emerged as a more mature adult. Having gained a lot of experience with cars as a kid, he got a job as a mechanic. He eventually saved up enough money to start his own repair shop in a high-crime area of South San Diego County. Because he felt he needed to protect himself, he kept a gun on the floor of his pick-up truck.

One evening, he was stopped for having a rear taillight out. As cops often do with younger black and Hispanic men, the officer asked if he had a fourth waiver. For those of you who don't know (as I didn't until I became a jail doctor), most felons are forced to give up their right to not be subjected to unreasonable search and seizure provided under the Fourth Amendment to U.S. Constitution. Knowing that the officer would probably search his car, he admitted having a loaded gun under the seat. This was a violation of his parole and landed him back in jail for a year.

He eventually got his business up and running again, married, and had two children. Now at the age of 35, he was again stopped for a minor infraction. Although most police departments deny doing this now, they certainly used to stop people based on racial profiling. Wanting to bust someone and put another arrest under their belt, they had a greater chance of finding drugs or guns on prior felons (and statistically younger black and Hispanic men are more likely to have been involved in the criminal justice system).

That's what happened again to Enrique. He occasionally smoked pot and had just been given a small zip-lock bag with marijuana in it by a friend whose car he had fixed. He was now back in jail again, this time facing his third strike and possible life imprisonment.

The three-strikes law was passed by the California legislature in attempt to deal with repeat offenders. The problem with it became clear to me when I encountered Enrique and other inmates like him. Because the law put such a severe restraint on judges in the sentencing phase, it was quite possible that he could end up with life, despite the circumstances of his case.

I think that most California voters were under the impression that the three-strikes law applied to violent repeat offenders like rapists and armed robbers. But the law was drafted so broadly and put such heavy constraints on judges that it seemed as though almost any three felony convictions would be enough to potentially put you away for life. In contrast, someone with a one-strike murder conviction could be on parole in 5 to 10 years. In Fall 2010, plenty of people in central California were quite disturbed to learn that a serial killer convicted of three murders in the 1990s was being released on parole to come back to their community. Politicians who passed the three-strikes law did it because they wanted to let everyone know that they were hard on drug users. One could interpret their laws another way—they are soft on murderers.

Perhaps Enrique could at least gain some comfort in knowing that he was not the only non-violent offender whose life has been ruined by the system in California (which was admittedly much more liberal than many states). Statistics from the mid 1990s (when I was working in the jails) showed that a third-strike conviction was four times more likely to occur as a result of marijuana possession than kidnapping, rape, and murder combined. It took a long time but people are finally waking up to our draconian treatment of drug users, especially those using marijuana. After a failed fall ballot measure to decriminalize possession of small amounts in 2010, the legislature passed a law effective in January of 2011 that essentially does the same. This is good news for small-time users but too late for Enrique and thousands of others in California.

History

Although many drugs I'm discussing in this book fall neatly into the category of stimulants, depressants, narcotics, or hallucinogens, marijuana doesn't really fit well into any single category. It is clearly not a narcotic but does have some stimulant, sedative, and hallucinogenic properties depending on how it is used. That is why it belongs in its own category of cannabis. It comes from the leaves and flowers of the Indian hemp plant, called Cannabis sativa.

One of the oldest non-food crops grown around the world, its use was probably first recorded by a Chinese emperor about five thousand years ago. Archeological evidence suggests that it was used there long before that, possibly 12,000 years ago. Although it was used primarily as a painkiller, the ancient Chinese were well aware of its mind-altering effects. It has always been represented by two characters that mean "big" and "numb." In Mandarin this is "Da Ma." (For those who have studied that language, that is fourth tone and second tone. Of interest is that fact that first tone "ma" means mother while third tone means horse.)

For thousands of years, the hemp plant has served a source of fiber, cloth, paper, and medicine. The first documented written record was in ancient Vedic Hindu scripture, probably around 1500 B.C. According to that, the god Shiva took pity on humans and gave them cannabis to make their lives more pleasant. It was widely used in ancient India in religious ceremonies, as well as by common people. It was called "the poor man's heaven." The leaves were brewed in water, to which milk and sugar were added. Because it is not water soluble, it requires the presence of fat, such as milk or cream, in order to get absorbed in the GI tract, just like the fat soluble vitamins A, D, E, and K. (This is an important point to note that many people don't realize. If you take your multiple vitamin supplements with water on an empty stomach, a lot of them won't get absorbed.)

From India and China, it eventually spread to the Middle East, North Africa, and most of the Roman Empire. A Greek physician in Rome, named Dioscorides, published a popular book in 70 A.D. in which he recommended cannabis as a treatment for earaches. This prescription was widely used for the next 1500 years. Like modern Americans, Brits, Canadians, Europeans, Australians, Russians, Japanese, and many others, the Romans preferred alcohol for intoxication and only occasionally used cannabis to get high. Hemp was far more important to them as a source of fiber and rope.

Ancient Arabs also used cannabis and developed a stronger form around 100 AD, called hashish, made from the resin of the hemp flowers. Arab physicians used marijuana to treat earaches, abdominal pain, headaches, and labor pain. Hashish didn't make it to Europe in a big way until the early 1800s when Napoleon conquered Egypt and his soldiers brought it back with them. By the mid 1800s, it had become popular in Paris and London.

At the start of the Renaissance in the 1500s, there was a huge demand for paper, fabric, and rope, all of which could be supplied by hemp. In making clothing, it was much more durable than cotton, linen, and wool. As the European powers competed with each other in trying to build navies, they found out that their warships required massive amounts of hemp. The production in their own countries was inadequate, so they turned to their colonies in the Americas in the 1600s and forced them to grow as much hemp as possible. By the end of the 1800s, 90% of American clothing was made from hemp, as were most textiles and paper. Washington and Jefferson grew thousands of acres of hemp on their estates. Washington had terrible problems with dental and gum infections and often used marijuana to relieve his pain.

By the mid-1800s, cotton began to replace hemp in clothing products. Hemp production was much more labor intensive and the invention of the cotton gin changed everything. We also began to move away from the big sailing ships to those run by steam engines. Although it was not needed to make clothing and sails to the extent it had been, another factor came into play. Until the late 1800s, almost all paper was made from hemp. It is a much better product than wood pulp and even much of today's money is still printed on cannabis paper.

Given the fact that much more cellulose can be produced from an acre of hemp than an acre of trees, why did we suddenly abandon hemp and favor cutting down our forests instead? Could it have anything to do with power, money, and greed? How did you guess? One major player in this transformation was William Randolph Hearst, the giant newspaper publisher. He was a rich kid who inherited the San Francisco Examiner from his father in 1887. About 40 years later, he owned a massive publishing industry, but apparently had a lot of personal and business problems.

His company did not do so well after the crash in 1929, and he was scrambling for money during the depression. Some of his biggest assets were forest lands in the Northwestern U.S. (Hearst Paper and Timber). Because going back to hemp production as a major source for paper would pose a substantial threat to him, he used all of his media power to demonize marijuana. In fact, it was called hemp and marihuana before he popularized the new spelling in his newspapers to make it sound like an evil Mexican drug. He teamed up with America's first drug czar, Henry Anslinger, and published a number of false stories that helped solidify public opinion against marijuana as a dangerous drug. In his best known big lie, Anslinger called marijuana "the assassin of youth." This movement led to its effective illegalization in 1937 with the Marijuana Tax Act.

The propaganda machine has been effective for more than 70 years now as demonstrated by the fact that it remains a Schedule 1 drug. This ban certainly has a lot of supporters among whom I would surmise might be the big players in the alcohol industry, although I have no evidence to support that guess. And who else doesn't want competition from any legal psychoactive drugs? Yes, the makers of psychoactive pharmaceutical drugs. In fact, I bet they would like to see a return to alcohol prohibition so that the only way you could get high would be with one of their prescription drugs like Valium (which used to be called whiskey in a pill). Hopefully you may start to realize that much of what you have been told about marijuana is largely based on propaganda after you read the rest of this chapter.

Cannabis Horticulture
The most powerful psychoactive ingredient in marijuana is called THC (delta-9 tetrahydrocannabinol). It comes from the golden resin produced by the hemp flowers (especially the female plants) to protect the plant from heat and keep it moist. It can grow in a wide variety of soils and climates around the world.

The two primary species producing a psychoactive resin are C. sativa and C. indica. Growers in California have developed a hybrid plant with a more potent resin called C. sativa x indica over the last 20 years or more. Many growers remove the male plants at some stage to prevent pollination of the female plants. The resulting plants are then seedless and produce a resin with a higher concentration of THC. This type of marijuana is called sinsemillia (meaning "without seeds" in Spanish). A potent version smoked by some U.S. soldiers in Vietnam, called Thai sticks, had about 6% THC. Some California products these days contain as much as 16% or sometimes more. A new variety developed in the Netherlands in the early 90s had concentrations of up to 30%.

Marijuana may be the largest crop grown in California. Why do so many people take the chance? Because they can get $70 a bushel for it, compared to less than $3 a bushel for corn. In fact, marijuana is the largest cash crop in the U.S., and at least 25% of the marijuana consumed in this country is grown here. American marijuana growers make $32 billion a year tax free (the corn crop only brings in $14 billion a year.)

Even though we produce a lot of marijuana in the U.S., it only supplies about a third of our domestic consumption. Much of the rest is imported from Mexico across the border by vehicle. Most of our homegrown marijuana comes from indoor cultivation. This allows year-round growth, makes it easier to hide from law enforcement, and provides a higher quality product because the environment can be carefully controlled. If you want to start your own home business, there are many suppliers on the Internet who can give you everything you need. But remember that although this could be a profitable business, it's still illegal most places.

Hashish is a more potent form made by a process of beating the dried resin off the flowers and mixing it with sugar. It usually has about 10% THC but can go up to 20%. Because it requires many man-hours to process, cheap labor is essential for its production. Most of it comes from Afghanistan, Pakistan, and Nepal. Because our homegrown marijuana has gotten more potent and importing hashish is a hassle, it is not nearly as popular in the U.S. as it is in many other countries.

The most potent form is hashish oil, which can contain as much as 70% THC. The black oil is made by mixing cannabis leaves and flowers with a fat solvent such as alcohol or gasoline and boiling the mixture. The sediment becomes a brown or black oil that usually contains about 15–30% THC. It is heat sensitive and must be stored in dark glass vials. A drop or two on a cigarette can make it as potent as a joint.

Medical Uses

As I mentioned earlier, marijuana has been recommended by doctors for centuries for a variety of problems. Looking at more recent history, hundreds of articles were published in the U.S. and Europe in the second half of the 19th century recommending it for sleep, pain relief, muscle relaxation, and appetite stimulation. One of America's pioneering physicians, William Osler, recommended it in the early 20th century as the best treatment for migraine headaches.

Because barbiturates and aspirin came along at about that time, doctors began recommending them instead of marijuana for many problems. During the 1920s, authorities became concerned about people who were simply using weed to get high, which fed right into the prohibition movement that had outlawed alcohol. Once the depression started, a lot of Americans felt that Mexican immigrants were stealing their jobs in an environment of massive unemployment. Because marijuana was seen as a Mexican drug, the hostility toward them led to a movement to ban it. As mentioned previously, the Congress passed the Marijuana Tax Act of 1937 that effectively made it illegal. The ban was temporarily lifted during World War II when all farmers were urged to grow hemp for making rope and other products needed for the war effort. As soon as the war ended, hemp was again outlawed. 65 years later, it's still illegal in most of the U.S. except for medical marijuana in some states.

This illegal status was basically cemented in place with the passage of the Controlled Substances Act of 1970, which established the Drug Enforcement Administration. The DEA created five categories into which drugs would be placed. Schedule I drugs were those with no medical use, highly addictive, and highly prone to abuse. Heroin, marijuana, LSD, and other hallucinogens were placed in this category. Schedule II drugs had some medical use and serious potential for abuse and addiction. These included cocaine, morphine, Demerol, PCP, and methamphetamines. Schedule III drugs had common medical use and were less prone to addiction and abuse, like Vicodin, codeine, barbiturates, and anabolic steroids. Schedule IV drugs, like Talwin, Valium, Xanax, and Darvon, were considered to be less addictive and less subject to abuse. Schedule V drugs were cough medicines containing codeine. Despite a few changes, this system remains pretty much the same 40 years later.

It might be reasonable to assume from the previous paragraph that according to the DEA, marijuana is one of the most dangerous drugs known to mankind (especially since it has left this drug in the same category the whole time). It certainly looks as though it is more dangerous than cocaine, morphine, and meth since doctors can't even prescribe it. Because it does actually have legitimate medical uses and a low potential for addiction, this rating certainly did not go unchallenged. Many physicians in the early 1980s asked that it be moved to Schedule II so that they could prescribe it for some patients. The DEA agreed to hold hearings and listened to many doctors testifying to its safety and efficacy over the next two years.

In 1988 Francis Young, the administrative law judge for the DEA, after reviewing all available evidence, said that "marihuana, in its natural form, is one of the safest therapeutically active substances known to man." He agreed with many doctors that it had useful medical potential and ordered that it be moved to Schedule II. End of story and beginning of a new era—right? Wrong. His order was overruled by the DEA. Although doctors can fill out an application to study marijuana under a compassionate use provision, few do it because the process is so complex. Most won't get involved with prescribing marijuana in any way because they are afraid of losing their licenses.

The DEA's answer to this is that we have a legal drug that works just as well as marijuana for chemotherapy side effects and other problems. This is Marinol, a synthetic preparation of THC. The only problem is that hundreds of physicians and patients disagree. Among the patients was Stephen Jay Gould, one of the most famous biologists of the 20th century. Diagnosed with a rare kind of mesothelioma in 1982, he received many bouts of chemotherapy over the next 20 years before he died. He was a strong proponent of medical marijuana because absolutely nothing else worked for him. A research study in New Mexico compared marijuana and Marinol in 260 patients on chemotherapy and found that marijuana was clearly superior in controlling nausea and vomiting. It was also more effective than a potent antiemetic sometimes used by doctors, chlorpromazine (which itself is far more toxic and potentially dangerous than marijuana in my opinion).

So why isn't synthetic THC just as effective as marijuana for nausea and other problems? The simple answer is that THC isn't the only ingredient. All variants of marijuana contain 61 cannabinoids that are not found in any other plants. THC is believed to be the major psychoactive ingredient, but no one is really sure what all the other components are doing. What we do know is that cannabis contains 421 chemicals in many different classes. The smoking process may release hundreds of additional compounds. As is true of many psychoactive drugs, we don't know that much about it. Remember that research has been quite restricted over the last half century because of its illegal status and unrelenting claims by the government that it has no medical use. Meanwhile scientists are foraging around the rain forests of the world trying to find new miracle drugs from plants. Why don't we spend some of that research money studying the ones we already have?

Nevertheless, using what studies have been done, the prestigious Institute of Medicine in the U.S. conducted a comprehensive review of marijuana in the late 1990s. The report they issued said that marijuana had great potential for the management of pain, nausea, and decreased appetite caused by medical illnesses and their treatment. A position statement in the mid-90s by the AMA said, "At present, the greatest danger in medical use of marihuana is its illegality, which imposes much anxiety and expense on suffering people, forces them to bargain with illicit drug dealers, and exposes them to the threat of criminal prosecution." Not much has changed since them, I'm sorry to say.

Drug Effects on the Brain

The effects begin within several minutes when the drug is smoked, peak in 15–45 minutes, and then taper off over the next two to six hours. The main effects include euphoria and decreased inhibition, much as you get with low-dose alcohol. Marijuana also increases appetite, as alcohol usually does, and may cause some to feel woozy or disoriented. Unlike alcohol in most people, marijuana often creates increased visual and auditory awareness. Some may experience visual hallucinations as I did the first time I used it. The most unpleasant effect, especially for non-smokers, is dry mouth and throat.

Besides smoking, the only other route is oral intake. But there is a catch. If you just add marijuana leaves to your salad, you probably won't notice much of anything. The active chemicals require heat to release them so you need to boil the leaves and drink it as a tea or make sure that you get those brownies hot in the oven before you eat them.

How and why marijuana works on the brain has only been partially figured out in the last 20 years. Israeli researchers discovered a nerve receptor in the early 1990s that was specific for cannabinoids. Why would such receptors exist? This was the same question I previously asked about receptors for opiates. It turns out that just as we make chemicals that fit into opiate receptors, we also make our own cannabinoids. The first one identified was named anandamide based on the Sanskrit word "ananda" meaning bliss. A second major one was subsequently discovered.

We are still in our infancy in understanding what plant cannabinoids and those that occur endogenously in our brains may or may not do to learning, memory, or anything else. The most striking finding so far has been that marijuana receptors seem to be more common than opiate receptors. The one exception occurs in the brain stem where no cannabinoid receptors have been found so far. That is where the control center for breathing lies. Narcotics can suppress breathing and cause respiratory arrest, which is usually the cause of death in their overdose. This may help explain why no one has ever died of a marijuana overdose.

Addiction and Withdrawal
Very few marijuana smokers, even those who have been using it a long time, experience any withdrawal symptoms. A few will complain of irritability, restlessness, insomnia, and so on, but not many. This is a far cry from the hundreds of people I treated who were addicted to narcotics. Most of them went through four or five days of something like a bad case of the flu—nausea, vomiting, diarrhea, sweats, and so on.

Not only does marijuana not cause withdrawal symptoms for most people who use it, but it seems to have a reverse tolerance effect in a lot of people. That is to say that many trying it for the first few times don't seem to experience much of any psychoactive effect. For some this appears to develop over time, quite the opposite of most mind-altering drugs. Just another mystery for scientists to try to figure out.

Whether marijuana causes addiction is another disputed topic. Many experts believe that it does not cause physiologic addiction for the reasons I mentioned in the last two paragraphs, but that it does cause psychological addiction. From my point of view, if that is true, then it falls in the category of taking melatonin for sleep or maybe even shopping. If it is addictive, then it is far less so than the benzos in Schedule IV or the antidepressants that the DEA doesn't even mess with.

Medical Effects

From a medical point of view, marijuana has two primary negative effects. Like tobacco, it causes some lung damage. It deposits more tar and releases more carbon monoxide, cyanide, and other toxic chemicals including those known to be carcinogenic than cigarettes. However, this effect is probably negligible for occasional users. Three to four joints a week might have the same effect on the lungs as one or maybe two packs of cigarettes a week. Because many marijuana smokers inhale deeply, they take in as much as five times the amount of tar and carbon monoxide as cigarette smokers. By the way this practice of "toking" or taking a deep breath and holding it in the lungs as long as possible probably doesn't really affect the amount of drug absorbed very much. So don't waste your time on that little ritual.

The big problem with trying to compare the harmful effects of smoking marijuana versus cigarettes is that almost all marijuana smokers are cigarette smokers too. Finding a group to study that only smokes marijuana has proven quite difficult. Of course, if you are a pothead and smoke from the time you get up until you go to bed, the lung and brain damage could potentially be significant over a prolonged period of time, but I don't know of hard data to support that.

The other main side effect is short-term memory loss in some people. But it is temporary. Whether it might have long-term effects on memory, cause lung cancer, or do anything else is not really known for sure. Because of its illegal status for more than 60 years in the U.S. and many other countries, relatively little research has been done when compared with legal drugs. Hopefully much more research will be done in the near future.

My Drug History

Before I end this chapter, let me tell you about my own personal experience with drugs. Don't get your hopes up; it's not very exciting. I've used quite a wide variety of them on patients but haven't tried many myself. In case you didn't know, the rate of drug addiction is much higher among physicians than in the general population. This is primarily a function of two things—a high stress job and easy access to drugs.

My drug of choice has always been the legal one—alcohol. I have never tried heroin, cocaine, or any other illicit drugs. This is probably kind of unusual, given that I went to college in the radical 1960s. Despite that, I never had LSD, methamphetamines, or anything else along those lines. I did smoke a few joints in college but only remember doing it once.

It was at the beginning of my third year, and I had just spent the summer hitchhiking around Europe and taking a course in 18th century French literature at the University of Paris (La Sorbonne) for six weeks. Although I was pre-med, I was a French major. Other than getting a minor in chemistry, I only took the science courses required for applying to medical school because I figured I would get enough science training there. One evening, I was sitting in a friend's dorm room talking when he asked me if I wanted to try some marijuana.

After I smoked the joint, I sat and watched a slide show of my summer in Europe. Only there wasn't any slide projector in the room, and I didn't even have a camera with me that summer. As I stared at a blank white wall, my brain provided the entertainment for about an hour. I'm not sure whether this was some really potent weed that created the hallucinogenic effect or whether it had been spiked with a hallucinogen. Realizing that I could never be sure what was in it or the effect that it might have on me, I was quite reluctant after that experience to ever smoke a joint or try any other psychoactive drugs.

As a doctor, I have had easy access to narcotics and other controlled substances for many years. For example, when I did rhinoplasty surgery, I used pure liquid cocaine to anesthetize the inside of the nose. It would have been easy to pilfer off my own supply if I wanted to use it. Despite the relatively easy access, the only potent narcotic I've ever had was Demerol, before a colonoscopy. To me, that high was not pleasant at all. Of course, this could have been influenced by the fact that some guy was shoving a colonoscope up my colon before the drugs even started kicking in. I warned you this wouldn't be very exciting.

Buyer Beware

Despite my rather benign experience with it, don't get the impression that smoking marijuana doesn't carry any serious risk. It can be dangerous, especially if you buy it off the street. As with all drugs that are illegal, there is no quality control in their production. You can't really be sure what you're smoking. Blunts are a good example. These are cigars made from a mixture of tobacco and marijuana. But you might end up with a version called "woolah," made with crack and marijuana mixed together. Or perhaps someone may have tossed in some angel dust (PCP). Even if you are just dealing with ordinary unadulterated marijuana, there is a great variability in the street product.

Some studies have shown that decreased reaction times can last five hours and the overall effects eight hours after smoking a single joint. You know that you shouldn't drink and drive. Don't smoke and drive either. One car accident is all it takes to possibly ruin your life and maybe those of many others. Don't ever start smoking joints if you have other things you need to get done the same day. It won't usually wear off in an hour or two like a beer or glass of wine (even though you may think so).

Speaking of alcohol, I have admonished readers to never even try many of the drugs that I talk about in this book. To take the same position with marijuana would be hypocritical since I drink alcohol. With moderate use, it is no more harmful than alcohol in my opinion. The big problem is that it's illegal in most places for recreational use. So unless you live somewhere like Holland where casual use is not prosecuted, then that must be a major factor in your decision.

Even if you think marijuana will be safe for you, jail may not be. It can sometimes get quite dangerous. Just ask some of the patients whose horrendous lacerations I had to repair in jails. If you're considering using it for a medical problem that it could help, ask your health-care provider if it might be beneficial to you. If you do use marijuana, do it in moderation and use the precautions you would with alcohol, but even more so because a joint takes longer to metabolize in many people than one or two drinks do.

8

Opium, Opiates, Opioids

Herman was a 50-year-old white male I saw during jail sick call one night for a possible infection in his right arm. Noting his partially amputated left arm, I asked what had happened. He said that he had lost the lower two-thirds of his left arm when a drunk-driving lawyer hit him as a pedestrian. "You must have gotten a really big settlement for that," I said.

"Not really very much," he responded. "Only a hundred thousand."

"Well that's something. What did you do with it?"

"I shot it in my arm," he said, indifferently.

After obtaining this initial information, I noted track marks on his right arm and asked, "How do you manage to inject yourself with only one arm?"

"My friends do it for me. If I'm alone, I inject myself in the leg or groin."

"How do you support your habit?" I asked. "It must be expensive."

"Usually I just stand at intersections with traffic lights."

"I see a lot of people doing that, but I hardly ever see anyone actually give them money."

"Oh, they do," he said. "I make good money, usually about $30 an hour. I just flap my bad arm around and get more than most of the women. Anyway, I don't need to steal to pay for my habit. I don't use all the time."

"That's a good thing." I said. "By the way, I'm just curious. What does it feel like after you shoot up?"

"God, doc. You should know. You have plenty of drugs to use."

"Yeah, I do. But I've never gotten into them."

"What you need to try is a speedball, man."

"What's that?" I asked.

"Heroin and cocaine mixed together. Since you've never used drugs, you would be blasted for probably twelve hours."

"Sounds good, but I think I'll pass," I said. "Anyway, that red area on your arm is an infection but not an abscess yet, so it should go away with some antibiotics. You'll get them three times a day, and we'll check you again in two days."

"OK, doc. But I may be getting out tomorrow. Can I take the pills with me?"

"Unfortunately, we can't do that. You'll need to go to public health or a free clinic if you get out." He had dealt with many infections at injection sites in the past, so I wasn't concerned.

History

Opium, which comes from sap of the unripe pods of the poppy plant, is the parent of all narcotic drugs. Its use dates back at least 6,000 years to the ancient Sumerians in the Middle East who called it "the joy plant." Egyptian doctors used opium mixtures in some of their drugs and recommended its use for many ailments as outlined in the Thebes papyrus of 1552 B.C. The famous Greek physician, Hippocrates, gave it to patients in the 5th century B.C. for pain and probably other conditions as well. The court physician to Marcus Aurelius in the second-century Roman Empire, Galen, whose teaching became the core of medicine around the world for the next 1,500 years, recommended "opium eating" for many illnesses. The Romans not only saw opium as a pain reliever but as a pleasant way to end life. The famous Carthaginian general, Hannibal, always kept some with him and used it to kill himself. In the 1500s, a Swiss chemist created a liquid preparation that he called laudanum (meaning to be praised) by mixing opium with alcohol. This became a popular health drink in Europe for the next four centuries. Opium was also often dissolved in red wine.

Along with tobacco, the Native Americans gave another gift to the rest of the world—the pipe. Although ancient peoples had gotten high on marijuana and other drugs by smoke inhalation for centuries, this required inhaling fumes over a fire or sitting in a room or tent filled with smoke. The long pipe was sacred to Native Americans and so were the substances they smoked, especially tobacco. It had a yin yang kind of symbolism to them with the bowl at the end representing the female element and the long stem the male counterpart.

Pipe smoking in Europe and Asia quickly became popular because of its highly effective mechanism of drug delivery. When a drug is taken orally, it is exposed to gastric acid and intestinal enzymes before it is then carried to the liver whose job is to eliminate toxic substances as best it can. Many drugs lose much of their effect in this process. As I explained in some detail in the chapter on nicotine, smoking a drug is the fastest way to get it to the brain. Many people see that as a big advantage when it comes to mind-altering drugs. The combustion process also causes release of some intoxicating components that wouldn't be experienced otherwise.

The European version of the pipe adapted from the Americas was much more like those now in use. Although they worked well for tobacco which has what many smokers perceive to be a pleasant smell, opium was a different story. Apparently burned opium creates quite unpleasant bitter fumes that kept opium smoking from becoming popular in Europe. The Chinese found a way to make the smoking more tolerable by doing what the Native Americans had done. They created a two-foot-long hollow tube of bamboo which allowed for cooling of the smoke and making it less irritating when inhaled.

Opium had originally come to China through Arab traders in the 700s. Smoking of the drug didn't really start to catch on there for almost a thousand years, but when it did, China became the first country to develop a serious problem with opium addiction. The Chinese started to smoke opium heavily for the first time after tobacco was banned in the mid 1600s. The Chinese rulers eventually banned opium smoking in the mid 1700s, but the measures were unsuccessful.

By the early 1800s, there was so much crime and corruption associated with the opium trade that the government tried to ban its importation. The problem was that this policy had a huge negative financial impact on England. The British were addicted to tea, most of which was coming from China. Since the Chinese weren't buying much from the British then, a large trade imbalance developed. Once the British got a foothold in India, they found a solution to the whole problem. Britain sold manufactured goods to India which in turn sold opium and cotton to China.

When the Chinese said no thanks to this deal, Britain launched its first opium war in 1840 (which they called The War for Free Trade). Once they had seized Shanghai within two years, China caved in and gave them full access to the country as well as possession of the port of Hong Kong. Because of further Chinese resistance, Britain launched the second opium war with the help of France in 1856 that lasted four years. By the end of the century, half of the males in China were opium addicts, causing major devastation for that country. The bitter taste this left played a big role later in the Communist revolution.

The American Experience
Perhaps because the American Colonials were having too much fun drinking alcohol day and night, opium didn't become widely popular with them in the 18ᵗʰ century. That isn't to say that nobody was using it. Opium poppies were cultivated starting in the 17ᵗʰ century and valued for their ability to relieve pain or coughing. The resin was often dissolved in whiskey. Benjamin Franklin started taking opium for gout in the last years of his life and was supposedly addicted to it when he died. Some have claimed that he used it much of his life, but I have no idea if that is true.

Thomas Jefferson grew not only hemp but opium poppies at his home in Monticello. The opium garden was maintained for almost 170 years after his death. Seeds from all his plants including the poppies were sold in the gift shop until the early 1990s when the board of directors destroyed all the plants and burned the seeds. They became somewhat paranoid following a drug raid at the nearby University of Virginia. Although not likely to have happened, technically the property itself could have been legally seized under RICO laws at any point in recent history. (Some amateur gardeners continue to raise opium poppies because of their beautiful flower blooms. Somebody better tell them about the RICO laws and the war on drugs. Their property is not that of a revered former president.)

Interest in narcotics in the U.S. began to change in the 19ᵗʰ century following a pivotal discovery made by a pharmacist in Germany who isolated the most important of the twenty ingredients in opium in 1803. It was named morphine, after the Greek god of dreams, Morpheus (son of Hypnos, the Greek god of sleep). It was prepared as a white powder that could be mixed with water or made into tablets. The next crucial discovery came in 1853 with the hypodermic syringe. Drugs could then be injected directly into the muscles or veins of the human body, creating a more potent effect with more rapid onset.

When the American Civil War started in 1861, doctors had few medicines to use on soldiers in the field hospitals. Antibiotics were still some 70 years away from being discovered. All they could do for many of the wounded was to stop bleeding, amputate limbs, and give them morphine for pain. By the end of the war, at least 300,000 men were allegedly suffering from "morphinism," or morphine addiction (although some historians think this problem was "invented" to support the ban on narcotics after passage of the Harrison act in 1914). It was called "soldiers disease." (It is interesting to note that a century later about 80,000 U.S. soldiers in Vietnam actually did become heroin addicts. However, most of them took the drug to relieve psychological, not physical pain.)

By 1870, both morphine and opium were less expensive than alcohol. During the rest of the 19th century, many other Americans became addicted to opium. It was used in a wide variety of "patent" medicines sold to everyone without prescriptions (none of these had actually ever been patented since the ingredients were never revealed). Babies who cried too much or teething children were often calmed down with "Mrs. Winslow's Soothing Syrup" or the "Infants Friend." These preparations became so popular that overdose deaths were common. Sears Roebuck sold the "White Star Secret Liquor Cure," which was supposed to help people with drinking problems. Besides patent medicines, many middle- and upper-class women became addicted to the opium-containing drugs prescribed by doctors for a variety of ailments.

Heroin
At the end of the 19th century, German chemists at the Beyer Company added an acetic acid group to a molecule found in willow-tree bark to create aspirin. Native Americans had been drinking tea made with willow bark for centuries to treat headache and arthritic pain. This is an example of a semi synthetic drug. Pharmacologists alter the chemical composition of a natural refined drug to create a drug with different or more potent effects.

In 1898, Beyer began to market another drug, called heroin, which was purported to be twenty times stronger than morphine. This was made by adding two acetic acid groups to morphine (diacetylmorphine). It was marketed not only as a cough suppressant (especially for the rampant tuberculosis of that time) and a strong pain reliever but also as a miracle cure for morphine addiction. Over the next seven years, 40 scientific studies supported its effectiveness. However, they forgot to mention that heroin was also highly addictive.

At a time when we had no drug laws in 1900, some have estimated that there were 250,000 narcotic addicts in the U.S. (about the same as now as a percentage of the population (500,000) when considering illegal drugs, mainly heroin). The Harrison Narcotics Act of 1914 severely restricted the amount of opium, heroin, and morphine that could be used in non-prescription medicines. It also put limits on how doctors could use it; they weren't supposed to allow their patients to become addicted.

Since addicts were now faced with having to kick their habit, many "treatment farms" cropped up all over the country. They had a poor success rate, and many users fell into the black market. Criminals rapidly got organized in running their profitable businesses to meet the new demand for drugs that were now essentially illegal. Because of its potency compared to opium and morphine, small amounts of heroin could be easily hidden and smuggled. Probably for the same reason, it remains the drug of choice among many narcotic addicts to this day.

To further the crusade against drugs, the Federal Bureau of Narcotics was established in 1930. It's first chief, Harry Anslinger, a true antidrug crusader, did have some success in suppressing narcotics use in the U.S. over his 32-year reign. Tough drug laws were passed in the 1950s, providing long sentences for drug use and capital punishment for some drug crimes.

You all know about the wild 1960s when some of my fellow baby boomers turned this country upside down. (I was a good boy and did not participate in the chaos and turbulence. I just drank a lot of beer at fraternity parties.) The economy was robust and people had money to spend. Then came the civil-rights and anti-war protest movements, and all hell broke loose. Rock stars glamorized drugs, and many people turned to them in order to escape from all of our society's problems. They also wanted to snub their nose at a government they hated by using illegal drugs, including heroin.

During the 1960s, the most serious problem we Americans had was called the Vietnam War. Protests during the late 60s became a major threat to the new Republican President, Richard Nixon. He wanted desperately to quell the dissent, but that pesky first-amendment right to free speech and assembly was getting in the way. Not to worry. J. Edgar Hoover sent a memorandum to Nixon explaining that there was a way to control these protesters. That was by going after them on drug charges. Because many of them were using drugs like pot, LSD, and even heroin, the government needed a way to severely criminalize those drugs. The war on drugs really started out as a war on dissent. This led to the Controlled Substances Act and formation of the DEA in 1970.

Narcotics
In the field of medicine, narcotics are the bedrock of the treatment of serious pain. This word comes from a Greek word meaning "to numb." Although it is often used to refer to any illegal drug, such as cocaine, I prefer to and will stick to its real meaning. Any drug that is derived from or behaves like opium can be called an opiate (or opioid) which interacts with the opioid receptors in the brain. In the strict sense, all narcotics are opiates. Calling other illegal drugs narcotics is like calling them all dope. Maybe that works OK on the street but not in a book trying to educate people about drugs. I must admit that even the DEA uses the word loosely so maybe I'm fighting a lost cause on proper terminology.

The plant that made opiate drugs possible is called Papaver somniferum (from the Greek word meaning "poppy" and the Latin word meaning "bearer of sleep"). Growing to a height of four feet after a three-month period of maturation, the flower petals fall off leaving a green seed pod. It is usually one to three inches wide and will ooze a milky fluid when cut. When scraped off, this gummy substance is called opium. If the plant is allowed to mature, the pod will turn brown and the seeds can be collected and used in cooking. It is the unripe pod that yields the active drug. (Please note that even though poppy seeds you buy in stores or eat on your bagel won't get you high, they can result in your testing positive for narcotics on sensitive drug tests.)

The sap is raw opium that can be dried and rolled into a ball or crushed into a powder. This requires a lot of human labor which is not a problem in a poor country like Afghanistan, the main supplier of illegal opium to the world. Legal opium powder is produced using machines on special farms licensed in various countries (mostly France, Spain, Australia, and Turkey) by the pharmaceutical companies. We Americans consume 45% of these legal opiate drugs even though we only have 6% of the world's population. I guess we have a lot more pain problems than the rest of the world despite having 25% of its wealth. Just something to think about.

Medical opium is usually broken down into its three main constituents—morphine (4–20% of dried opium), codeine (1–5%), and thebaine (less than 1%). Each of those is then converted into one or two other drugs that are used in their own right. Morphine was the first drug extracted from a plant and serves as the gold standard for the treatment of pain, although it also has other important medical uses. Even though morphine is used in medicine on a wide scale, most of the opium is synthesized into codeine and other opiates. Although codeine can be refined directly from opium, that's not where most of it comes from.

I'm sure that many of you have taken codeine (methylmorphine), which is often useful orally for pain but not nearly as strong as morphine. It is clearly the most common narcotic used in the world. (Codeine is the most effective safe treatment for a horrible, persistent cough; I took it one time for a few weeks after I broke two ribs when I was first learning to snowboard and then developed a bad bronchitis. Coughing when you have broken ribs and are trying to treat patients or operate is not a lot of fun).

Other commonly used narcotics are hydrocodone (probably best known as Vicodin), and hydromorphone (Dilaudid). Although hydrocodone is six times as strong as codeine, hydromorphone is six times stronger than morphine. The latter is often obtained illegally to use as a substitute for heroin. Oxycodone (Percodan) is another commonly abused prescription drug which I will deal with shortly in its sustained released form Oxycontin.

Some narcotics are purely synthetic, like Demerol, which is not derived from opium. These are usually referred to as opioids because they are made in laboratories rather than being produced directly or indirectly from opium as is true of the opiates I just discussed. One of these drugs that is not used in medicine because it is way too potent is etorphine. Ten thousand times as strong as morphine, it is used primarily in dart guns to immobilize huge animals like rhinos and elephants.

Another synthetic opioid is fentanyl which is a hundred times more potent than morphine but still safe for humans when used properly, both in anesthesia and for pain relief. Other opioids include propoxyphene (Darvon) which is about half the strength of codeine and used for mild pain. I won't get into the subject of opioids used mainly as maintenance drugs for narcotics addicts such as LAAM and methadone.

Attempts to produce designer drugs in illegal labs have not been very successful and have unfortunately led to development of analog drugs that are often sold on the street as fentanyl and other narcotics. These can be extremely dangerous. I wouldn't ever take anything like that unless you have a strong death wish. Sorry to keep repeating myself, but don't buy street drugs unless you're not concerned about toxic reactions, brain damage, or possibly death. If you think your life sucks now, just wait—street drugs can take you to a whole new level of pain.

Lock and Key

The mechanism of action of the opiates wasn't really understood at all until the 1970s when the so-called lock and key interaction between various opiate drugs and the corresponding receptors in the brain were discovered. Three subtypes of opiate receptors called mu, delta, and kappa are widely distributed throughout the body. Pain relief was initially thought to be localized to or mediated through the brain, but subsequent research demonstrated that it not only involved the spinal cord but more peripheral sites. For example, morphine injected into the knee can relieve pain without any brain involvement.

If this lock and key explanation seems as simple to you as putting key in a lock and opening a door, it's not. This is a radical oversimplification of something that is far from being well understood. Although many scientists try to make it sound that way, take it from a pharmacologist and physician who has been a leading researcher in this field his whole life, Avram Goldstein, M.D. In his book *Addiction*, at the end of his chapter on this topic, he admits that "scientific knowledge about brain receptors is still a work in progress." I would consider that to be a huge understatement as I will discuss at greater length later in this book.

Street Science

In addition to pain relief, their primary effect is to cause relaxation, drowsiness, and suppression of the cough reflex. Narcotics make the pupils constrict and can cause sweating and nausea (they stimulate the vomiting center). Some heroin users know that they've gotten a good batch when they puke after they shoot up. Wow, that's exactly how I'd like to start getting high. And the way you can tell that you overdosed is if you wake up on a cold metal table hearing a coroner describing your body. You see, you can be quite scientific when figuring out how to use street drugs.

Addiction and Withdrawal

The model of drug dependence came from observing opiate addicts who exhibit the three characteristic features of physiologic addiction—craving for the drug, tolerance, and withdrawal symptoms. I will talk about the sedative-hypnotic drugs later in the book such as sleeping pills (barbiturates like Seconal and non-barbiturates like Quaaludes) and the minor tranquilizers (like Valium and Xanax). However, I would like to point out that heroin and other narcotics are safer than many drugs in the sedative-hypnotic class, especially when talking about long-term use.

One reason for this is that a narcotic user develops rapid tolerance to both the active dose and the lethal dose at the same time. This means that it is easy to get addicted but hard to overdose. A patient after surgery receiving morphine every four hours could develop mild dependence within a couple of days. This might result in symptoms of sweating, nausea, headache, or restlessness after the drug is stopped.

Tolerance to narcotics can develop quickly and reach striking levels. Tincture of opium (laudanum) was popular in Europe and England during the 18th and 19th century. Approximately 100 drops a day in divided doses would be effective for relief of pain. Thomas De Quincey, who published his book *Confessions of an Opium Eater* in 1824, used up to 8,000 drops each day. This would kill anyone who did not have tolerance for the drug. He first used opium for a toothache in his early 20s and remained addicted his whole life until his death at the age of 73.

Tolerance to the lethal dose develops more slowly in many sedative-hypnotic drugs, making overdose a more common problem. Heroin addicts who die of overdoses usually do so because of the poor quality of street drugs and many dangerous contaminants that may be in them. Or they may accidentally get a batch that is almost pure heroin, exposing them to a huge dose that they can't handle. (Drug dealers sometimes sell pure drugs or contaminated drugs in the territory of their competitors. The competing drug dealer then gets a bad name on the street after some of his usual buyers die of an overdose. Yet another good reason not to buy and use street drugs.)

Here is another big advantage heroin has over many of the drugs in the sedative category. The withdrawal symptoms are not that serious and certainly not life threatening. Having treated hundreds of heroin addicts in jail, I can assure you that their four- or five-day withdrawal period is no worse than having a bad case of the flu. They feel like crap—nausea, vomiting, sweating, diarrhea, and body aches. Some drugs (like clonidine and compazine) will help alleviate the symptoms, and usually on the fifth or sixth day, they are back to normal and drug-free. (Just as is true with the flu, some people may still not feel completely normal for a week or so after the major symptoms go away.)

In contrast to narcotics, many of the other depressant drugs like alcohol, barbiturates, and benzodiazepines can create violent withdrawal symptoms, including convulsions, and sometimes even end in death. As far as organ damage goes, opium (taken orally) would be my drug of choice if I were forced to become chronically addicted to one drug for the rest of my life. Perhaps this will be a punishment for crimes in a future society. Except for the brain, it does not damage other organs.

As far as brain damage goes, I have taken care of many long-term heroin users who did not display any obvious mental impairment or neurological abnormalities. Sensitive nuclear medicine brain scans might pick up some abnormalities in certain people, but you certainly do not get the same kind of obvious brain impairment that often comes with alcohol abuse. The only peripheral target organ affected by narcotics is the colon. Chronic alcohol abuse can cause cerebral and cerebellar degeneration, heart disease, cirrhosis, pancreatitis, and a host of other diseases. Narcotics cause constipation because they inhibit bowel function—that's pretty much it. An occasional laxative and you're good to go.

As you can see, heroin's portrayal for many years starting in the tumultuous 60s as the "devil drug," the most evil and dangerous of all drugs is pure crap. This is just more propaganda from the drug warriors who are knocking down those harmless martinis at their fancy Washington parties. Because it is a Schedule 1 drug (along with marijuana and LSD), it can't be prescribed by doctors in the U.S.

However, it can be legally prescribed in England and almost 50 other countries, where doctors often use it instead of morphine. Because of its greater potency, lower doses can be used to avoid the unpleasant and sometimes severe nausea that comes with morphine. I can tell you from experience that no surgeon who has just closed up someone's midline incision following abdominal trauma wants to see his patient vomiting his guts out postoperatively and possibly opening up the incision. It is also commonly used in the treatment of cancer patients with chronic pain. Because it is more potent than morphine, it can sometimes relieve severe pain without having to knock the person out with the higher, more sedative doses of morphine.

Now, do I recommend that people try heroin as a recreational drug? Hell no. I will say the same thing I said about cocaine. The first rush you get may be all it takes to drag you into a very expensive and dangerous habit (because it is illegal, you may end up in jail, and dirty needles lead to bad diseases).

Oxycontin

Oxycontin is probably the most widely abused prescription medication in the U.S. Its active narcotic drug is oxycodone which is the same drug found in Percodan. The difference is that Oxycontin is designed to create a controlled release of the drug over a prolonged period. It is mainly indicated in the treatment of severe chronic pain such as metastatic bone cancer. It should not be used for short-term problems such as postoperative pain or chronic pain of indeterminate origin, such as many musculoskeletal problems. Those who really need narcotics are better treated with drugs like Percodan or Vicodin.

An Oxycontin pill bought on the street could be five times what it costs from a pharmacy. Although it has sometimes been referred to as the poor man's heroin, it is actually often more expensive when purchased illicitly. Many people begin abusing Oxycontin that their doctors have prescribed for some medical problem. As long as the doctor keeps doing this and an insurance company pays most of the drug cost, it can be a cheap addiction. However, when the supply is cut off, some of these people then start using heroin to avoid withdrawal.

One might think that Oxycontin would be safer than heroin or other street drugs because it is a high-quality, pharmaceutical-grade product. Alas, such is not the case since most users are not well versed in pharmacology. When you crush the pill to snort, drink, or shoot it up, the controlled release effect is destroyed. You get the full dose all at once, thereby increasing the prospect of adverse effects or overdose.

The Halsted Legacy

Before I tell you about a great surgeon, let me talk about one who wasn't so great. When I was a junior resident in general surgery assigned to neurosurgery, I learned about the resident supervising me during my first day on the job from the nurses. He was a neurosurgery resident who had supposedly just returned from a vacation. It turned out that he wasn't really on vacation but in some kind of drug rehab program. And this wasn't the first time he had left under similar conditions.

Apparently he was a Talwin addict. Talwin is a potent synthetic narcotic that he was taking both in pill form and by intravenous injection. He was taking drugs at work and, according to rumor, frequently went to the operating room high. He was not very secretive about his problem; the nurses would sometimes find broken glass from the i.v. Talwin containers on the bathroom floor after he'd been seen coming out. Sometimes he prescribed Talwin to patients who were being discharged and then would take half of their pills to keep for himself before they left the hospital. He never completed the program and like many doctors with drug addictions didn't do so well in his medical career.

In contrast, William Halsted was a brilliant young surgeon practicing in New York City in the 1880s. As Freud had already begun doing, he started experimenting with cocaine on his patients, primarily to test its effectiveness as a local anesthetic. As happened with Freud, he began using it himself and became addicted. During his recovery period, he was invited to come to the newly created Johns Hopkins University to do research. When the hospital opened in 1893, he was appointed the first chief of surgery.

Over the years, he went on to develop an entire new approach to surgery, which is now widely practiced throughout the world. He also played a major role in getting American surgeons to accept the concept of antisepsis and the germ theory of disease that the great Scottish surgeon Joseph Lister had been mostly unsuccessful at doing for many years in England and Europe. Halsted was the first to introduce the practice of using rubber gloves in surgery.

So why would I include this story in this section on narcotics? After his death in 1952, a shocking secret was revealed, much to the surprise of the hundreds of so-called Halstedian surgeons trained by his residents, many of whom had gone into academics and become famous in their own right. It turned out that Halsted had continued abusing drugs throughout much of his professional career. He didn't go back to cocaine but instead developed a liking for morphine. This pioneer in surgery was a chronic drug abuser. So I don't want to hear any more propaganda about the inevitable slide into hell that always follows any kind of drug use or addiction.

But let's look at something else. How did Halsted's chronic drug abuse differ from that of the average heroin addict? The answer is this. He had access to a high-quality, uncontaminated pharmaceutical-grade narcotic that he could correctly dose and thereby avoid any adverse consequences. Not only were his colleagues unaware of what he was doing, but he also managed to have a more productive and accomplished life than most people who have never used either drugs or alcohol.

I am not suggesting that the average person should try using drugs to become more productive or creative, but under the right circumstances, some people can remain quite functional despite a drug or alcohol "problem." To avoid any confusion about this last statement with my actual belief about the use of psychoactive drugs, let me say this. No one should look to any mind-altering drugs to transform his or her life in some magical way to avoid life's trials and tribulations. On the other hand, if you have as much intelligence and talent as Halstead did, then maybe you can deal with a chronic drug habit. But don't get your hopes up—not many have succeeded in that attempt.

9

Hallucinogens

One day at the start of my shift in an ER, a man was brought in by paramedics with a full-blown psychosis. He has been placed in restraints and was yelling incoherently on his gurney. Fortunately his girl friend was with him and able to provide a detailed account of what had happened. She was a librarian at a local college where he was a history professor. They had been invited to a party by some of his students who asked him if he wanted to try a marijuana cigar. His girlfriend explained that he had smoked marijuana a few times in the past but never got much of an effect from it so he thought it would be harmless to do this time.

She was inside talking to several students drinking a glass of wine while he sat outside on a balcony smoking. A short while later, he came inside and seemed disoriented and confused. When things quickly got worse, she panicked and called 911.

I explained to her that his cigar had obviously been laced with something besides marijuana. We kept him restrained as he continued to hallucinate for the next several hours. We closely monitored his vital signs and gave him small doses of benzodiazepines occasionally to try to calm him down. We kept him in a dimly lit room and asked his girlfriend to stay with him and constantly reassure him that he was being taken care of and would be OK in order to minimize the potential paranoia that an ER and lots of strangers would create.

When he finally came out of his trip and was coherent, I explained what had happened. He was embarrassed and profusely apologetic for having caused such a major scene. I told him that he was lucky nothing worse had happened and related my own experience with a marijuana cigarette in college. My hallucinatory experience was actually calm and somewhat pleasant, but he had obviously smoked something much more potent than just marijuana. The students who gave it to him probably had no idea what was in it either. I doubt that he ever repeated that experience.

LSD

Hallucinogens are drugs that generate or cause hallucinations. Supposedly the word hallucination is derived from the Latin word alucinare, meaning "to wander in mind or talk idly." Since that's what a lot of us do everyday free of drugs, I think they should have picked a better word. But I guess we're stuck with it.

They are also called psychedelics. You may know that psyche comes from Greek meaning mind. The entire word means "mind manifesting" or "mind revealing." Do psychedelic drugs really reveal something profound about the mind itself other than it can hallucinate? Do we really need to take such drugs to find that out? I don't think so on either count. People experiencing various forms of psychosis, and most notably schizophrenia, frequently have hallucinations of all sorts with no drugs in their brains. Although we haven't identified them precisely as we have with some neurotransmitters, it seems reasonable to assume that we might make our own hallucinogens.

Early man may have discovered hallucinogenic plants even before alcohol. Most of these plants are indigenous to the Americas, where natives have been using them for thousands of years.

The pharmacological effects of these drugs are widely variable in terms of their ability to induce hallucination. The circumstances under which they are used have a big effect on the experience. What they have in common is that they are potent stimulants. I will only focus on several of them and have chosen to split them into two major categories. The LSD-type drugs are less dangerous physically and more likely to cause just psychological problems. Those in the belladonna family of drugs can certainly have adverse psychological effects but are also much more likely to cause dangerous physiological changes with intoxication. If you must take a trip, I would suggest the former group unless your goal is to end up in a wheelchair or a coffin.

The drugs that fall into the first category would be LSD, mescaline (from peyote cactus), psilocybin (from mushrooms), and dimethyltryptamine (DMT). DMT gives the shortest trip of an hour or so, while psilocybin usually lasts two to four hours. LSD can last eight hours or more and mescaline somewhat less time. Something interesting to note is that the chemical structure of mescaline is not like LSD, psilocybin, or other hallucinogens that resemble serotonin. The structure is closer to that of amphetamine. More about the chemistry issue shortly.

First, I want to dispel some myths. People do not overdose on these drugs; they do not get addicted to them; and they do not suffer from damage to body organs. Although the DEA must have a secret but logical reason for making drugs like LSD Schedule I drugs that are supposed to be very addictive and highly prone to abuse, I haven't been let in on it.

History

The first mention of hallucinogenic substances dates back to Hindu Vedic scriptures (some written as far back as 1500 B.C.) in which they not only proclaimed the virtues of marijuana but magic mushrooms as well, especially Amanita muscaria. Somewhat later circa 500 B.C., a cult developed in Greece centered around the Temple of Eleusis in Athens. Relatively few people were initiated into the secret organization including such notables as Sophocles, Plato, and Aristotle. It continued for centuries and included famous Romans such as Cicero, Marcus Aurelius, Hadrian, and others. The rites were kept secret by a threat of death to those who joined the organization and then later revealed them.

The secret was never uncovered until the 1950s when a possible explanation was suggested by a Swiss chemist named Albert Hofmann. He was studying a mold that sometimes grew on rye and wheat. It was believed to be the cause of a number of poisonings throughout Europe at that time as well as in many previous centuries when it was called "St. Anthony's fire." The offending drug in the fungus was ergot. This drug was also probably responsible for the strange behavior that led to the burning of hundreds of thousands of "witches" in the middle ages. What Hoffman discovered was that ergot contained at least 30 alkaloids, many of which he synthesized. The Eleusian mystery had been solved. The ancients were drinking a potion that contained hallucinogens. The likely culprit was ergonovine, one of the few components that can be easily extracted in water. It is used in obstetrics to stimulate uterine contraction, but much higher doses than those used medically can produce LSD-like effects.

The most famous drug that Hoffman discovered was LSD, the story of which he later recounted in a book called *LSD, My Problem Child*. Working for the Sandoz pharmaceutical company in Switzerland in 1943, he had sudden strange effects overtake him one day. He went home and experienced a dreamlike state seeing incredible pictures and colors. He decided that the LSD-25 he had been working with had somehow gotten absorbed through his fingers. He then went back a few days later to conduct an experiment on himself. He took what he thought would be the smallest possible dose that could cause any effect, dissolved it in water, and drank it.

Within a half hour, the visual distortions he had experienced a few days before returned. He asked his assistant to ride home with him on their bicycles (which was the main mode of transportation because of wartime gas rationing). Although he experienced gross perceptual distortions on the way home, his assistant later told him that he appeared quite normal. He went on to have a fantastic but at the same time somewhat terrifying trip.

This is not surprising given that he took what would be considered these days to be a rather large dose (250 micrograms). When it was released for experimental clinical use in psychotherapy as a tablet and injection several years later, the dose was reduced to 10% of what Hoffman took.

It was used through the 1950s and early 60s in several ways. The first was as an adjunct to psychotherapy, presumably to help break through inhibitions and repressions or maybe precipitate a major breakthrough for the patient. How well this worked, I don't know. It was also used extensively as a treatment of alcoholism. Bill Wilson, the father of AA, took it a number of times himself. Although its use may have yielded positive results for some people, the U.S. government put an end to the whole experiment by outlawing LSD for any use when it was made a Schedule I drug in 1970, along with heroin and marijuana.

LSD and other hallucinogens were also used in the 50s and 60s to create mystical experiences. This concept was popularized by Aldous Huxley who associated these drugs with the *Tibetan Book of the Dead*. His own book *Doors of Perception* later became a guidebook to Timothy Leary and many of the hippies in the 1960s. LSD was also used with those suffering terminal illness. Huxley himself took his last trip on his death bed (from throat cancer) when his wife gave him his final dose.

That same 25 microgram dose in the original pills would be a reasonable starting dose for someone trying out LSD for the first time now (although experienced users might take 5–10 times that much or more). Some researchers maintain that the psychedelic effects don't kick in until 50 µg and are proportional to the dose up to about 500 µg. People don't

OD with higher doses but the trip may last longer. (There was one possible overdose in someone who injected 320 mg intravenously, which is a hundred times what would be considered a high dose for anyone taken orally.) However the effects can differ widely from person to person using the same dose. Similarly the same person may have dramatically different effects with the same dose at different times.

Because of its incredible potency, a few drops can be applied to blank paper which is often then printed with cool designs or cartoons and perforated into small squares called tabs, each of which constitutes one dose. Remember that these are all produced in illegal labs, and unlike cocaine and some other drugs, it is a complex drug to manufacture. The usual dose is about 20–50 μg per tab as measured by police agencies. However as is true of all illegal drugs, they come with no guarantees and you can't buy them with pay pal or credit cards and request a refund if you're not happy with the product.

To put its potency in perspective, LSD is hundreds to thousands of times more potent than most other hallucinogens. Compared to the original 25 μg dose, an average postage stamp weighs 60,000 μg or the equivalent of 2,400 doses of LSD. Two gallons would be enough to stone two to three hundred million people.

Unlike most other mind-altering drugs, tolerance to LSD develops rapidly. For example, if someone used 100 μg two days in a row, he might need 200 μg the next day to get the same effect. Cross tolerance develops between LSD and mescaline which is hard to explain since they are chemically quite different. However there is no cross tolerance to other drugs such as amphetamines, marijuana, and PCP that have substantially different mechanisms of action. This tolerance is lost quickly, usually within 3–4 days.

The duration of action goes something like this. The initial sympathetic effects begin shortly after taking an oral dose but may not start for two hours and peak at 4–5 hours. Most people feel these effects for about eight hours although it may take 12 hours to get back to normal, at which time a lot of people just crash and sleep for a long time. Many feel bummed out the next day. For all these reasons, most people don't use LSD more than once a week, once a month, or just occasionally.

Pharmacology

Unfortunately, I (we) don't know much about this. However according to the experts, LSD, mescaline, DMT and other psychedelics work their magic by overwhelming the serotonin receptors in the brain. Specifically they bind to both the type 1 and type 2 hydroxy-tryptamine (serotonin) receptors in the locus ceruleus and cortex. LSD also binds to a different receptor (5-HT1A) that the others don't, which scientists think may account for some of its unique characteristics.

But the bottom line is that they all work by inhibiting the action of serotonin in a major part of the brain. In medical terminology, they are serotonin antagonists. What really happens is that when these drugs first hit the receptors, they cause a massive release of serotonin which is then followed by a prolonged depletion of the neurotransmitter. But wait a second. I thought that decreased serotonin in the brain leads to depression. Now they're saying that it causes hallucinations for up to eight hours or more. I'm so confused by this brain chemistry stuff. Could somebody out there please help me?

Trust Me—I'm a Witchdoctor

One of the hallucinogenic drugs coming out of the jungle plants of South America goes by various names but is commonly called Yage. Here is a small part of a letter that William Burroughs wrote to Allen Ginsberg in 1953 about his first few experiences with that drug: "I have taken it three times (1st time came near dying). A large dose of Yage is sheer horror. I was completely delirious for hours and vomiting at 10-minute intervals... The old bastard who prepared this potion specializes in poisoning gringos who turn up and want Yage."

So you see. You can't always trust witch doctors. Maybe they're more trustworthy than those supplying illegal drugs on the street, but I wouldn't bank on it. After all the warnings I've given, you're hopefully starting to get a little paranoid about taking any street drugs. But wait until you get to the chapters on legal prescription drugs. Hopefully if I have done my job, you'll be leery of taking those too without a lot of information about what you may be getting into.

Sorry to be a party pooper and sound a little negative, but all drugs are potentially dangerous (some obviously more than others). Maybe if you think that when you take a legal pharmaceutical drug prescribed by a doctor, you're completely safe and sound. Wrong. Thousands of people in the U.S. die every year because of adverse reactions to drugs they were given by mistake. Thousands more die from reactions to drugs that were prescribed but not indicated for the problem they had. Yet thousands more die from reactions to drugs that were appropriately prescribed but which happened to cause an unexpected allergic reaction.

The danger levels go up dramatically with street drugs, but all drugs can be potentially dangerous and even fatal. Don't take them causally. Just so you know that I practice what I preach, the only drugs I've taken in the last ten years (besides alcohol) have been antibiotics a couple of times for dental infections. I'm not opposed to drugs if they are taken appropriately and carefully, but that's not what many people taking legal or illegal drugs are doing.

Nightshade Plants
This family of plants contains some harmless and even healthy foods such as potatoes, tomatoes, peppers, and eggplant. A less healthy member is tobacco and dangerous plants in this group are datura, henbane, and mandrake. Probably the best known is a plant called Datura stramonium (Jimsonweed), which got its common name from a mass poisoning of settlers in the Virginia colony of Jamestown in the 1600s. The new colonists were not familiar with many of the New World plants and put some of these Datura leaves in their salads. Although the plant was originally called Jamestown weed, it eventually was corrupted into Jimsonweed.

The active ingredients are atropine and scopolamine, the so-called belladonna alkaloids. (Belladonna means beautiful woman in Italian; apparently females in the Middle Ages were considered pretty if their pupils were dilated. Atropine causes the pupils to dilate.) The major brain effects are due to scopolamine which easily crosses the blood-brain barrier. What are these effects? They often induce what can only be called a strange delirium or dream. (For this reason, some experts place them in a separate category from hallucinogens, called deliriants.) What's really great about this kind of high is that most users develop amnesia for much of the experience. What more could you want? Instead of getting high on LSD and recalling most or all of the experience later, you may risk your life to have a hallucinatory experience that you won't even remember.

Am I exaggerating here? No. These drugs can cause a shutdown of the entire parasympathetic nervous system. The user gets a tachycardia, extreme dry mouth and thirst, hot, dry skin, dilated pupils making bright light painful, and sometimes a dangerous rise in body temperature in addition to the agitation, disorientation, and hallucinogenic effects. The physical effects may take 12 to as long as 48 hours to wear off. By the way, Jimsonweed and mandrake are not illegal in the U.S. (despite the fact that you can go to prison for growing a vastly safer drug, marijuana). The most common use for scopolamine as a medical drug is in skin patches used to prevent motion sickness. Even though the nightshade plants are legal, do not ever take these "natural" drugs for a mind-altering experience.

Peyote and Mescaline
The molecular structure of mescaline is almost identical to that of amphetamine which itself is closely related to methamphetamine. Ecstasy, which I will talk about next, is also closely related to amphetamines. Nevertheless, the effects of these two drugs are quite different for reasons that elude me.

Although archeological evidence suggests that peyote has been used in North America since about 8,500 B.C., it didn't come to the attention of the Europeans until Cortez launched his conquest of the Aztecs in the early 1500s. The conquistadors were not happy about this drug that supposedly made the natives they wanted to conquer fearless. Later that century, these drugs and all religious practices were severely suppressed. Although its use became less widespread, it continued for the next few centuries.

In the late 1800s, dried buttons from a peyote plant were sent to chemists in Germany. One of them spent a great deal of time isolating the many alkaloids and then ingested them himself to determine what effects they had. He named the psychoactive compound mescaline. It was synthesized a little more than 20 years later, which led to its first widespread use outside of Native Americans. Most other people were turned off by the terrible taste and nausea and vomiting that comes with ingesting peyote buttons. The pure drug avoided the nasty side effects, prompting various artists and writers such as Allen Ginsberg and Aldous Huxley to start using it. Mescaline never caught on in a big way though because it was difficult to make; it was overtaken by more readily available hallucinogens like LSD and psilocybin. They are not only much easier to make but vastly more potent as well. When people buy what they think is mescaline off the streets, they are usually not getting what they think they are; most of the samples tested have proven to be LSD or LSD mixed with PCP.

Although it is legal to grow the deadly nightshade drugs in the U.S., that is not true of the much less dangerous peyote plant. It is legal in many parts of Europe but not used very much for reasons mentioned previously (most people do not enjoy copious vomiting). However, there are some exceptions allowing its use legally in the U.S. Many states protect religious users of peyote such as members of the Native American Church. Even the U.S. military permits its almost ten thousand American Indian soldiers to use peyote if they want to. They are also allowed to answer "no" when asked if they use any illegal drugs. A pentagon spokesperson explained the policy this way in the late 1990s: "If they're using peyote in their religious practice, it's a sacrament, not a drug, just as sacramental wine is not considered a drug." Wow, I'm glad I learned that. I always thought that alcohol was a drug regardless of why it was being consumed. Meanwhile non Native Americans can go to jail for growing or using peyote for any reason in many U.S. states. If you want me to explain this policy to you, forget about it.

MDMA (Ecstasy)
After the discovery of amphetamines in the late 1800s, pharmaceutical companies were interested in creating variant drugs that might have potential use in humans. MDA was synthesized in 1910 and in 1912 Merck took out a patent on a related molecule called MDMA (the MA stands for methamphetamine). Although they were hopeful that this could be used as an appetite suppressant, animal tests didn't seem to bear this out, so it never got used on humans.

It was forgotten about for the next 40 years until the CIA decided to investigate psychoactive drugs as potential agents for use in interrogation and possibly warfare. They were not impressed with it. The next time MDMA came to light was in 1978 when a chemist described its ability to make people become more sociable and friendly. Psychiatrists started to use it in therapy and especially marriage counseling. Although they called the drug "empathy" initially, it was later given the name "Ecstasy." Because of widespread street abuse and testing showing possible brain damage in animal studies, the DEA made it illegal by putting it in Schedule 1 in 1986.

Since Ecstasy is not approved for any medical use and illegal, many designer derivative drugs have been developed, often by amateur chemists, and sold for many years on the streets. More than 200 such drugs have been synthesized and given many names such as STP (for serenity, tranquility, peace), Eve, DOB, DOET, 2C-B, and so on. Very few of them are still being used and some of the most toxic were only abandoned after a number of deaths were well publicized. How could you possibly know which variant of Ecstasy you are getting? A biochemist at Dow Chemical named Shulgin synthesized many of these drugs and tried them on himself. That's the only way I know of that you could really be sure of what you were taking.

Most of the Ecstasy drugs are made in Europe and smuggled into the U.S. This is a much more profitable business than heroin because the cost of production is less than one cent per tablet. The wholesale price is around a dollar or two and the street price twenty times that. Almost half of pills sold as Ecstasy are something else. A common substitute is dextromethorphan, a cough suppressant that causes hallucinations and sometimes psychosis in high dose ranges; doses of 130 mg are sometimes found in fake Ecstasy pills (that is 13 times the dose you take for a cough). It has another side effect of inhibiting sweating, which can lead to heat stroke as young people dance the night away at a rave party.

Mechanism of Action
Although MDMA increases brain levels of dopamine, serotonin, and noradrenalin, it appears to release more serotonin than the other two. It acts partly like an amphetamine but also like a hallucinogen; wild hallucinations or dramatic changes in visual perception don't usually occur in lower doses but can in high doses. How does this drug cause a feeling of intimacy with others in addition to euphoria in lower doses? Take your best guess. I have no idea.

What we do know scientifically is that sudden death can occur in people who lack a specific enzyme (cytochrome P450-246) required to properly metabolize MDMA. One British study showed that 1 in 12 people are missing this enzyme. Could you be one of them? (14 Ecstasy pills are enough to kill most people; in someone susceptible, one will do the job.)

One of the big issues with these drugs is the question of nerve damage and neuron death. Although amphetamines can potentially kill neurons in high doses, it appears that MDMA and its variants can do this in normal doses based on animal studies. Although this question of brain damage is far from resolved, chronic heavy use may lead to memory impairment, which has led to the labeling of some users as "E-tards" by their friends and fellow drug users.

The fun doesn't always end after a rave weekend. Then you can look forward to what many users call Terrible Tuesdays. The symptoms can include abdominal pain, anxiety, muscle aches, extreme hunger, exhaustion, serious depression, and even suicidal ideation. Doesn't that sound like a great way to end a weekend of partying? I haven't had a hangover in years, but I'll take a Terrible Monday anytime.

To counteract the potential problem of neuronal damage, some drug experts have suggested that you combine your Ecstasy with Prozac to help decrease the damage to serotonin-releasing neurons. I have no idea why they think that would work or be beneficial, but my recommendation is that you don't take either of these drugs for any recreational purposes.

Magic Mushrooms
Plants are not the only place you can find hallucinogenic drugs. They also are found in the fruiting body of a fungus, commonly called a mushroom. The main hallucinogenic drug coming from them is psilocybin, whose name is derived from the Greek words "psilo" meaning bald and "cybe" meaning head. About a hundred species of mushroom contain this drug. One of the most commonly used in the U.S. is Psilocybe mexicana.

Although the Spanish explorers were aware that the Aztecs were using such mushrooms for various rituals, not much was known about their history until the mid 1950s. A wealthy banker named Gordon Wasson became obsessed with this topic and discovered that psychoactive mushrooms had been used extensively in Europe, Asia, and North America for the last ten thousand years. Hoffman, who discovered LSD, got interested in Wasson's studies and extracted the two psychoactive ingredients psilocybin and psilocin. He was still employed by the Sandoz Company who manufactured psilocybin for use in psychiatry. Although the pharmacology is different, the mind-altering effects are similar to LSD.

Just as people were starting to enjoy these mushrooms in the 1960s, they were made illegal when psilocybin and psilocin were made Schedule I drugs under the Controlled Substances Act of 1970 (along with LSD, heroin, and marijuana). There is a loophole in the law in most states, although California closed it in the mid 80s. The spores from which the mushrooms grow do not contain these drugs, so they are legal to buy and grow yourself (but not in California). Even the mushrooms are not illegal per se, unless you are growing them or in possession for the express purpose of getting high. You can buy complete kits on the Internet. It takes about six weeks to grow them.

I do not recommend the use of any hallucinogenic drugs and would caution you about trying to grow mushrooms yourself. Unless you are an expert in this area (or know someone who is), what you end up with may not be what you are expecting. Even an expert can't guarantee you anything. Cultivated and wild mushrooms can vary greatly in drug potency. The strain you grow because you got such a good high from your buddy's mushrooms may have ten or twenty times the potency his did.

This is the same reason you shouldn't try to pick these mushrooms where they grow wild. Also many mushrooms contain toxic poisons. Do you know how the Buddha died? As the story goes, someone accidentally put poisonous mushrooms in his dinner bowl when he was 80 years old.

The main safeguards against poison ingestion for humans and other animals are smell and taste. If something smells bad or tastes bitter, you won't eat it if you're smart. But not only does a poisonous mushroom often smell and taste just fine, you sometimes can't tell there's a problem even after it's been in your body for a while. For example, Amanita phalloides can cause severe liver damage within a few hours. You might not have any idea there's a problem until you start to go into a hepatic coma a few days later. Unless you can line up an emergency liver transplant, you're pretty much dead.

Drugs sold on the street as a specific psychedelic may actually be contaminated with other drugs. Or the drug may be completely different from the one you think you're getting. Studies from ERs in some US cities have shown that about half of the people who thought they had taken LSD actually had been exposed to something else. Magic mushrooms often turn out to be mushrooms from a grocery store that have been laced with LSD or PCP. One study showed that less than a third of street-bought mushrooms actually contained psilocybin; about a third were tainted with other drugs, and more than a third had no drugs in them (that's the kind I like to ingest). If you got a magic mushroom with LSD instead, your trip would be longer than expected. If you got PCP, you might end up deciding to take a nap on some train tracks. I hate to bore you to death by repeating myself, but this is why illegal drugs are so dangerous. Do not buy street drugs or accept them from friends or anyone else. That's my advice. Take it or be ready to suffer the consequences.

10

Inhalants and Anesthetics

During the last few months of my six-year general surgery training program, I faced my greatest challenge of the entire residency. The newly opened trauma unit at UCSD became the responsibility of the surgical service I was in charge of. Although trauma was a recognized subspecialty of general surgery, we had no trauma surgeons on our faculty at that time. The chief of surgery overseeing the service hadn't done much trauma surgery in quite a while. The unit became my responsibility, and the staff surgeons trusted me enough to run the entire show with their backup when I asked for it.

Although I took care of many patients with major multiple trauma during that experience, one of the most frustrating was a young man who had a rather bad experience while on PCP. He was a 20-year-old Mexican male who had been in the San Diego area for a few months living with friends while he worked at whatever jobs he could find. One of his buddies introduced him to PCP. Although we never found out the exact circumstances of what happened, he was brought to the trauma unit in critical condition. The paramedics reported that he had been lying down with his legs across one track when a train came by and ran over him.

Needless to say, he had severe crush injuries to both legs requiring amputations. He went on to develop adult respiratory distress syndrome that took him to the brink of death, but we managed to get him through it. After months in the hospital, he was eventually well enough to be sent back to Mexico. The hospital was reimbursed very little by the county or any other organizations and took a massive loss in providing his care.

That was hardly the first time I had seen what tremendous problems we had with our U.S. health-care system. However, I didn't fully understand until then what a huge financial drain trauma patients are on the hospitals. That was 32 years ago, and we still have major trauma centers being forced to close because of inadequate funding for the critical but very expensive care they provide. As far as I'm concerned, trauma surgeons are some of the greatest heroes of medicine and deserve much more respect than they currently receive in our society. Their patients also deserve better access to care than they now have many places.

Inhalants

Organic solvents that can produce psychoactive effects when inhaled are widely available as glues, paint thinner, lighter fluid, and gasoline. These are the first drugs many children experiment with and sometimes get addicted to. Adults consider it a cheap high and have much better options. Another thing that people of any age should keep in mind is that organic solvents are highly flammable. Facial and body burns are not pleasant and the after effects can last a lifetime.

Most inhalant sniffers are between the ages of ten and seventeen, with some as young as five or six. Children should be taught that using inhalants is bad for them. However, parents should know that from a practical medical view, occasional minimal use of inhalants is not likely to cause any serious medical problems in most cases. Chronic long-term exposure is a different matter (such as that experienced by factory workers in poor countries who may breathe toxic fumes for years). As is true with other depressant drugs, inhaling solvent fumes can impair judgment and coordination as well as cause disorientation, frequently leading to accidents. Overdoses can sometimes lead to unconsciousness and death.

Adults do use some inhalants. The most common ones are generally called poppers (amyl or butyl nitrite). Amyl nitrite is a potent vasodilator originally used by doctors to treat symptoms of coronary artery disease. It was discovered by a Scottish physician in the 1800s. Other better drugs like nitroglycerine pills and paste are now used for people with chest pain. Amyl nitrite is also an antidote to cyanide poisoning and is carried for that purpose by first responders. Although using these drugs to get high was outlawed by Congress in 1990, they are sold without regulation over the counter as a "room odorizer." A hit from a popper causes the veins and arteries to quickly dilate, often resulting in a drop in blood pressure, a throbbing sensation in the head (or even a bad headache), and sometimes dizziness. Doesn't that sound really cool?

It is commonly used, especially among gay men, to enhance sexual arousal. This is mainly true among young gay men. Why would healthy young guys need to use a drug to get an erection? Don't ask stupid questions. It's because they are high on uppers.

Methamphetamine is a vasoconstrictor, which means that it shrinks down arteries and veins. In order to get hard, the penis needs a good blood flow into the dorsal artery so that the veins can get engorged. So if a guy is high on a vasoconstrictor drug, he needs to take a vasodilator to compensate for that. In order to be absolutely sure things will work, especially if he's really cranked up, he might also decide to take a Viagra pill (also a potent vasodilator) a half hour before he has sex.

Combine all these drugs with some alcohol and wild dancing and guess what happens? His blood pressure may suddenly drop out, causing him to lose consciousness. Or his heart might develop a fatal arrhythmia, and he may finally get to come out to his parents—lying on a slab in the morgue. Whatever happened to just having sex without taking drugs? For most people, it's pretty good all by itself. Don't use any of these drugs.

Dissociative Anesthetics
Although general anesthetics used in surgery are mind-altering drugs, most of them are not used recreationally. The first general anesthetic was nitrous oxide, or laughing gas, discovered in the late 1700s. It creates a light anesthesia and was not suitable for major surgery. Chloroform and ether were discovered within the next 60 years and ushered in the era of true general anesthesia. Parties using all these drugs were popular during the 1800s.

Two synthetic drugs that first came into use in the 1950s in anesthesia have now become popular illegal drugs; these are PCP (phencyclidine) and Ketamine. PCP acts by causing a dissociation of the mind from the body. Under its anesthetic effect, people still retained some degree of consciousness, but were not concerned that someone was taking out their gallbladder, for example. Because many complained about their bizarre state of consciousness and postop psychosis occurred in some people, its use was discontinued in humans in the early 1960s. (It continued to be used in animals—they don't complain).

It soon appeared on the black market and was sold as a pill or in powder form. It got its street name "angel dust" because many users experience a feeling of power and invulnerability along with decreased or sometimes no sensitivity to pain. Many young and especially poor people use it because they like the effect of being disconnected from reality. The dissociative state comes with higher doses and the user often becomes oblivious to the environment around him. This may be accompanied by visual and auditory hallucinations and sometimes violent behavior. Many cops consider people on PCP to be the most dangerous drug users to deal with. Users who overdose can rapidly go from acting crazy to being poorly responsive to coma. The user often has amnesia for the entire event, as was true for my patient that I described in the beginning of this chapter. Some may remain in a delusional state for a week or more after their trip.

Although it may sound appealing to some, feeling no pain and being disconnected from your body can produce some quite unpleasant outcomes. As if the story I related at the outset wasn't bad enough, one of the most horrifying things I ever saw was a well-documented case of a teenager who had mutilated himself while high on PCP. This kid got a knife and began carving off pieces of his face. As he threw each piece of flesh on the floor, his two dogs ate it. When he was done, most of his face was a bloody skeleton. Now that was a really bad trip. Don't ever use PCP.

Because it is cheap and easy to make, it is often substituted for other drugs to the unsuspecting buyer or put in ordinary mushrooms, which are sold as expensive magic mushrooms. Or maybe the joint someone gives you at a party has been sprinkled with PCP. Most of the labs making it in the U.S. are controlled by gangs, and they aren't known for their excellent quality control. Don't take PCP unless you have a death wish. Even then, don't do it—you may just end up with fewer body parts and decide you want to live. Also take note of the fact that some users experience auditory or visual hallucinations for years.

Ketamine, also called Special K and many other names, is a middle- and upper-class version of PCP. It is still used as a human anesthetic agent despite the fact that its pharmacology and action are much the same as PCP. It comes in an injectable form producing an altered state of consciousness within a few minutes and lasting about an hour. When I worked in burn units, anesthesiologists used it frequently, especially with children when we did quick, painful procedures.

Recreational users of ketamine are sometimes professional people who are able to take precise doses of pure material. It was legal and not a controlled substance until the DEA put in the Schedule III in 1999 because of widespread abuse. Nevertheless it is relatively easy for people with money to obtain and is popular from Bangkok to Moscow to New York, especially among teenagers. As is true for PCP, ketamine can be swallowed, smoked, or snorted (as it is at many rave parties and gay dance clubs). Why can't people just get high on the house music and dancing (or maybe some alcohol)? I guess that's asking too much of a lot of people. Hopefully you're not one of them.

Some ketamine users have described the feeling of being cut off from reality as "going into a K-hole." The FBI used to publicize what they thought was a catchy phrase that would appeal to kids and teenagers: "Only losers use drugs." Some people responded with this: "Only users lose drugs." Here's my contribution to the world of witty phrases: Why be an A-hole by trying to go down into a K-hole when you won't even remember what happened later anyway?

11

Depressants

Maria was Hispanic female speaking pretty good English who came into sick call for chest pain and palpitations a day after she was arrested. After talking to her briefly, I realized that she was there to get me to prescribe Valium. She said she had been taking it for a year for depression and anxiety. Following a careful history and physical exam, I did an EKG. Everything was normal. I told her I would put her in the infirmary next to the nursing station so that the nurses could watch her for the next 24 hours and run another EKG anytime she was having palpitations. I asked the nurses to try to verify her story by obtaining medical records. Unfortunately she said that her doctor was in Mexico making it highly unlikely that we would be able to get records and verify her story.

When I saw her the next day, she had not complained about any more palpitations. I asked her exactly how much medication she had been taking and she seemed to be clearer on it than the day before. She had been taking 10 mg about four times a day. That's a large dose, and, if true, it meant that she was probably addicted and tolerant. However there were several factors that decreased my concern. First of all, I found out from the deputies that she was in for a minor charge related to prostitution and would probably be out in a few days. Secondly she was taking a long acting benzo (if her story was true), and she would be unlikely to have any significant withdrawal symptoms during her time in jail. If she was going to be in for a month, I would have much more concern because she could develop serious problems during that time, possibly requiring hospitalization. My suspicion was that she really was taking Valium as she claimed but probably getting them off the street or from a drug store in Mexico, not from a doctor. When she got out, she would be able to get them again. Problem solved. Not hers, but mine. As a jail doctor, you want to do the right thing but also be practical.

The topic in this chapter is the treatment of anxiety—with drugs of course. Or maybe you are having a problem sleeping. From a medical point of view, I'm talking about what is usually classified as sedative or hypnotic drugs. By far the most common in this group are the benzodiazepines like Valium and Xanax, followed by the more potent ones like the barbiturates that are much less commonly prescribed these days. Many of these drugs fall into a category called minor tranquilizers that stand in stark contrast to the major tranquilizers like Haldol and Thorazine that are used to treat various mental disorders, usually falling into the category of psychosis of one kind or another. I will not get into the issues of major tranquilizers or the treatment of psychosis in this book. (However I will refer you to books that do deal in depth with that subject on my website for those of you wanting to know more about it.)

My main focus here is benzodiazepines (less formally known as benzos) because they have been and continue to be some of the most commonly prescribed drugs by all physicians, not just psychiatrists. Even though they are also called minor tranquilizers, there is nothing minor about their intended effects and side effects as you will see. The name comes from the fact that the chemical structure involves the fusion of a benzene ring with a diazepine ring. I had a minor in chemistry in college and have extensively studied the chemistry and pharmacology of the drugs I am writing about. However I doubt that many readers will be all that interested in those details. That's why I haven't made a big issue of chemistry and molecular structure in this book. My goal is not to impress you with what I know but with what I don't know, despite my education, training, and experience.

Humans have been plagued for centuries and even millennia with sleeping problems, stress, and anxiety. A thousand years ago, some people in the Americas may have been awakened or kept awake by howling wolves. Now it is more likely to be the trains coming through town all night blasting their horns every half hour. Not being able to sleep leads to stress and anxiety. And most people can't blame their insomnia on wolves or trains. It's the chattering mind that keeps them awake. The most commonly used drug to relieve such problems for the last few thousand years has been alcohol for most people. Other natural drugs like marijuana and opium were also used for such purposes.

Nowadays, we refer to pharmaceutical drugs used for anxiety and sleep problems as hypnotics or sedatives. When you are awake and alert functioning normally, your brain waves usually operate in a range of 10–20 Hertz (cycles per second). The fully awake beta brain-wave state is usually 13–30 Hertz. In order to fall asleep, you must go through a transition into a state of self-hypnosis moving from the beta state into the slower alpha state of 8–12 Hertz. This alpha state can be achieved through various techniques of meditation and self-hypnosis. You can still remain aware of what's going on around you in this relaxed state. However if you fall asleep, you have usually moved into the theta and delta states of less than 8 Hertz. This is what sedative and hypnotic drugs help you do pharmacologically. You take a pill and get relaxed or maybe fall asleep depending on the drug and its dose. (By the way, you can also accomplish this without drugs using breathing techniques and self-hypnosis. I do this whenever I have trouble sleeping. It doesn't always work but usually does.)

What kind of pill should you take if you just want to relax or feel less anxious, but you have to stay highly functional (at work, for example)? Therein lies the problem with all sedative/hypnotic drugs, including alcohol. The transition from being relaxed, to getting sedated or stoned, or maybe even falling asleep (aka passing out) is a slippery slope. It is easy with many of these drugs to go way beyond just getting relaxed, especially if you are not being extremely careful of how much you consume and how often.

Since most of you have familiarity with alcohol and its effects (even if you don't drink), you know what I'm talking about. One or two beers will relax you, but five or six may knock you out, depending on your sex, body size, tolerance, and other factors. When a pharmaceutical company claims that their new drug was developed strictly for sleep, they are giving themselves way too much credit. Sedative hypnotic drugs relax you in lower doses and put you to sleep in higher doses. Very high doses lead to coma and sometimes death.

The sedative drugs were dominated by the barbiturates during much of the 20th century after first being introduced in the early 1900s. Many have been synthesized and marketed but relatively few of these are still in use as sedatives, hypnotics, general anesthetics, and anticonvulsants. They fall into several categories related to their onset and duration of action. The ultra-short acting drugs such as Pentothal can induce general anesthesia within a minute of i.v. injection. Short and intermediate acting drugs like Seconal are used for sedation or sleep. Longer acting ones are usually prescribed for seizure disorders.

Much like alcohol, when excessive doses are taken, they can cause impaired judgment, loss of motor coordination, and slurring of speech. In contrast to what I discussed in the chapter on narcotics, once someone becomes addicted and tolerant to most barbiturates, the margin of safety gets very narrow. In other words, the effective dose and the lethal dose come closer and closer together. Then when you increase your dose because you're not getting the effect you want, you can overdose or maybe even die by accident. More than a few celebrities have done this.

When benzodiazepines were first marketed in the 1960s as Librium and Valium, they were touted as being much safer than the barbiturates. Although they did not cause the same level of respiratory depression or risk of overdose, a lot of other things turned out over time to be similar. Chronic high-dose use can cause irritability, hostility, confusion, impaired memory, amnesia, and depression. Withdrawal symptoms from most sedative drugs can be severe.

At the lower end of the spectrum come anxiety and insomnia, usually the reasons the drugs were started in the first place. The most severe withdrawal syndrome is delirium tremens, a truly life-threatening problem, unlike those seen with narcotics like heroin and stimulants like cocaine. Although I used these drugs frequently for sedation when doing surgery under local anesthesia, I'm not going to talk about such uses in this book since their utilization in a hospital setting is not relevant to most people taking them as prescription or recreational drugs.

No Longer Popular or Illegal

Chloral hydrate, the oldest pharmaceutical sedative, was first synthesized in 1832. It was sometimes added to alcohol to create the infamous "Mickey Finn" (preceding current date-rape drugs by perhaps 150 years). It is still used widely in children to sedate them before various medical or dental procedures.

Methaqualone (aka Quaalude) was released in 1955 as another sedative alternative to barbiturates that was supposed to be much safer. It did well for a few decades but fell into disrepute with the American government because it was frequently abused by young people, often college students, who just wanted to "lude out" by mixing it with alcohol. The DEA then moved it into Schedule 1 of the Controlled Substances Act in the mid 1980s, making it illegal for doctors to prescribe any more.

What remains out of favor but still widely abused as an illegal street drug is GHB (gamma hydroxybutyric acid). It is often used by bodybuilders because it supposedly helps increase muscle mass by causing release of growth hormone from the pituitary gland. Whether that is true, I have no idea. It is also used to get high or drug others. Sometimes people at raves or nightclubs just add it to their alcoholic drinks to make them more potent. This may be the most commonly used date-rape drug in 2010 since Rohypnol (aka roofies) has never been legal in the U.S. and may not be as easy to get (usually through Mexico where it can be easily obtained).

Duration of Action
The short-acting benzos have a half-life of 1–8 hours (like Versed and Halcion). They are the ones usually used for sleep problems. People using the intermediate longer-acting ones may experience residual effects the next day feeling lethargic. On the rare occasions when I have taken benzos marketed for sleep (when I had an injury), I felt as though I had a mild hangover the next morning. Librium and Valium are the longest acting and can stay in some people's systems a week or more with a half-life ranging from 40–200 hours.

The longer acting benzos are often used in the treatment of panic disorder or generalized anxiety disorder, but treatment should be limited to a few weeks in most people. Long-term therapy with these drugs is generally not effective according to many studies and can result in many problems with dependence and withdrawal.

There are many other medical reasons to use benzos besides anxiety and insomnia. These include seizure disorders, sedation of patients on ventilators, to prepare people for general anesthesia, to minimally sedate people undergoing procedures under local anesthesia, and others. Those are the main reasons I have used them throughout my medical career. I must admit that I can't remember ever giving a prescription to a patient who was simply having problems with anxiety, so I don't have personal experience treating anxiety disorders with anything other than talk therapy (usually with friends or family members).

Side effects and Withdrawal Problems
The most common side effect is decreased mental alertness or even drowsiness. Remember, these drugs are CNS depressants. They can interfere with learning and remembering new material and sometimes cause

amnesia. Older people are prone to develop dizziness and coordination problems that may result in injuries. People who are mildly depressed may go into more serious depression when taking these drugs. As is true of alcohol, driving skill can be seriously impaired.

Tolerance and dependence to benzos can develop within a short period of time in some people. Even after a relatively short course of a few weeks, sudden dose reduction or discontinuation of the drug can result in rebound or withdrawal symptoms. Rebound is something you may have experienced before with sprays you used for nasal congestion. When you stop using the spray, you might end up with more congestion than you had before you started using it. Similarly if you start taking benzos for panic attacks, they might come back and get even worse after you quit.

Withdrawal symptoms can range from mild to dangerous. Many doctors are not familiar with the serious withdrawal problems and handle the drug discontinuation inappropriately or poorly. Patients should be advised to not just stop cold turkey because they run out of meds. These drugs need to be tapered off to prevent problems. The most common symptoms are insomnia, agitation, GI symptoms, and anxiety. Even when the medicine is slowly tapered, about 10% of people will experience a prolonged period of withdrawal that may last for months, but sometimes a year or more.

The same thing sometimes occurs with people trying to get off of antidepressants. If you are on both kinds of drugs and trying to get off of them, it can become a long nightmare. Even after some people have gotten off of benzos, they may have some mental or neurological impairment for a year or more. Be very careful before you start taking sedative drugs and have an end point established within a few weeks of starting if at all possible. A number of people who have become addicted to these drugs have ruined marriages, lost businesses, declared bankruptcy, or worst of all ended up committing suicide. Don't get on them casually for a few weeks to deal with life problems that you could handle in other ways without drugs.

12

Antidepressants—The New Cocaine

Several years ago, one of my friends called me just to talk, as we did every few weeks. He had gone through a bad divorce and a child custody battle that he lost about five years before that but had gotten through it all and been OK since then. All of a sudden, he said that he had an embarrassing problem that he wanted to ask me about.

"What's going on?" I asked.

"I can't come."

"What are you talking about?"

"I like to jack off at least once a day, but I haven't been able to come for the last week."

Without hesitating for a second, I asked, "Are you taking an antidepressant?"

"How in the hell did you know that?"

"You didn't say anything about this the last time we talked."

"I know. I was too embarrassed to tell you."

"How long have you been on it?"

"A month."

He told me the whole story at that point. Because of a change in insurance providers, he had to switch to a new internist who would perform his annual exams. He didn't have any medical problems at that time. When he went to her, his blood pressure was mildly elevated and he mentioned that he had been feeling a little down the last couple of weeks because he was going to have to switch jobs. She told him that he had hypertension and was depressed. She wrote him a prescription for an antihypertensive drug and an antidepressant.

"Your new doctor doesn't know what she's doing. You do not have hypertension or depression and you should not be on any drugs. I'll find someone else who takes your insurance for you to see."

I knew a lot about hypertension because I had developed a protocol for treating that problem within the entire San Diego jail system after I was put in charge of quality assurance and supervising all the physicians working in the system. Every doctor seemed to have his own way of treating high blood pressure and we needed more consistency. One of the cardiology residents, who moonlighted with us, told me that my protocol was better than the one they had at the University Hospital.

I had worked closely with psychiatrists in the jails and seen many patients being treated for depression. I had also done a lot of research for many years on that subject because of all the psychological problems my mother had. Long story short, I told my friend to get a blood pressure cuff and monitor himself for several months to establish whether or not he had hypertension. If he did, I would recommend further tests to see if there was any cause that could be corrected. If not, I would start him on a diet and exercise program to see if he could get rid of it without resorting to drugs. I also told him how to quickly taper off his antidepressant. His ejaculation and blood pressure problems quickly disappeared.

However when he sent me copies of his records, I noticed a slight abnormality on one of his blood tests that his doctor had dismissed as insignificant. It jumped out at me the moment I saw it. When I spoke to the internist I referred him to, he agreed to do a complete workup. It turned out that my friend had a serious but treatable liver disease and was referred to a hematologist. He has undergone extensive medical treatment but fortunately is still doing well some seven years later.

Although the name antidepressant sounds as though these drugs are targeted at the treatment of depression, they are also used to treat a wide variety of other problems. These include anxiety disorders, eating disorders, OCD, and various chronic pain syndromes, to name some of the most common ones. They are also sometimes used to supplement stimulant drugs in ADHD. Many people with substance abuse problems of all kinds are put on them. I have read that antidepressants are almost passed out like candy in some alcohol rehab clinics. They are even used to treat minor problems such as snoring. So it would seem that they must be very useful medicines that pose relatively little risk to those using them (low risk-to-benefit ratio). Before we consider whether that is actually true, let's look at a little history of the treatment of depression and other psychiatric problems.

History

As I mentioned earlier, cocaine was touted as a miracle drug for depression by a man who suffered from that problem himself, Sigmund Freud. It was widely prescribed in Europe in the late 1800s and early 1900s for everything from severe depression to shyness, making it the first prescription antidepressant of modern times. It eventually fell out of favor because it was found to be addictive. This also occurred because it became a drug of abuse when people began to snort it or use it intravenously, not for any therapeutic reason, but to get high.

From the early 1900s into the 1950s, psychiatrists in the U.S. developed far more toxic ways to treat psychiatric illness. They spent those years conducting experiments on patients in insane asylums and then extended that practice into the general population. Although schizophrenia did not respond very well to many treatments they developed, depression seemed to. They started with insulin shock and then stumbled on drug-induced convulsive therapy (because epileptics don't appear to get depressed, it only seemed to make sense to turn depressed people into epileptics with drug-induced shock therapy.) Then they discovered the miracle of electroshock therapy that was much easier to administer, although many patients got broken bones and other injuries during their seizures that were sometimes induced several times a day over a period of weeks.

The doctors were able to show in the many people who died that various kinds of injury occurred to the brain as result of these treatments. A leading psychiatrist of the day in the 1930s coined the term "therapeutic brain damage" to explain how and why these treatments were successful for a variety of psychiatric illnesses. They finally found a way to better control the area of damage when a Portuguese doctor named Moniz published his results with frontal lobotomy. (He later won a Nobel Prize for that great discovery.)

This operation proved a big boon for many neurosurgeons who had a hard time finding enough patients to support their practices. They started off by drilling holes in the temples and inserting instruments to lacerate the brain tissue at various points in the frontal lobe to separate it from the rest of the brain. (They didn't actually open up the head and remove the frontal lobes of the brain, as the name might suggest to some people.)

Although these were relatively short operations, one neurosurgeon developed a technique that would allow him to do it in less than twenty minutes. First he shocked the patient, and then during the postictal (unconscious) period after the seizure, he stuck an instrument that looked like an ice pick through the boney orbit above the eye and moved it around to lacerate the frontal lobe (first on one side, then the other). Because it was easy and he had more business than he could handle in the mental hospitals, he started teaching psychiatrists with no surgical training to do the procedure.

Although you might assume that this practice was confined to dark wards with hopeless patients locked away in mental hospitals, you would be mistaken. The medical profession and the press touted frontal lobotomy as a miracle cure for depression and other psychiatric illnesses. Doctors published glowing papers about the incredible recoveries that many patients experienced with almost no serious side effects. The depression went away and they were back to normal, having suffered no ill effects from major damage to their frontal lobes.

Consent was almost never required for these procedures. Whether the patient wanted it was often not a consideration. This was even true for outpatients. For example, if parents were concerned about their 22-year-old daughter's mild depression for a month after breaking up with her boyfriend, they could take her to a doctor and request a lobotomy. Her consent was not required and the procedure was sometimes done for such problems.

During the 1940s and early 50s, more than 20,000 people underwent lobotomies in the U.S. Eventually the truth came out about all of the lies being used to promote this procedure (although it was still used somewhat more selectively for several more decades). Many of the people suffered permanent debilitating side effects, as you would expect when a major part of the brain that makes us human is at least partially destroyed. (If you want to read a much more complete history of our horrifying treatment of the mentally ill in the United States of America since its inception, get Robert Whitaker's well-written and well-documented book *Mad in America*. It's on my list of recommended books on donaldchapin.com with a link along with his new book, *Anatomy of an Epidemic,* the epidemic being psychiatric illness.)

New Era
Thank God, we finally came out of that dark era and got back where we were fifty years before that—treating psychiatric problems with drugs. We

initially started using methamphetamine-like drugs such as Benzedrine and Ritalin (methylphenidate). Then we developed the major tranquilizers (also called neuroleptics) like Thorazine for psychosis and schizophrenia. Having seen many patients taking those drugs as a jail doctor (not to mention my own mother), I can say confidently that they create a temporary chemical lobotomy. The person often goes from saying and doing crazy things to being a compliant zombie.

Our armamentarium continued to grow with minor tranquilizers (benzodiazepines like Librium and Valium for anxiety). These were marketed as being better and safer than the barbiturates that had been used for anxiety, pain, sleep, depression, and so on for fifty years. During the 50s and 60s, we developed the MAO inhibitors and tricyclic antidepressants. However, the real breakthrough didn't come until 1988 with the release of Prozac. For the next ten years this was touted by most psychiatrists and almost the entire media as a miracle drug, with occasional serious dissent that was mostly ignored.

What did this new class of drug do? It was called an SSRI, which stands for selective serotonin reuptake inhibitor. Here's what happens. Neuron A releases serotonin into the synapse with neuron B. After it has stimulated neuron B, the neurotransmitter is then reabsorbed into neuron A so that neuron B does not get over stimulated. If you block the reuptake of serotonin, then stimulation continues. Because many neuroscientists believe that depression results from an inadequate release of certain neurotransmitters, it only makes sense that increasing their presence will cure the problem.

As was true of the many papers proclaiming the miracle cure for depression called frontal lobotomy, some facts were missing with Prozac and subsequent SSRIs. These are called side effects and long-term effects. Since the clinical trials testing these drugs rarely last more than 6–8 weeks (sometimes only 4 weeks), long-term effects may not become apparent for many years. Nor can scientists determine whether they are addictive and associated with withdrawal symptoms since the patients are rarely followed after the trial stops. Such problems are usually not discovered until years later.

Another interesting dilemma to consider is this. Many doctors will tell you that antidepressants will take 3–4 weeks to kick in. Ask them why and they can't explain it. (At least I can't.) But if the trial that proved it's effectiveness only lasted 4–8 weeks, how does that work? Have you ever had a doctor tell you that it was going to take a few weeks for your insulin, antibiotic, benzo, or sleeping pill to kick in?

As for long-term effects, time has shown that these drugs cause many problems besides just significant withdrawal symptoms; such side effects include anxiety, depression, and suicidal ideation, often mistaken for persistence of the original problem for which the drug was started. The percentage of patients experiencing withdrawal symptoms varies from a low of 14% with Prozac to a high of almost 80% with some of the newer drugs. The drug companies have paid millions of dollars in secret settlements following trials involving terrible problems that were directly related to these drugs, the worst examples being suicide and homicide.

Even though SSRIs caused some problems, the next breakthrough came with antidepressants that not only block the reuptake of serotonin but noradrenalin (norepinephrine) as well, such as Effexor and Serzone. Now if we could just find one that affects dopamine. Hooray, we did it—Wellbutrin (as well as Zoloft—don't want to shortchange that company). Now if you take a two-drug cocktail such as Wellbutrin and Effexor, you've got the big three feel-good neurotransmitters kicked up in one package. What could be better than that?

SAD

How about only one drug that does that? That is going to be the next big breakthrough—a drug that blocks the reuptake of all three neurotransmitters (and a cash cow for the first company that releases it). Let's call it the Super Antidepressant Drug. But wait a second—we already have that. It's called cocaine. It blocks the reuptake of dopamine, serotonin, and noradrenalin. It also supposedly directly stimulates their release, and when it comes to feel-good neurotransmitters, more is better (at least according to a lot of the biopsychiatrists). And now that we know that all of the current antidepressants are addictive and have associated withdrawal symptoms of varying degrees, we don't need to worry about that issue as some kind of negative problem.

If you want me to convince you that all this BS about neurotransmitters and depression is mostly hype and marketing by the pharmaceutical companies, consider this. Some of the tricyclic antidepressants in wide use before Prozac were touted as blocking reuptake of two of the big three neurotransmitters (serotonin and noradrenalin). In fact when Prozac was introduced, the pitch was that it was a selective blocker that only affected serotonin. This made it sound somehow safer with less of a shotgun approach.

But then along came Zoloft that not only blocked reuptake of serotonin but dopamine as well. In order to compete, it was marketed as Prozac with a punch. And so it went with new drugs like Effexor that blocked noradrenalin uptake as well as serotonin (just like eight of the tricyclics had done for many years previously, such as Elavil). Are you beginning to see that the marketing of these drugs is all smoke and mirrors designed to confuse and deceive not only the public but many physicians as well? The fact is that nobody really knows much about brain biology and biochemistry. Certainly I don't. There are at least a hundred (maybe two hundred) other documented neurotransmitters besides the four or five always mentioned, as well as many probably yet to be discovered.

If you do a little research, you will find that SSRIs are now just one of the many categories of antidepressants you can choose from. Depending on what kind of neurotransmitters they affect in the brain, you can take SNRIs, NRIs, SSREs, as well as the so-called augmenter drugs that are tacked on to some of the others to give you a combo that's even better than any single drug. (I'll say more about these wonder drugs in the next chapter.) Then there are the older drugs like the MAOIs, the TCAs, and even more.

But let's get back to the original "miracle" antidepressant. The leading medical textbook on pharmacology, *Goodman and Gilman's The Pharmacological Basis of Therapeutics* says that when cocaine is taken orally in reasonable prescription doses, it produces alertness, ability to concentrate, increased energy, self-confidence, and a sense of well-being. It does not cause craving, as is seen with abuse of high doses taken by snorting or injection, but can cause withdrawal symptoms if stopped abruptly (true for most or maybe all current antidepressant drugs). By the way, in case you didn't know it, some antidepressants have become street drugs and are snorted and injected by many people who just want to get high. (I would bet that Prozac probably tops the list since its patent has expired and it is now available much more cheaply as a generic drug.)

So since we may already have the miracle drug, why not conduct huge clinical trials to determine its effectiveness in depression. The answer is simple—it might turn out to be safer and more effective than current drugs. Since no one owns the patent for cocaine, the competition of a cheap, effective drug would be a disaster for the giant pharmaceutical companies currently making billions of dollars from the sales of antidepressants. The economy of countries like the U.S. would suffer from a loss of tax revenue and jobs, not to mention money donated to the politicians by the drug companies. It could never happen.

Be Wary

My advice is simple: Don't start taking any of these drugs unless it is under the guidance of a really good physician or psychiatrist. On the other hand, if you are already taking psychiatric drugs of any kind, do not simply try to stop them cold turkey. It's easy to get started on most of these drugs but not easy and perhaps even difficult or impossible for some people to get off of them. Withdrawal problems are quite variable from drug to drug and person to person. Trying to get off some drugs can be dangerous and even lethal. You must do it under the supervision of a competent health-care provider who will be supportive and stay in close contact with you during the period of withdrawal from any psychiatric drug.

I should also point out that many children and adolescents have been put on various psychiatric drugs during the last ten years or more in the U.S., often in addition to ADD methamphetamine-type drugs. The fact that the UK and other nations have essentially banned the use of antidepressants in children under 18 doesn't seem to bother the more sophisticated American psychiatrists (many of whom receive a lot of money from the pharmaceutical companies in one way or another).

If you or your children are already on these drugs and would like to get off, a good place to start would be *The Antidepressant Solution* by psychiatrist Joseph Glenmullen, M.D. or with Dr. Breggin's book *Your Drug May Be Your Problem*. If you want a current book aimed at professionals but still quite readable to the nonprofessional, then check out Peter Breggin's book *Brain-disabling Treatments in Psychiatry: drugs, electroshock, and the psychopharmaceutical complex* (or any of his many other books). If you think that I am being too hard on the drug companies, then listen to what Harvard professor Marcia Angell, M.D. has to say. As a longtime editor of the prestigious *New England Journal of Medicine (NEJM)*, she is one of the most experienced doctors in medical peer review in the world. Read her book: *The Truth About the Drug Companies: How They Deceive Us and What to Do About It.*

The most interesting story she told in that book described how the *NEJM* attempted to recruit psychiatrists to write a major review article on antidepressants. They had strict criteria on ethical issues and wouldn't allow anyone with financial ties to the pharmaceutical industry to participate in such a sweeping review of the subject that they wanted to present in their journal. Guess what? Although many psychiatrists from prestigious medical institutions were probably chomping at the bit to participate in the project, the editorial board had to reject everyone who expressed interest because of their ties to the psychotropic drug industry. It would appear that many psychiatrists are not operating without outside conflicts of interest any more than many politicians in Washington who are beholden to the lobbyists who help keep them in office. Quite a depressing situation if you ask me.

In or Out—On or Off
Although I put a disclaimer in the front of this book, I'm going to repeat it here so that no one can say that they didn't see it. Here is a basic life lesson that I have learned through my own experiences as well as those of my friends and patients over many years. It is easier to get in than to get out. As far as drugs go, we could rephrase that to say that it's usually very easy to get started on any given psychoactive drug (legal or illegal, prescribed by a doctor or bought on the streets or from friends). On the other hand, it can be and often is very difficult to get off of the same drug.

Besides drugs, one of the main sources of human suffering is relationships with other people. The same rule applies here. It is usually easy to get in but often difficult to get out. This is especially true if the relationship is sanctioned by whatever your personal religion dictates and perhaps even more so if the government you live under codifies it under its laws. The best example would be marriage. Most societies make it easy to get married but often quite difficult to get divorced, especially if you have younger children. Even if you don't get married, and especially if you have any children, the task of separating from someone can be not only difficult but emotionally traumatic at the very least.

No Lawsuits Please

Since I'm talking about psychoactive drugs in this book, let's stick with that issue. Even if you decide to get off of some drug, especially one that has been prescribed, you need to be very careful. Do not do it based on anything you read in this book. I am not your doctor and don't know anything about you. Don't try to say that you stopped some prescription drug because I advised it. I only give advice to patients if I have taken a complete history, performed a thorough physical exam, and run any tests that may be required to analyze their problems. If I reach a definitive diagnosis, I will inform them of that. Then I will explain what all of the potential treatments might be. If they are unsure what to do at that point and ask for my advice, that is the only time I will offer it.

No one reading this book is in that position. You are not my patients and I am not giving any of you advice about your particular problem, whatever it may be. I am only expressing my opinions about a variety of topics in this book. I don't want you to blindly accept anything that I say. If a doctor has started you on a psychoactive drug and you think you might want to try to get off of it, then you need to discuss that with your healthcare provider. If you don't like his or her advice, then you should look for someone else. Unfortunately I cannot be your doctor or help you withdraw from drugs if that's what you think you should do.

If you are a psychoactive drug virgin (except maybe for moderate alcohol intake), then I think you should seriously consider staying that way. I won't tell you to stop drugs without professional help if you are already on them, but be very careful before you start them in the future if you are drug free right now.

Some psychiatrists may say that this might prevent people from seeking help when they have various life problems. That's not what I'm saying at all. If you need help, go get it wherever you can. If you are experiencing depression or anxiety or any number of other psychological problems, this book isn't the final answer for you. All I'm doing is telling you to be careful before you start taking psychoactive drugs of any kind. You can certainly show this book to anyone you want, but he or she may tell you that I don't know what I'm talking about. Remember that I am not formally trained as a brain doctor (I haven't done a residency in neurology). Nor am I formally trained as what might be called a mind doctor (I haven't done a residency in psychiatry and don't have a PhD or any degree in psychology). Maybe I have a lot of insight into how the mind works, and maybe I don't. Many of you reading this book may not be in a good position to make that assessment. Sorry to have to repeat here what was said earlier in the initial disclaimer at the beginning, but I have a phobia for adverse interactions with attorneys.

Risk-benefit Ratio

This is a basic question you need to ask yourself before taking any psychoactive drugs. Am I exposing myself to a low risk with a high potential benefit? This is the same question to ask before having any kind of surgery—even a mole removal. The same analysis would even be appropriate before trying a new sport. How likely are you to get injured as opposed to having a good time and staying healthy? I thought about going helicopter skiing about 15 years ago but then changed my mind after doing some research. The place where I wanted to go had a record over the previous several years of skier deaths from helicopter crashes and avalanches that came to one percent. Would you like to ski down virgin powder on a beautiful mountain when doing that carried a 1% mortality rate? I wouldn't. That's more risky than having a lot of open heart surgery operations which you are usually not choosing to do for the fun of it.

Big Head/Little Head

Hopefully you realize now that there are potentially significant risks of taking antidepressants. I would like for the moment to focus on a frequent side effect that I mentioned at the outset of this chapter. Sexual problems are common with many antidepressants, especially SSRIs. This usually involves decreased sexual desire and trouble having orgasms. Although these effects are usually reversible as they were with my friend, in some people they can last months or perhaps even years after the drug is stopped. Some studies suggest that sexual dysfunction may occur with some SSRIs in as many as 30 or 40% of people taking them for extended periods.

This problem raises another interesting dilemma for drug companies about the best marketing strategy for their products. Could this sexual dysfunction problem actually prove useful to some people? The answer turns out to be yes. That would be someone with the opposite problem of what my friend had—premature ejaculation (PE). But how are you going to market your antidepressant for the treatment of PE and still keep other potential customers with depression from finding out that it causes sexual dysfunction in many people? I can't think of a good way in mass marketing, and it would be too risky given that the huge market is with depression, not PE.

On second thought, the best strategy would be to secretly promote your drug to urologists who are the ones most likely to see men with PE. Problem solved, but there is still one last question. How does an SSRI work for premature ejaculation? It just came to me. Depression is caused by inadequate serotonin in the big head and PE by low levels in the little head. There you have it. I'm a genius.

More Bad News
Many people on SSRIs and their cousins, especially those on high doses for some time, complain of emotional blunting or numbness. Some become apathetic, indifferent, or feel detached from what is going on around them in their lives. These are often emotions they have not experienced previously. Many antidepressants dramatically suppress REM sleep leaving some patients feeling chronically fatigued. More serious side effects have been well documented including substantially increased risk of suicide (over and above that resulting from depression alone). This prompted the FDA to issue Black Box warnings on all SSRIs in 2004.

Beyond the side effects, we need to look at the therapeutic benefits. Do antidepressants work as advertised? There are many reputable studies that show that they are only marginally better than placebos and certainly not the magic pills portrayed by some of the press and certainly the pharmaceutical manufacturers for 10–15 years after Prozac first arrived on the scene in 1988. If you want to know a lot more about that subject, then turn the page.

13

Please the Master

After having worked several years in the jail system, I treated an obese 42-year-old white woman who only spent about a week in jail until her attorney was able to bail her out on some kind of fraud charge. She had a history of chronic back pain for many years without a definitive diagnosis and, although able to walk, was confined to a wheelchair because walking was too painful for her. Our dilemma was that her physician had been prescribing morphine, which she injected herself.

After doing a careful history and physical on her day of arrival, I was convinced that Candy was what some doctors might refer to as a crock or, to put it in kinder terms, just a legal drug addict. During my six-year general surgery residency, I had treated many patients with chronic pain stemming from a variety of injuries, including gunshot wounds, as well as chronic cancer patients. I spent one month as the only resident taking care of thirty patients on a pain ward run by a psychologist and a neurosurgeon. Those patients, many of whom had chronic pain for years including some who had been treated unsuccessfully with neurosurgical pain-relieving procedures, were never given any drugs stronger than Tylenol or aspirin.

As this patient pleaded with me to give her morphine, I explained that we didn't have any because of the security problems that would create in jail. But I told her that we did have another option. She immediately asked if it was Demerol or Talwin, because those just didn't work for her. I knew that she had probably taken every narcotic or synthetic narcotic known to man, so I told her that we had a new drug that had just been released. After warning her that it might be somewhat painful when injected, she agreed to accept that.

After the patient was put in the infirmary, I asked a nurse to draw up a solution of sterile saline mixed with a local anesthetic to make it sting. Feeling quite confident that Candy's pain was psychological and not physical in origin, I had laid the foundation for a strong placebo effect. Thirty minutes later, I went in to ask how she was doing. She was quite satisfied and said that this new medicine had relieved her pain almost better than the morphine. We continued this course of therapy until she was released about five days later.

There was certainly some risk to me in doing this. If any of the nurses had decided to confront Candy with her malingering, she and her attorney could have raised holy hell and possibly accused me of violating her eighth amendment rights. But that didn't happen, and she was soon able to get back to real drugs. (To be certain, if this woman had serious documented disease such as metastatic breast cancer with severe bone pain, I would have given her whatever drug it took to relieve it. We would have obtained morphine regardless of any logistical or security problems that might have ensued.)

Do Antidepressants Work?

Hopefully I managed to convince some of you in the last chapter that the hype surrounding how antidepressants actually work is mostly propaganda from the drug companies that sell them. But an important question remains to be answered. Do antidepressants work? Specifically, do they get rid of or at least improve the mental state of a majority of people who are diagnosed with and treated for depression? I can absolutely, positively, give you a completely unequivocal answer to that critical question—yes and no.

Even the average lay person should be able to feel confident about answering that question based on logic alone. Obviously antidepressants must work because otherwise doctors would not be treating millions of people with them. Also the government regulators in various countries would not have approved their release into the market place if the trials required for drug approval didn't show clearly that they work.

A better question to ask than just if they work is how and why they work. If you believe what I said earlier, then you know that SSRIs don't work just because they increase serotonin levels in brain synapses. The fact is that large trials over many years have shown that the old MAOI and tricyclic antidepressants introduced in the 1950s and 60s work just as well for depression as SSRIs and all of their variants that first appeared in the late 1980s. The problem with the older drugs was that they were "dirty." That's medical lingo meaning that they had too many undesirable side effects. The reason was that they not only affected the brain amines like serotonin and noradrenalin, but they also affected acetylcholine and histamine which play major roles all over the body.

Enter Biopsychiatry

Prozac was touted as a breakthrough drug because it was so selective in its effect. It supposedly only affected serotonin and left everything else alone. It also fit perfectly into the medical model of psychiatry as a biological science with its main tenet being that psychological problems were simply a result of a biochemical imbalance in the brain. And not surprisingly, many of the biopsychiatrists seemed sure that depression was simply the result of inadequate serotonin in the brain, much as diabetes is caused by insufficient insulin production by the pancreas.

I'll give you my brief explanation of how psychiatrists went from being therapists to biologists. Show me a person who honestly doesn't need any respect from other people and I'll show you a potential Zen Master. Psychiatrists, like most people, want to be respected. Because of some of the history of the first half of the 20th century that I talked about previously, they didn't get the respect they wanted. In the 1950s and 60s, this became even more problematic as non-M.D.s such as psychologists and social workers began to assume the same roles and took on more and more responsibility in treating people with mental problems. Many psychiatrists felt threatened by this and were worried that this would further degrade their position among their fellow physicians who already held them in low regard for the most part. This was certainly the case when I was a medical student in the late 1960s. I respected some of the psychiatrists I encountered but many of my classmates didn't. They certainly fell below every other specialty in medicine on the respect scale.

What began to slowly turn this around starting in the 1950s was the development of drugs that could be used to treat various psychiatric disorders. This expanded dramatically in the 70s and 80s and created the field of biopsychiatry. Now they could be just like their fellow internists. They would evaluate patients, make a diagnosis, and then prescribe a drug that would alleviate or maybe even cure the problem. When the pharmaceutical industry began to realize what a huge market there was for psychiatric drugs, they had to come up with a way to sell it to both the general population and doctors. That is how the theory of the biochemical imbalance came into being. That theory was readily accepted by many psychiatrists because it made them seem to be more like their fellow physicians who treated patients with drugs like insulin and antibiotics.

Holes in the Theory

Over the more than twenty years since Prozac was released, we have learned a lot about antidepressants. During the 1990s, there was a mad race by pharmaceutical companies to develop something that could be marketed as bigger and better. Now well into the new millennium, we have a lot of drugs to look at. We have noradrenalin RIs, dopamine RIs, and various combinations in terms of their supposed mechanisms of action. And how well do they work? Pretty much the same in terms of giving a positive response in the range of 60% in people who are depressed.

But how could that be if the original theory was correct that depression was caused by inadequate serotonin in the brain? The answer is that this theory of biochemical imbalance in neurotransmitters was made up by the pharmaceutical companies and accepted lock, stock, and barrel by many psychiatrists and other doctors even though there was no scientific evidence to support it. The media jumped on board with a winning story as they usually do, and the U.S. became what a major magazine called Prozac Nation on its cover. If this sounds to you in any way similar to the media hype about the miracle of frontal lobotomy in the 1940s, I wouldn't be surprised. History does repeat itself—over and over.

A recent addition to the SSRI armamentarium is a new drug developed in France and now sold in many European countries as an anti-SSRI. It is an SSRE, a serotonin reuptake enhancer. That means that its mechanism of action is to decrease levels of serotonin in the brain. But wait a second; that seems crazy since we know that depression is caused by a serotonin deficiency. What is going on here? Obviously, this drug must have proven to be a failure in the treatment of depression and even made it worse in most people. Oops—wrong. It works just as well as the SSRIs and the rest of the drugs in that league. OK, if you're starting to get confused, here's what you need to know.

Psychiatry is not Surgery

There has been a great attempt to make psychiatry appear to be as scientific as surgery and clinical medicine over the last 30 years or so. The propaganda machine probably started by the pharmaceutical companies but widely embraced by many in psychiatry has been quite effective at convincing the lay public as well as many physicians that they have this brain thing all figured out scientifically. But the fact of the matter is this: Not one disorder, which many think are diseases, described in the official manual used by all American psychiatrists, called the DSM-IV, has any documented biological or biochemical basis to explain it, including schizophrenia.

I would simply like to emphasize what I will discuss at great length in an upcoming book. The brain is not the mind. The mind is vastly greater. Brain disease may or may not impair the mind. This is why the DSM refers to psychiatric problems as disorders, not diseases. But most lay people don't understand the distinction. A mental disorder is really just a diagnosis and that is nothing other than an opinion. Can the diagnosis of depression or ADHD be backed up with hard science as diabetes and cancer can? No.

The psychiatrists and many other doctors just want you to believe that so that they can treat all these so-called brain diseases with brain drugs. Writing a prescription takes a lot less time than psychotherapy. The HMOs and the pharmaceutical companies want to keep the status quo mostly for that reason to enhance their profits, despite the sometimes unfortunate consequences for you, the consumer of their drugs and propaganda. I'm not saying that real biological and biochemically-based brain diseases don't exist. They certainly do, but they are treated by neurologists, not psychiatrists (Parkinson's disease, dementia, organic brain syndromes, etc).

Here's something else few people know. Not one psychiatric disease can be diagnosed by a laboratory test, brain scan, or any other kind of diagnostic test. If I take a history, examine someone, and then arrive at a possible diagnosis of cancer of the pancreas, that is just my opinion (my best guess based on the information I have so far.) Because the diagnoses of mental disorders cannot be confirmed scientifically, psychiatrists can make any diagnosis they want with little fear of medical malpractice. Unlike most doctors practicing medicine, they are relatively immune to the adverse consequences of misdiagnosis and subsequent inappropriate treatment. Lawyers find it difficult to use science to absolutely confirm or refute their diagnoses and related treatment programs.

Depression is not Diabetes
Many years ago, prolific self-help author, Wayne Dyer, recounted a story that I could definitely relate to. He said that he lived for a while next to a

woman who had eight children. He saw her running around all the time, hanging clothes out in the yard, and so on, but had only casual contact with her. One day he asked her how she could deal with all the stress of having to take care of so many kids. When he specifically asked if she ever got depressed, she was quite surprised by the question, saying "Are you kidding me? I don't have time to get depressed." Have you ever met anyone who said that she didn't have time to get diabetes? I can certainly relate to that woman's statement. During medical school and my brutal surgery residency, I never suffered from depression serious enough to cause me to miss a day of school or work on that account, even though I was admittedly often a very unhappy camper (sometimes mildly to moderately depressed).

Before I go on, I need to clarify something. When I talk about biochemical causes of depression referring to current neurotransmitter theory, I am making some major assumptions. Specifically I assume that people given a psychiatric diagnosis of depression have already undergone a medical workup to rule out possible underlying organic disease as the cause of their problem. For example endocrine problems such as those originating in thyroid or adrenal diseases must be ruled out.

Hypothyroidism can cause serious depression associated with inadequate output of thyroid hormone from the thyroid gland. So can adrenocortical insufficiency associated with inadequate circulating cortisol from the adrenal glands (as in Addison's disease, which President Kennedy had). Too much thyroid hormone and cortisol can cause anxiety and mood disorders but also sometimes depression. The treatment for this kind of depression is not antidepressants or psychotherapy. It is to correct the underlying disease. In hypothyroidism this may require taking thyroid hormone for the rest of your life. Unlike antidepressants, that will correct an underlying hormonal imbalance and prevent recurrent depression caused by the deficiency of thyroid hormone.

Another thing that must be ruled out in anyone with depression is side effects from drugs. People who become depressed while taking any medicine need to find out if depression can be a side effect of a drug they may be on. For example, beta blockers such as propranalol can cause depression. These are often prescribed to treat heart problems but have other uses as well such as chronic headaches. Anyone taking this drug who becomes depressed should be switched to something else, not just started on antidepressants (which some doctors may do almost as a reflex).

You should do your homework on the drugs you are taking if you become depressed. Some doctors may not bother to take the time. If you see your doctor and relate that your research and perhaps a discussion with a local pharmacist shows that the drug you're on may cause depression (such as Aldomet, Accutane, steroids, Lipitor, Tagamet, Valium, etc.), he will be much more likely to try to switch drugs to see if that helps before considering anything else. Obviously you should insist on a medical work-up if you're not on any drugs. Because of cost constraints, many doctors may refuse to do this and just start antidepressants.

Although this has happened to many people, you don't want to be someone who takes antidepressants for a year or two, has many side effects and withdrawal problems, only to eventually discover that your depression was caused by hypothyroidism or some other easily treatable medical problem. Certainly before the modern era, many of the people locked up in insane asylums for years simply had untreated medical problems.

Chestnut Lodge

Now I have an interesting case to discuss that may have changed the practice of psychiatry in the U.S. It caused great turmoil in the psychiatric community in the 1980s centered on a 42-year-old medical doctor named Raphael Osheroff. He was admitted to Chestnut Lodge in Rockville, Maryland in 1979 for depression. (This mental hospital has a special place in my memory because I used to walk by it every day on my way to elementary school. When I asked what it was, my parents explained to me that it was where crazy people were sent.) He had been treated for two years with tricyclic antidepressants by a well known and respected psychiatrist who thought that Raphael was getting better.

Osheroff decided to stop his meds and go into Chestnut Lodge which only treated depression with psychoanalysis (or at least some type of psychotherapy—I'm not sure what kind). After seven months there, his life was in the toilet. His medical partners had abandoned him and he had lost his hospital privileges. His first wife had obtained custody of their two children, and his second wife had left him. At that point, he was moved to a hospital in Connecticut where he was diagnosed with a psychotic depression and placed back on tricyclics in addition to antipsychotic medication. Appearing to have improved significantly, he was discharged a few months later.

In 1982 he brought a lawsuit against Chestnut Lodge. His lawyer claimed that failing to put him on drugs instead of just giving him talk therapy had been negligent. After the usual five years of arbitration and appeals in our legal system, an out-of-court settlement was reached in his favor. Although no legal precedent was set because the case never went to trial, it sent a chill of paranoia down the spines of psychiatrists all over the U.S. This may have been the turning point when they began to distance themselves from psychotherapy and become biopsychiatrists who just make diagnoses and write prescriptions for psychotropic drugs.

Although the Chestnut Lodge case was settled against a hospital, the same did not follow with individual practitioners. In a research study done in 2000, there had been no cases of any psychiatrist or psychologist successfully sued in the U.S. for making a mistaken diagnosis causing injury to a patient that resulted in awarded damages. This is pretty incredible given that a large proportion of people hospitalized over the last 50 years of the 20th century were there because they had been diagnosed with a mental illness that was serious enough to require inpatient treatment. Is the explanation for this that psychiatric diagnosis and treatment and psychotherapy are so accurate and safe? No way.

Not So Crazy

Thousands of people have been wrongly diagnosed as being psychotic or schizophrenic and placed on major tranquilizers like Thorazine. Some of these people have later developed a neurological disease called tardive dyskinesia that is a direct side effect of these drugs. It can be mildly or seriously disabling and sometimes go on for the rest of the person's life. I am quite familiar with this problem since it happened to my mother.

Let's compare making a psychiatric diagnosis to standard medical or surgical treatment. What if I decided to perform emergency surgery on someone with acute abdominal pain based on a preop diagnosis of acute cholecystitis (inflamed gallbladder), which I concluded after just talking to and examining the patient. In my operative report, I say that the gallbladder is acutely inflamed and describe its removal. However, the patient continues to have pain over the next week and the pathology report comes back as "normal gallbladder." In that situation, I have a problem, don't I?

And so does the patient. However, such misdiagnosis and inappropriate treatment can rarely be documented in psychiatry.

The reality is that there is not only no scientific basis for calling depression a biochemical disorder of the brain but also no evidence for the biochemical imbalance theory in general. As psychiatrist Peter Breggin has said, the only people with a biochemical imbalance in their brains are those taking psychiatric drugs (or illegal psychoactive drugs). Medical science pretends to be able to explain depression as a simple neurotransmitter depletion problem. It sounds so scientific, but a lot of what they claim is BS, folks. Many psychiatrists will not tell you the truth, but I will. I don't know what causes depression, drug addiction or drug tolerance in the brain, or any psychiatric disorder (and I'm not exactly mentally handicapped).

I Shall Please the Master

Let's get back to the issue I raised earlier. Do antidepressants work? The answer is yes (to some extent). But a more important question is this: how and why do they work? As you might have guessed from the opening story, I'm going to talk about placebo effects. Pretty much everyone has heard about them, but not many people really understand them.

Before I get into my discussion of placebos, let me point out something else about my patient. Not only was her pain completely relieved with saline, but it was also remarkable that she did not show any kind of withdrawal symptoms from her morphine. I am sure this would have happened if she had simply been refused any medicine for her pain. I saw patients every day who were addicted to street narcotics and going through withdrawal for five or six days after they came into jail. Why didn't that happen to Candy? As best as I can figure, this was a second placebo effect. She was convinced that she was getting a potent narcotic, so the mind told the body not to worry about having nausea, vomiting, diarrhea, sweating, and so on.

The origin of the word placebo is interesting. It supposedly means "I shall please" in Latin. Anyway that's what I've read. (I speak a couple of the romance languages derived from Latin but never studied that language at all until very recently.) I would guess that it would not be unlikely to have heard priests in the Catholic Church over the centuries saying

"Placebo Domino," meaning I shall please the Lord (or Master).

So what does this have to do with drugs? Who are you trying to please when you are experiencing a placebo effect? The doctor, of course. (It could be any kind of health-care provider, or therapist, or even a witch doctor who gives you his special brew.) For some who seem to believe that medical doctors are gods, then the Latin phrase fits perfectly. Before the nurse gave Candy her injection of salt water, I had already established a good rapport with my new patient. I actually am a good doctor and most of my patients have liked and trusted me over the years. She wanted to make me happy by responding to my treatment—and she did. I was pleased to be able to relieve her pain by giving her something that couldn't possibly hurt her in any way while she was under my care. I was also pleasantly surprised not to see her experience any narcotic withdrawal problems.

The placebo effect only started playing a significant role in the evaluation of drugs in the second half of the 20th century. When Freud began treating patients for depression with cocaine, he didn't have two groups, one of whom was getting a placebo. He just knew that cocaine helped him with his own depression, and so he started giving it to his patients. If they didn't get better, they got more. (This is the same thing many doctors do now with antidepressants.) As the founder of psychoanalysis, I presume he also gave them some form of psychotherapy, but I would guess that he wasn't a very empathetic person. My favorite quote attributed to him is this: I have met many people in my life, and most of them were trash. (Bad day or Freudian slip?)

Government regulatory organizations didn't start requiring controlled trials using placebos in the U.S. until the 1950s. What exactly is a placebo? Commonly called a sugar pill, it is just an inert substance that doesn't have any chemical effects. Because glucose is the primary metabolic substrate in the body, there is no human being who can't take it. Too much or too little can cause some problems, but a little a few times a day should have no biochemical effect.

So why did placebos become such an important issue? The reason is that you need to sort out what is a biochemical effect and what is a psychological effect. After all, nobody is willing to buy or take a prescription drug if the drug or drugs in it aren't doing something to help them with a specific problem. It was only in recent history that doctors started appreciating how powerful the placebo effect could be with drugs. But where does this come from? It is the power of belief. How strong is that? Let me tell you another personal story to give you an idea of what I'm talking about.

Fire Walking

The power of the mind can do incredible things for your body and your life. Or is it the brain that does these things? Many neuroscientists view the brain and mind as being the same thing. I don't. Although the brain is incomprehensibly complex, the mind is even more miraculous (providing you are in control of it, which I will have much more to say about in an upcoming book).

The brain and mind are intertwined but not the same. If you have ever experienced telepathy, remote viewing, or had an out of body experience, you are already aware of this. The brain is local. It's confined to the cranial cavity. Your mind is both local and non-local. It has the capacity to perceive things far away from your physical body, even thousands of miles.

Many people think such psychic phenomena are bunk. If so, why did the CIA and KGB spend years studying remote viewing and other psychic powers for their potential use in spying? In fact they found that some remote viewers were astoundingly accurate in describing places thousands of miles away. The problem was that they couldn't do it with the same consistency, reliability, and reproducibility of other scientific technologies such as spy plane photos and satellite images, especially as they became more sophisticated in the last part of the 20th century (not to mention spies on the ground).

Like profound spiritual experiences, these kinds of abilities can only be appreciated through direct personal experience. I'll give you a more concrete example. Do you believe you can walk on fire without getting burned? I didn't until I actually did it. Before I talk about that, let me give you a little background.

When I was a surgery resident, I spent an entire month as the only person running a burn unit, under the supervision of a staff surgeon. I was on call every day that entire month. After spending the first two days in the hospital, I begged another resident to cover my patients for an hour so that I could go home and get some clothes and a few other things. It was fortunate I did that because I wasn't able to leave the hospital again for another five days.

Spending a month taking care of very sick people with major body burns was a horrifying experience, as you will learn if you read my book *Boy to Man.* The excruciating pain the patients experienced during the daily dressing changes was barely touched by the morphine we gave them. The psychological trauma I experienced, especially in taking care of children, was immense, although probably little compared to theirs. After that month, my greatest fear in life was sustaining a serious burn injury. I felt I could handle major trauma or serious illness, but not a bad burn.

Fast-forward almost 15 years to my early forties when I was on a kind of spiritual journey. I went to a Tony Robbins weekend seminar where the main event was a fire walk the first evening. Having used hypnosis quite a bit myself with some patients for pain control (especially kids), I was amazed at what a masterful hypnotist Tony was. He was able to convince me and a thousand other people that we could walk on a hot bed of coals without getting burned.

Once that belief was firmly planted in my mind, I was able to fearlessly go outside and walk in my bare feet over a fifteen-foot bed of hot burning coals. Not one person got burned as they walked across coals that were probably over a thousand degrees.

Despite the fact that this experience defies all logic and science, it happened. So when people give me a host of reasons why fire walking is a scam and can't really be done, I just nod and say, "Maybe you're right." It can't be done unless you've done it. The same goes for remote viewing and telepathy. It doesn't exist unless you have experienced it yourself.

By the way, I love reading about scientists who say that they can explain fire walking easily with basic physics. I've treated a lot of burn patients and some of them only had high heat exposure for a second or less. Have you ever touched a hot stove with your finger and developed a blister. And why did you pull your finger away so fast—because it hurt like hell. With less than a second of contact of a temperature much lower than burning embers, you got a second degree burn. Now try putting your full body weight on hot coals repeatedly over a distance of 15 or 20 feet. Wouldn't you be surprised not only to have no blisters but not even any pain? However, under other circumstances, the outcome could be quite different. For example, I would not recommend trying fire walking at your next backyard barbecue with friends after a few beers. Can you spell skin graft?

A week after the seminar, I went out of my house to get something on my wood deck. It was a hot summer day and I was barefoot. After I took three steps, my feet were on fire, and I had to run back in the house to get shoes. The deck was probably 115 degrees. Why was the deck hot but not the coals? Because when I walked on the hot coals, I believed that I could do it without feeling any pain or getting burned. This is a manifestation of the amazing power the mind has over your body. Although many theories have been proposed, this simply cannot be explained with science (at least not to my satisfaction).

The Power of Belief
Is the power of belief that often manifests itself in the placebo effect something that was just discovered in the last 50 years? No, it's at least a hundred years old. Henry Ford said, "If you believe you can or believe you can't, you are right." But even before him, the father of American psychology, William James, said, "Belief will help create the fact." So was anyone on to this secret before that? Well, let's go back to the first century B.C. when the great Roman poet, Virgil, wrote this: They can because they think they can. Another famous Roman, Seneca, around the same time, said something similar in more negative terms: I was shipwrecked before I got aboard. I'm pretty sure that this secret didn't escape Lao Tzu or the Buddha some five hundred years earlier.

But wait a second, some of you might say. Am I trying to convince you that beliefs can have effects like chemicals? Exactly, and sometimes they can be much more powerful. Let's start with some simple examples that aren't all that impressive. When people who say that they are sensitive to coffee and get jittery after two cups are placed in a study, they often feel fine after 3 cups—when they have been told that the coffee is decaffeinated, even though it isn't. Many people who are given what they are told are strong caffeine pills report feeling a pronounced stimulant effect even though the pills have nothing in them.

Not that impressive to you? How about people who are given amphetamine stimulants like Benzedrine but are told they are sedatives and feel relaxed by them. Or the people who are given sedatives that they believe are stimulants and report feeling hyper. These are drugs that have genuine chemical effects on the body, but those effects can not only be negated but completely overridden by the mind in its power over the body. This is especially true when dealing with issues like pain that may sometimes be largely or even completely in the mind to begin with, as was the case in my patient I described at the beginning of this chapter.

Placebo under the Knife

Although the placebo effect is generally stronger in people with anxiety, pain, or depression, it is certainly present in surgery as well. In the 1950s, someone theorized that tying off the internal mammary arteries that run down either side of the breast bone would increase blood flow to the coronary arteries and thereby help people with narrowing of their vessels that was causing anginal chest pain. Thoracic surgeons began doing this operation and found the results to be impressive. Many patients experienced dramatic relief of their symptoms.

Because this was the period in which investigating placebo effects started to catch on in medicine, someone suggested that a double-blind trial should be done. In some patients, the standard operation was carried out while in others, the chest was just opened and closed. The results of the study were astounding. The placebo group experienced almost the same results in terms of relief from their chronic chest pain. Some followed up for many years continued to say how wonderful the operation had been for them, even though they had been in the placebo group. Once these results became clear, the operation was abandoned.

Can you imagine such a study being done in our current legal environment in the U.S.? The strict protocols for obtaining informed consent would prohibit it. How many of you with chronic anginal chest pain would agree to become part of a study in which half of the patients would only have their chest opened and closed? As someone who opened and closed many chests as a surgery resident, I can assure you that just having your breastbone sawed apart and wired back together will create quite a bit of pain for at least a few weeks. If you've ever had broken ribs, that will give you an idea of what I'm talking about. In fact, that pain may have been what created such a strong effect in the placebo group. It convinced them that they had the real operation.

What would be the equivalent of post-operative pain creating a placebo effect in patients only taking pills in a double-blind study? The answer is side effects caused by the drug that convince the patient they are getting the active drug rather than a placebo. As I mentioned earlier, that's why I gave my patient Candy a shot that would sting in order to convince her that this was caused by the potent drug she was getting.

Drug Trials
So how do we get around this problem in trying to establish double-blind trials, especially when psychoactive drugs are being tested? Although many researchers might deny this, we really can't, and I'll explain why. The reason is that experimental protocols for such studies require that the people involved have a full and complete informed consent. This is also required for any medical or surgical procedure, as it should be in those cases. Unfortunately it really screws up studies of drugs, especially those that are psychoactive.

How would I conduct such a study if my primary goal was to minimize the placebo effect as much as possible? I would simply tell my group of volunteers that some of them would be receiving the drug being studied and some would be receiving something different. Some might experience side effects and some may not. I would not even mention anything about placebos and ask them to answer all of our questions honestly and completely during the course of the study. People would be left somewhat confused and many might not have any specific expectations (that would be my goal). Some could even conclude that they are in what is called a comparative trial where two similar drugs are being tested against each other. So what's wrong with this? Nothing except for one minor issue. No hospital ethics board or research committee would approve such a study.

OK, so I admit that we've made progress since the frontal lobotomists of the 1930s and 40s performed their human experiments without necessarily obtaining any kind of permission or providing an informed consent about the procedure. On the other end of the spectrum, the details that must be provided for testing antidepressants need to be incredibly complete, perhaps excessively so. For example, you must let everyone know that they will either be getting a real drug or a placebo. Then you have to tell them what the side effects of the real drug are such as dry mouth, sweating, diarrhea, sexual dysfunction, and so on. You don't need to say what the side effects of the placebo are because they are chemically inert and should not cause any.

Are you starting to see the problem? How hard is it going to be for the average person to tell whether he or she is getting the real drug or a placebo? Not very. Many studies have confirmed this fact by showing that 80% of people "break blind," meaning that they are able to correctly guess whether they have been taking a real drug or placebo before the trial ends, and for many this occurs in the early stages. Doctors are able to figure this out with greater accuracy based on what the patients are telling them. So much for the double-blind trial.

For some kinds of trials, this isn't too much of a concern because the placebo effect is small. However with antidepressants, the placebo effect is huge. Once the placebo effect is factored in, the difference may be small enough that the researchers find it hard to get a statistical difference between them. Although they often can, it may not be a clinically significant difference. In other words, 60% of patients with depression may have a positive response to the real antidepressant compared with 50% on placebo. I'm not pulling these numbers out of a hat; they are pretty standard for such trials.

That kind of difference may be plenty for the drug companies sponsoring the studies and even satisfy the government regulators overseeing them before the drug is approved for release. But I wouldn't want to take a drug that is only 20% better than placebo. Compare this with a study of a real biochemical disease in the human body—diabetes. If the real oral medication is effective for type II adult-onset diabetes in keeping the blood sugar in a normal range, those taking placebo will have little or no effect. Their blood sugar levels will remain elevated throughout the study. The placebo effect will not be an issue.

Not so for mind-altering drugs. I mentioned side effects, which muddies the water even more. If you are told in advance of the study that the active drug being used causes a variety of side effects and you start experiencing some of them early on, what will your reaction be? If you're depressed, you'll probably be happy to figure out that you're getting the real drug that might actually relieve your depression. This would especially be true if you believe it to be the latest greatest drug for this problem. If it didn't at least have that potential, why would they be testing it on people? Most people don't want to be part of a drug trial of this sort to help the rest of the world. They want to get better themselves.

Super Placebos

What kind of effect does thinking that you are getting the real drug have on you? Since placebo effect explains most of what antidepressants do anyway, it just magnifies that. In other words, it creates a super placebo effect. Believing that you are on the real drug will only enhance the effect that you would already have if you had no idea whether you were taking the real drug or a placebo. In many trials, that may explain the small advantage that the drug under evaluation actually has over placebos. In other words, the entire effect of the drug being tested is nothing more than a standard placebo effect augmented by a super placebo effect related to side effects.

Some researchers may counter this statement saying that people on placebos do sometimes experience side effects. They would be right. However not many do and when they do, it is also a placebo effect. Actually in the medical literature, this is called a nocebo effect, meaning a negative or unwanted effect of the placebo. But just think about it. If you are depressed and would much prefer to be in the real drug group, wouldn't you be unconsciously motivated to experience some side effects that let you know you are getting the active drug. You might think your mouth feels a little dry or you have some nausea after taking the drug for a week. Now you feel fantastic because you know you are not getting a placebo. You may continue to experience such side effects throughout the trial that will just serve to enhance the placebo effect for you.

Other than these psychological effects, are there other problems with these drug trials? I will respond with an unequivocal yes, and in this case I really mean it. Many of these trials are designed by and paid for by the drug companies who sponsor them. They want to do everything possible to make sure that their drug being tested performs much better than a placebo. In order to assure this, many trials have an initial two week period called a placebo washout before the actual trial begins. This is kind of like the voir dire process in jury selection where opposing attorneys want to get rid of people who may tend to oppose their position during the trial. They ask them a lot of questions about their experiences and beliefs and then exclude some based on their responses from participating on the jury for the actual trial. The drug companies similarly want to exclude anyone who they think may be prone to a placebo effect.

Although I don't have any idea how well the voir dire process works

in selecting juries, I can tell you this. You can't wash out people susceptible to placebo effects—because almost everyone falls under its spell. So if
they can't prevent the placebo effect, what else can they do? Well, several
things. First of all, they can try to structure the study in the best possible
way to get the result they want. Then they can find people who will help
them interpret the data in a way that will be most favorable to them. Then
if the data don't give them what they want, they can disregard the study
and do another one.

If they get a couple of studies that show their drug works better than
placebo, they will publish them. Studies showing no significant benefit
or negative results are rarely published. Researchers who want to dispute
the drug companies' findings usually find it very difficult to ever dig up
the negative studies. The government regulators are supposed to get everything but sometimes downplay or ignore some of the studies that don't
confirm the drug's effectiveness. Am I being too negative here? Not at
all—just realistic. Many drugs have passed the approval process that are
later discovered to be little better than placebos. Some of them have been
pulled off of the market after release because of severe side effects.

Even the supposedly unbiased medical journals get caught up in this
mess of making a new drug appear much better than it really is. This results from something called publishing bias. Nobody is all that interested
in publishing studies that have failed to yield positive results of some kind.
If I were to submit an article to a journal dealing with cosmetic surgery
indicating that my three-month study using dog poop as a wrinkle reducer
didn't work, no one will even consider publishing it, no matter how good
the study was. On the other hand, if I were to conduct a study that con-
cludes that using a cream containing aloe vera and ginseng reduces wrinkles by 60% in 30 days, that would stand a reasonable chance of getting
accepted if a decent protocol was followed (or perhaps even if not).

Although placebo controlled trials didn't become commonplace in
medicine until the second half of the 20th century, they were used by the
Catholic Church some 500 years earlier in the exorcism of demons. For
example, people who were suspected of being possessed might undergo
a treatment that would involve splattering holy water on them. If they
went into convulsions, then they were deemed to be possessed. However,
the priests developed an ingenious method of detecting fraud in people
pretending to be possessed. They splattered them with ordinary water that

had not been blessed. Those who convulsed or experienced other manifestations of demon possession were then exposed as fakers. If that seems a little unscientific to you, I've got bad news. Things aren't that much better as we head into the second decade of the 21st century when it comes to testing of new pharmaceutical psychoactive drugs.

Are You Really Depressed?

Why is it that we have so many problems accurately assessing the effectiveness of antidepressants? Many forms of bias come into play. First of all, the drug manufacturers are just like movie producers and book publishers—they are always looking for the next blockbuster that will bring in huge profits to their company. And just as many of the movie and publishing moguls don't really care whether their huge hit movie or book is actually a piece of trash, neither do some of the people running pharmaceutical companies mind if their drug doesn't really do much to help people. The big difference with this analogy is that nobody gets hurt by a lousy book or movie (other than wasting their time and money). But people can and do get seriously hurt by some of the psychiatric drugs that don't deliver what they are supposed to and actually cause some people to suffer with bad side effects and then experience serious withdrawal problems when they try to get off of them.

It should be obvious that the pharmaceutical companies are highly motivated to create trials that will make their drugs look as safe and effective as possible. What about the psychiatrists who are conducting the trials for psychoactive drugs? Are they totally impartial? In a perfect world, the answer would be yes, but that's not where we live. People criticizing drug trials have alleged that many doctors take anything but an unbiased position. First of all, it is hard to gather patients with depression who will be good candidates for a study. For example, maybe the protocol only calls for patients who are severely or very severely depressed.

Now let me give you a little background on the money issue. The way these trials are often structured is this. The doctor conducting the trial on his patients is paid a certain amount of money for each patient who goes through the trial. Although there is nothing wrong with that since he will have to spend time with each patient, it does create some temptations. Honestly I haven't met many doctors who feel that they make plenty of money and are perfectly happy with what they are getting. Even those who are already worth several million or perhaps have family money don't usually feel that way (at least in my experience). Doctors, like most people, would always like to have more money if they can find a way to get it.

Now imagine you are a psychiatrist who doesn't have enough people in his practice to qualify for the drug company study, but you really want to participate. Is it possible that you might consider fudging your patient selection process a little bit? In other words, why not say that ten of your patients who are only moderately depressed are actually severely depressed so that they can qualify for the study? If some doctors are willing to do this in the beginning, they might also be tempted to do it later in the study after they realize which patients are on placebos. Perhaps even subconsciously, they might rate the improvement as better than it is in those on the real drug. Just as patients want to please their physicians, some of the doctors may want or possibly just be tempted to please the company sponsoring the trial so that they can get involved in the next one. I'm not saying that this process takes place intentionally, which would be considered unethical at the very least. But it may happen quite at bit. The end result would be data that are seriously compromised.

Gold Standard
Even if doctors involved in the studies of antidepressants are the most ethical, honest, and unbiased people in the field of medicine, they are still dealing with a highly subjective problem—human emotions manifesting in a variety of mental states that may be quite fluid. The screening test they often use for evaluation of depression is called the Hamilton scale. It consists of 51 questions. The examiner asks you each question and then rates your response according to his or her opinion. Even if this was precisely consistent from one examiner to another, which it isn't, then the accuracy would still depend on the patient to be entirely honest in answering each question. Sorry to tell you, but a lot of patients lie, distort the truth, or simply give answers that are not truthful even though they may believe that they are.

The patient racks up a certain number of points for each answer and is then placed into some category. The higher the score, the worse it is. A low score means that the patient is not depressed. Then the categories move into mildly depressed, moderately depressed, severely depressed, or very severely depressed. Although the evaluation may be fairly accurate on either extreme, I have serious doubt about the middle range. Again there is a lot of room for error or difference of opinion. Now here's the reason this is significant. If a patient improves by only three points on the scale, that is considered a positive response to the therapy. The trouble is that such an improvement doesn't require any dramatic changes in how the patient really feels.

The Hamilton Depression Rating Scale is better known to psychiatrists and psychologists as the HAM-D. It was developed in the 1950s by Max Hamilton, a British psychiatrist. He was treating people with severe major clinical depression who required hospitalization and wanted to create a way to better standardize their mental and physical symptoms. This system was developed based on evaluation of people who were already severely depressed and was not intended to be used as a tool to figure out whether normal people were depressed or not. Nevertheless it has become the standard instrument for that. Other depression scales have been developed but this remains the so-called Gold Standard. (For those of you interested in returning to the gold standard, this has nothing to do with economic policy. It was just named after a guy whose last name was Gold.)

I think that even Dr. Hamilton might not approve of the fact that his scale is used to evaluate people's response to antidepressants in trials lasting only 4–6 weeks. I read an article in a psychiatric journal written about five years ago questioning whether this was still the gold standard or had become a lead weight. To me this test seems highly subjective and not all that reliable, but what do I know. That is a debate for the psychiatrists and psychologists to have. In the meantime it has been a linchpin in the drug industry studies of antidepressants over the last thirty years or more.

Now let's compare depression trials with medical trials that don't have all this subjectivity in them. For example, a pill taken once a day for adult-onset diabetes. Prior to the trial, the average daily blood sugar in all patients is 150 mg% in the morning before eating (normal being around 100). Four weeks later, those on placebos have maintained an average of 152 and those on the pill are 110. You don't need to spend a lot of time trying to figure out whether there is not only a significant statistical difference but a remarkable clinical difference. If the drug has few side effects, it is a winner. This kind of clear-cut result has never been demonstrated with antidepressant studies—ever.

Time Heals All Wounds

It has been said that time heals all wounds. As a surgeon I can tell you that when it comes to flesh wounds, that is true most of the time. But just as some soft tissue wounds never heal, the same can be said of emotional states occasionally. All therapy, whether medical or psychological, has to be compared against what the passage of time would accomplish by itself. If a leg wound takes three weeks to heal with no treatment but one week to heal with dressing changes, then the therapy can be deemed effective. Let's say a witch doctor gives the person a potion to drink on the day the wound is incurred and tells him this will make the it heal very quickly. If it heals in a week, then we could say that this placebo treatment was just as effective as dressing changes would have been and more effective than time alone.

So placebo effect is simply the difference between what happens with placebo compared to time alone or no treatment. The effect of a drug or other form of therapy must then be measured against the placebo effect rather than simply no treatment. In this example, dressing changes were no better than placebo. If the patient was given a pill twice a day and the wound healed in five days, then the improved outcome could be attributed to drug effect. But note that we can only compare the drug to the placebo, not to no treatment at all.

In the case of a wound that is not infected, pills are not going to speed up healing through any drug effect. Let's say the drug was an antibiotic and doubled the rate of wound healing. Even though the person is taking an active drug, that doesn't mean that the drug is responsible for the faster wound healing. It would have to be attributed to placebo effect and compared against an inert sugar pill to confirm this suspicion. Even just local wound care every day could have a placebo effect on top of whatever beneficial effect the dressing changes were having. If the person changing the dressing was telling the patient what a fast healer he was, this could possibly accelerate the rate of healing.

The power of the mind to heal the body can never be disregarded in the evaluation of any kind of therapy. Everyone is looking for a magic pill that will cure whatever problem they have. But a lot of times, the magic is not in the pill or its active ingredient but in the person's own mind. The same is true with non medical forms of therapy. In many people, psychotherapy of various kinds may be working mainly through a placebo effect.

In the case of any kind of talk therapy, the only thing you can really compare it to is time. This might be done with depressed patients by comparing a group put on a waiting list for several months after a diagnosis is made with those who start therapy right away. Unfortunately that happens a lot even in the wealthiest countries where psychotherapy resources are often limited. That is one of the big reasons antidepressant pills are so popular. It doesn't take much time to write a prescription.

Active Placebos
One possible way around the problem of using a sugar pill as placebo is to use what is called an active placebo. This is a drug that will cause side effects in the patient but should have absolutely no biochemical effect similar to the drug being tested. For an antidepressant, this means that it should not possibly have any positive effect on depression based on its chemical structure and action. A common drug used for this is atropine, which in medical terms is an anticholinergic drug. That means that it blocks the stimulation of acetylcholine receptors. In the heart as an example, the vagus nerve releases acetylcholine which causes the heart rate to slow down. Atropine does just the opposite causing the heart rate to speed up.

In other words, if atropine is the active placebo, some patients might notice that their heart rate is faster than normal. They also might experience dry mouth and other effects caused by the atropine. This could reasonably lead someone in a trial to think that he was getting the real drug, not a sugar pill. Not many such trials have been done with antidepressants, but in nine that used this protocol, seven showed no difference between the real drug and atropine. In other words, active placebos are much more likely to point to the placebo effect of the drug being tested than sugar pills. That's why they aren't used much in drug trials.

This active placebo effect also helps explain why a number of non-antidepressant drugs have been found to be effective in the treatment of depression in drug trials. One such trial tested a barbiturate, another a benzodiazepine, and yet another thyroid hormone (in patients with normal thyroid function). They were all just as effective as antidepressants used in other trials and more effective than placebos. Yet other studies have used antipsychotics, stimulant drugs like amphetamines, opiates, and herbal drugs. Again all of these proved more effective than placebos in the treatment of depression. In other words, stimulant drugs, depressive drugs, herbs, or pretty much anything you throw at depression seems to work better than placebo sugar pills. Why is that? Because they all have side effects. The mind that has been placed in a trial is always on the lookout for them, whether you the person are aware of that or not.

But this can backfire for the drug companies. Remember that the SSRIs and their successors were hailed as great new drugs because they weren't as "dirty" as the old MAOIs or tricyclics. But what if the new drug has very few side effects? Some drugs that were initially great hopefuls of the drug companies ended up failing to do any better than placebo in clinical trials for just that reason. They had to be abandoned because they were too clean. In fact, many trials have shown that the correlation between side effects and improvement is incredibly strong. In other words, the more side effects a drug has, the better the results it shows in clinical trials against placebos. That is why comparator trials between competing active drugs for depression usually show little difference. If they both have lots of side effects, they end up getting rated as equally effective. In general, the only time you see really drastic differences between psychoactive drugs being compared is when one drug company does a study comparing its drug to that of a competitor. Then you may see something like this: Our drug is effective in 60% of patients while the competitor's is only effective in 30%.

Doctors under the Gun

Most prescriptions for antidepressants are written by family doctors. Many of them resent being forced to do this by their HMOs and medical groups instead of being allowed to refer depressed patients to therapists or psychiatrists. In the UK and other countries with national health care, they can be put on a referral waiting list for many months. In the U.S., the millions who currently have no health-care coverage don't even get to see a doctor to begin with. They just cope with their depression in any way they can. Some turn to alcohol or street drugs for relief. Even many people with decent insurance never get past a gate keeper who may just write them a prescription for an antidepressant or some other psychiatric drug.

A large percentage of family doctors in the U.S. (ten years ago, it was at least 70%) know little about antidepressant withdrawal problems, and many of them feel uncomfortable or just unable to competently help wean patients off of their drugs when they request it. That leaves many patients in a bad position of not being able to find anyone to help them get off of antidepressants. Many have simply tried to go cold turkey, sometimes with disastrous results. Although I don't have any accurate current statistics, a few years ago, it was estimated that about 20 million Americans were taking antidepressants, including a million children. People should be wary about agreeing to start taking antidepressants unless their doctor gives them some kind of clear exit strategy. Either he or she will help you taper off when you want to or refer you to someone who can.

As for kids on these drugs, in 2003 the British regulatory agency controlling medicines virtually banned all antidepressants in children. Officials found that as well as not being significantly more effective than placebos, they cause many children to become agitated, aggressive, hostile, and even suicidal. In 2004 the FDA created a black box warning for antidepressants in children indicating that they would increase the likelihood of suicide over and above that of the baseline depression. The warning went on most of the popular antidepressants including Cymbalta, Zoloft, Paxil, Effexor, Luvox, Prozac, and others. Although they did not ban any of them, they maintained their previous position that only Prozac was approved by the FDA for use in children with depression.

Meanwhile, many American doctors continued to prescribe a variety of antidepressants for children in what is called "off label" prescribing. It is entirely legal and here's how it works. If I believe that thyroid hormone is effective for the treatment of depression (despite no studies showing its effectiveness for that), I can prescribe it to my patients with depression even though they have no problems with their thyroid function. As long as the drug is legal for something, any doctor can use it for whatever he or she wants with little risk of problems as long as their patients stay under the radar (don't suffer severe adverse consequences from the drug). Doctors have a lot of power and are often poorly regulated. Many of them get away with incompetent practices for a long time. I've seen plenty of examples.

Truth in Advertising
Although their antidepressants don't work as advertised to treat depression, ads by the drug companies do work very well. Some of them spend

much more on advertising their drugs than they do on research and development. Research on drug ads reveals that they are quite effective in selling their products. One study showed that on average every dollar spent on the ads brings in about $1.37 in drug sales. In 2007 more than 500,000 people in the U.S. scheduled visits with their doctors as a direct result of seeing antidepressant ads. The companies and some psychiatrists would pitch this to the public as a good thing. People with depression are being prompted to get help. I see it differently. People who are unhappy because of their life problems are looking for a drug to magically get rid of them. What many of them will get is just more problems.

In fact it's even worse than it sounds. The researcher from Harvard who found that half a million people sought antidepressants as a result of ads estimated using epidemiological data that only about 7% of them actually had clinical depression. Fortunately the doctors just sent the rest of them away—right? Wrong. Other studies show that probably half of them or more got prescriptions for antidepressants. This is the same problem I mentioned elsewhere. Many doctors will give patients what they ask for even if it's not indicated. No need to take time to explain why they don't need an antibiotic for a viral flu or engage in confrontation. Just give them what they ask for so that you can get on to the next patient.

A study was done using actors who went on almost 300 doctor visits a few years ago. They were trained to simulate major depressive disorder and adjustment disorder with depressed mood. The first group should be diagnosed with depression and get some form of treatment while the second group should not. The doctors missed the diagnosis of depression in 20% of patients with it but diagnosed 40% of the people who were not depressed with depression. The number of people in each group diagnosed with depression increased dramatically when the patient asked for drugs. Overall about 75% of those who asked for drugs got them. Of those given drugs, most who specifically asked for one brand got it.

Consider that these were actors who were not depressed. Try faking a diagnosis of hypertension or diabetes and walking away with a prescription. After you watch a few ads on depression, you kind of learn to fake the diagnosis. Just say you have the symptoms they mention in the ad and you get the magic pill (This could be done intentionally or subconsciously). All this is great for drug company profits but not so good for the non-depressed people who end up getting addicted to antidepressants that they didn't need to be on in the first place. When they really push hard with their marketing, they can turn a drug with poor sales into a huge winner. 90% of prescriptions for one such drug several years ago were off label.

Whistleblower?

Many readers may be incredulous that they haven't previously heard what I'm saying about antidepressants and drug trials, but let me assure you that I am not exposing anything that hasn't been well known for at least the last 20 years. The drug companies and the government agencies that regulate them and review their drug trials have known very well for many years that antidepressants performed little better than placebos. Many psychiatrists, especially those involved in drug trials, were also aware of this problem. So who didn't know? Pretty much everyone else it seems.

Certainly I never knew anything about all this until I started doing a lot of research on this subject over the last five years. My mother was treated by psychiatrists for what they diagnosed as manic-depression throughout the time I was in college, medical school, and surgery residency. I got more involved in helping her out as she got older and had frequent contact with a number of her psychiatrists over many years. I always assumed that they must know what they were doing and that the drugs they were giving her would help her with what they diagnosed as chronic depression. To me she seemed OK and quite functional much of the time. I thought this was due to her medication. Now I have a different view. She was doing all right in spite of her meds.

When they told me in the early 90s that the new SSRIs would work much better for her than the tricyclics like Elavil that she had taken for many years, I believed them. I thought that they were also being sincere and that what they were doing was the best thing for her. They never attempted any serious psychotherapy. They would just chit chat for a little while each time she went in to get her prescription renewed. The psychotherapy was left up to me. I was the one my mother talked to incessantly about her problems. I could usually make her temporarily feel better, but certainly never felt as though I made much headway. I just kept hoping that her psychiatrists and their drugs were actually helping her.

Looking back nine years after her death, I don't think they ever did much for her. I know that some of their drugs led to tardive dyskinesia that gave her incessant problems that no one could do anything about. My mother was a passive patient like most people are and went along with pretty much whatever doctors recommended. She relied on me to let her know if her doctors were doing anything that might be wrong or inappropriate. Although I frequently advised friends and family members over the years not to follow medical or surgical advice given to them, I didn't know enough about psychiatry to be able to do that. Now that I do know something, I want to share that knowledge with as many people as possible so that they don't end up casually accepting advice to start taking various psychoactive drugs for their life problems.

So I was in the dark when it came to many psychiatric drugs and especially antidepressants for many years. Was I alone? Not at all. With the exception of many psychiatrists, most other doctors were not aware of the poor results of antidepressant drug trials. Nor were they aware of the many of the common side effects and serious withdrawal problems that these drugs caused. Remember that psychiatrists are in a minority when it comes to prescribing psychoactive drugs. Probably most of the doctors prescribing antidepressants over the last fifteen years have been as much in the dark as I was. And of course the other people who didn't know what some drug company insiders have referred to as their "dirty little secret" were the millions of patients taking these drugs.

Have some people with inside knowledge been trying to get word out for the last twenty years or more? Absolutely, but unfortunately their voices have been pretty much drowned out by the corporations and media. The winners have been the big drug companies who continue to make billions of dollars selling mind-altering drugs to millions of people, many of whom are adversely affected by them. Peter Breggin wrote a book called *Toxic Psychiatry* in 1991 as well as many other books before and since then. They are a profound indictment of the entire psychoactive drug industry and the collusion of psychiatry with them. He was the major whistleblower but never had his message taken seriously (especially not by the media) as far as I am concerned. I hope to change that if I can.

Psychotherapy
Before I start talking about alternatives to drugs for various psychiatric problems in the next chapter, I want to clarify what I mean by psychotherapy. Does any conversation with someone who calls him or herself a

therapist count? No. There are different kinds of psychotherapy. First of all, there is Freudian psychoanalysis started by the most famous cocaine addict in history. It was probably all the rage in the early and mid-1900s for many people (at least those who could afford it). In the U.S., behaviorism became popular as a form of therapy in the 1920s and 30s, championed by psychologists such as B.F. Skinner. By the 1960s, both behavioral psychology and psychoanalysis began to fall out of favor. The new approach was a kind of cognitive therapy, pioneered by the late Albert Ellis with rational emotive therapy. Aaron Beck followed on soon after with cognitive therapy.

That remains the workhorse of psychotherapy to this day in the form of cognitive-behavioral therapy (CBT). There are still many psychoanalysts, but they are probably catering to wealthier people who find their lives so difficult and want to spend a few years trying to figure out why. A newer shorter form of therapy called psychodynamics was spawned by psychoanalysis with the same ideas of dredging up problems from childhood. I don't know anything about it, but it supposedly only takes a few months, rather than years, to complete.

Cognition refers to thinking, and behavior refers to—well, behavior. So therapy is aimed at helping you to change both thinking and behavior. They both influence each other, sometimes dramatically. To give you several simplistic examples, if you think that you have no athletic ability, you're not likely to sign up for tennis lessons. If someone can convince that you do have athletic potential, then you might start exercising and try to get into shape. Or you could try to change your thinking by creating a change in behavior first. If someone can convince a person to start exercising regularly and encourage him to keep doing it, this may lead him to start seeing himself as having athletic potential. I'll talk more about psychotherapy as well as other alternatives to drugs in the next chapter.

14

What Happened to My Drugs?

When I was a plastic surgery resident, I developed a great interest in malignant melanoma, a dangerous form of skin cancer that originates in moles. I researched the literature extensively looking for the answer to a question that perplexed me. Why was it necessary to perform wide excisions around moles that proved to be malignant? This was not necessary for squamous-cell cancer of the skin, also highly malignant.

Back then, every surgery textbook recommended wide local excision of normal skin (3–4 cm or 1.5–2 inches) around the tumor as the only acceptable way to be sure that no malignant cells were left behind. This often required a big operation and resulted in a serious deformity, just to remove a small mole. The explanation given was that these tumors were usually associated with microscopic deposits of metastatic tumor around the primary tumor, sometimes out as far as two inches or more.

In the many journal articles spanning almost 80 years, most referred back to a doctor named Handley, who first discovered these microscopic deposits. When I dug up his article, written in the British medical journal, *The Lancet*, in 1903, I was astounded. His study was based on the autopsy of a woman who had died of malignant melanoma. He was studying metastatic lesions, not primary tumors, when he came up with his findings and recommended wide local excision.

Many brilliant surgeons followed Hanley's advice for the next 75 years, but apparently nobody bothered to go back and read the original article. If they did, they couldn't have read it very carefully or really thought about it much. As a result, thousands of people over many years may have undergone overly aggressive and sometimes unnecessary disfiguring operations.

I started giving lectures recommending that the standard policy of wide local excision for primary malignant melanoma be re-evaluated. During my plastic surgery practice, I gave a one-hour talk in Surgery Grand Rounds at UCSD Medical Center to a large group of surgeons, residents, and medical students. In the audience was a cancer surgeon reputed to be one of the world's foremost experts on malignant melanoma.

After my lecture, the Chief of Surgery said that the talk had been pro-vocative and then asked the expert to get up and set things straight. He came to the microphone and said, "That was the best talk I have ever heard in my life on malignant melanoma. I have nothing to add to what Dr. Chapin said."

What does that have to do with depression and psychiatric drugs? Not much except this. The biochemical imbalance theory of psychiatric disorders is to psychiatry what Handley's work was to surgery and the treatment of malignant melanoma for most of the 20th century. Just as a lot of people may have undergone unnecessary disfiguring operations for melanoma (and I did some of them), many people have been harmed by taking certain psychiatric drugs that never really had much of a chance of helping them. Scientists and medical doctors need to take a more serious look at this theory and where it came from. (By the way, the debate over wide local excision in melanoma continues some 25 years later.)

The rationale for the radical treatment of melanoma originally came from a study that had nothing to do with the disease in most people (pri-mary malignant melanoma), but the origin of the theory of the biochemi-cal imbalance in the brain is much worse than that. It was intentionally created by the pharmaceutical industry in order to sell drugs. Over time it was accepted by many psychiatrists and subsequently other physicians, the media, and the general public.

Even though science does not support it, it is still the prevailing theory among physicians who frequently tell their patients with depression and other psychiatric disorders that they have a biochemical imbalance in their brains and need drugs to correct them, possibly or maybe even probably, for the rest of their lives. Scientists who have been trying to verify this theory for the last forty years have been unable to. I can't help but quote from President Kennedy: The great enemy of truth is very often not the lie—deliberate, contrived, and dishonest—but the myth—persistent, per-suasive, and unrealistic. (Maybe that's where British psychiatrist Joanna Moncrief got the idea for the title of her excellent book *The Myth of the Chemical Cure*.)

Pharmaceuticals and Cosmeceuticals

If drugs aren't so great for a lot of people, are there really any alternative ways to treat psychiatric and psychological problems without them? In the first half of the 20th century, we had somewhat limited options other than illegal drugs for the treatment of problems like anxiety and depression. These included (in chronological order) barbiturates, insulin shock therapy, electroconvulsive therapy, frontal lobotomy, and then amphetamines. During the second half, we progressed to major tranquilizers, minor tranquilizers, and antidepressants.

If I have managed to cast some doubt about whether these procedures and drugs work as advertised, what are we left with that doesn't involve drugs or procedures that can or possibly might cause some degree of brain function disruption or damage? I've mentioned psychotherapy and also said that its main effectiveness for some people might well be attributed to a placebo effect as is true of antidepressants.

So what if many of these things work primarily through a placebo effect some physicians might say. What difference does it make as long as they work? People with anxiety and depression need help. Just give it to them in whatever way you can. Here's the problem with that. Just as I pointed out that psychiatry is not surgery, neither are drugs the same as cosmeceuticals. Most doctors know a lot about drugs but little about cosmeceuticals. As a plastic surgeon, I know a lot about both.

A cosmeceutical is a skin-care product that contains active ingredients that are supposed to have an effect on the skin. You see them in all beauty stores, spas, drug stores, and the offices of many dermatologists and plastic surgeons. Unlike drugs that go into your body, they are not under the oversight of the FDA or any regulatory agency with respect to quality control or effectiveness. The only thing they will sometimes go after is false or misleading advertising of these products, which is easy to avoid.

Let's say that I start my own line of cosmeceuticals. The first one I come out with is a vitamin cream that goes under your eyes to help smooth out the skin and decrease wrinkles and aging changes over time. In order to market it, I say it contains Vitamin L (the L stands for love). Nobody knows what's in it except me, but let's say it contains some B and C vitamins. I have conducted tests on patients in my cosmetic surgery practice. One group got placebo which was just an ordinary moisturizer that you could buy cheaply at any drug or grocery store. The other was the same except with some vitamins added. Being conscientious, I followed the patients for six months and found absolutely no difference in the two groups.

However, because I need money, I decide to go ahead and market Dr. Chapin's L Cream for beautiful eyes. I put it in a really small (tiny) tinted glass container and sell it for $50. Because you're paying so much for so little, it must be good. That's what a lot of my customers would think. I will guarantee you that if I did a good job of marketing it that most of the customers would swear that their eyes looked better within a short period of time.

Would I be doing anything wrong here? Certainly some people might consider this to be a little unethical, but welcome to the world of cosmetics and skin-care products. The thing that really bothers some of you is that I know for a fact that my product doesn't really do anything when I market and sell it for outrageous prices. Any perceived improvement by people using it will be a placebo effect. But so what? I'm not really hurting anybody.

I hate to break the news to you, folks, but this is exactly the attitude that many physicians and psychiatrists have about prescribing benzos, antidepressants, and some of the other psychiatric drugs. Some of them refer to their patients as the "walking wounded." I'm not exactly sure what that means since when I hear the word "wounded" as a surgeon, psychological problems aren't usually what pop into my mind first. I think many who use the phrase do so mockingly, referring to people who just don't seem to be able to deal with ordinary life problems effectively. It's kind of like the derogatory word sometimes used by doctors in emergency medicine when referring to street people, drug addicts, and other undesirables—gomers (which stands for "get out of my ER"). So much for compassion.

I have read major players in psychiatry quoted as feeling that they don't see any problem with treating the walking wounded with antidepressants. They may not really have serious depression, but what the hell—a lot of them get better on these drugs. So why not prescribe them? Well here's the problem. These are drugs that you take into your body, not creams that you are putting on your skin. In my example, the only problem anyone might have with my skin cream could be an allergic reaction manifested by a skin rash. I would make sure that everyone knew to test for that before they started using the product.

All drugs ingested internally can be dangerous or fatal. Thousands of people in the U.S. and around the world die every month as a reaction to such drugs as I have mentioned previously. Psychoactive drugs are no exception. Although relatively few people die as a result of using them, many become addicted and have great difficulty getting off of them. These drugs do not correct biochemical imbalances or deranged brain function as many experts claim. In fact they may sometimes cause them, as I have already said.

In one of Peter Breggin's recent books, *Medication Madness*, he recounts the sad story of a man who had several young kids and wanted to quit his habit of having several drinks every evening. He mentioned some anxiety about giving up alcohol altogether to his doctor who suggested he take the SSRI Paxil to help him with this. Three days after he started taking the lowest dose possible, he committed a violent murder suicide by drowning himself and his young children in his bathtub. He had an exemplary work record at a high-tech firm and had never had any psychiatric problems, treatment, or counseling in his life. So when you hear that these drugs are basically harmless, especially in low doses, don't believe it for a second.

Since drugs have some serious problems and may not be the best way to deal with depression in many people, what are the alternatives? First let's look at psychotherapy.

Cognitive Therapy

The fact is that not much has changed since the late 1800s. Freud treated depression with a drug (cocaine) for several years and then decided to go back to psychotherapy. He developed psychoanalysis and continued to use that therapy for the rest of his life and passed it on to his protégés. Although various kinds of therapy have evolved over the last hundred years, the one most commonly used now is some form of cognitive or cognitive-behavioral therapy. Two of the big pioneers in this field of psychology in the 20th century were Albert Ellis and Aaron Beck. Ellis died several years ago at the age of 94 and Beck is in his late 80s.

Cognitive therapy is quite different from psychoanalysis. In fact Beck's membership application to The American Psychoanalytic Institute was rejected years ago because the organization said that "his mere desire to conduct scientific studies signaled that he had been improperly analyzed." (Ouch—as a psychoanalytically trained psychiatrist, that must have really pissed him off.) I don't know much about psychoanalysis, but when I refer to psychotherapy for the treatment of depression, that's not what I'm talking about. In head-to-head studies comparing antidepressants with psychotherapy, talk therapy either comes out as effective or sometimes more effective. However this is only true in reference to some form of cognitive-behavioral therapy.

I have discussed this issue elsewhere in the book and the potential problems associated with psychotherapy—the big ones being the time required and the expense involved (given that many insurance companies have poor or no coverage). I also pointed out that improvement for many people may be largely a placebo effect, as is true of all antidepressants. However good talk therapy does something that drugs don't do. It teaches people how to better cope with their life problems. That's why relapse rates are often significantly higher for people who have drug treatment without any psychotherapy once they get off the drugs.

Why should this be true? Because they haven't gotten at the core problem. First of all, if the patients really had a biochemical imbalance that was causing their depression, then they should never get off the drugs. (Once you've been diagnosed with diabetes, do you just take your pills for a year and then stop them to see how things go?) That's exactly what the pharmaceutical companies want everyone to believe and why they fabricated the theory to begin with. Unfortunately many physicians and lay people have accepted the bogus theory as gospel, which works out perfectly for the drug companies but not so well for many patients taking their pills.

The people I am trying to reach in this book who think they are depressed are those with mild to moderate depression. Many famous people have suffered with severe recurrent major depression, which used to be called melancholia. I believe this was eliminated as a diagnostic category when the DSM III became the DSM IV in 1994. A few psychiatrists would like to see it brought back with the DSM V due out in 2012.

I think this would be a good idea because severe debilitating major clinical depression should be in its own category. There should be some way to clearly distinguish the following two people suffering from "depression." The first one is a teenage girl talking to her friend: "I'm so depressed because my cat just got run over by a car." The second is a man talking to another friend who also has a lot of problems. "I don't know what's wrong with me. Things seem to be OK for a while and then I just can't function at all. I have been in bed for most of the last two weeks but can't sleep much. I've hardly eaten anything and all I can think about is whether it would be better to take pills or use my gun." His friend says, "I hear you, man."

The girl just needs emotional support from her parents and friends. The man needs more help than he can get from just reading this book or maybe any book. I'm glad there are therapists and clinicians who are willing to help such people. My focus is on the majority of people with depression who fall in between these extremes. The problem many, if not most of them, have is not a biochemical disorder but a thought disorder. A famous motivational speaker frequently used the phrase "stinking thinking" to describe what kept people from achieving big goals. That is also a major cause of depression and lots of other psychological problems in many people.

Psychoactive pills have two problems. They not only don't balance the chemicals in your brain but do often unbalance them. Secondly in the treatment of depression and anxiety, they don't do anything to change your stinking thinking. That is where good cognitive-behavioral therapy (CBT) comes in and is exactly what it is supposed to do. How helpful it is depends on how capable the therapist is and how willing and determined the patient is to critically look at the way he or she deals with life problems. If the patient can't relate to or doesn't like the psychotherapist, then the outcome may not be so great. If, on the other hand, the patient admires and looks up to the therapist, the outcome may be positive, even if the therapy isn't all that good (the placebo effect). Obviously the best combination is a receptive patient and a good therapist who get along well.

Even if you end up with mostly a placebo effect, how does that compare to the same thing with an antidepressant drug? The answer is simple. Psychotherapy doesn't carry the risk of side effects, addiction, and withdrawal problems, not to mention an increased risk of suicide associated with some of the drugs. I'm not saying that therapists can't ever do damage to people. One of my cousins with an eating disorder and other serious psychological problems went to a therapist who helped her recover repressed memories when that was a big fad in the U.S. back in the 1990s. That therapy was a total disaster and tore her family apart. Although maybe some former patients might disagree with me, I would think that outcomes like this are rare. In contrast, such devastating outcomes with drugs are not rare.

Even if the psychotherapy isn't that good and doesn't really help some people more effectively deal with their life problems, it's still safer than drugs by a long shot. I would liken it to my Vitamin L cream that I mentioned earlier. It's expensive and doesn't really do what it was supposed to, but at least nobody gets hurt by it. It would be a lot safer to use my eye cream and think your eyes look better than to have surgery done by a incompetent surgeon followed by terrible complications that could make your eyelids look worse for a long time.

You need to judge all therapy based on a risk-benefit ratio. You should be looking for extremely low risk with high potential benefit. Good CBT could give that to you and possibly dramatically improve your life and ability to cope with its problems. Psychoactive drugs will not do that for very many people. Some people may swear that such drugs saved their lives just as the patients who had the bogus chest surgery I talked about in the placebo chapter said the same thing. Changing your thinking and ability to deal with your emotions and reactions to them really can transform your life for the long term, not just temporarily.

Inexpensive Therapy

What if you are mildly to moderately depressed and don't want to take drugs, but your insurance won't pay for psychotherapy (or you don't have any health insurance like millions of Americans). Yes, it is actually possible for some people to work through the problem themselves, maybe with the help of friends or perhaps self-help groups. I have mentioned some books previously and recommend many on my web site. You can get them from a library if you can't afford to buy them. For example, you could read books by a woman called Byron Katie.

She is not a psychologist but has developed an abbreviated but effective form of cognitive therapy that she calls The Work that has helped thousands of people all over the world with a variety of psychological problems including depression. In fact she suffered from severe major depression for many years until she had a revelation one day: Her depression was caused by believing her own thoughts. If you want to know more about her personal story, you can read it in her books such as *I Need Your Love—Is That True?* or *Loving What Is* (written with her husband, Stephen

Mitchell, a great author in his own right). You can also learn more about her kind of therapy from her web site TheWork.com.

If you like what she has to say, you could attend one of her seminars if you can afford to do that. She also has an audio program available from Nightingale-Conant. I have not attended any of her seminars or heard the audio program but know from her books that she demands excellence from herself (and others). You can check out some of her videos on youtube.

Seminars I have attended and can recommend that teach you how to deal with your life problems are those of the Sedona Method. Founded by Lester Levinson 40 years ago, the company was taken over by Hale Dwoskin after Lester's death. You can start out with the core book, *The Sedona Method*, and go from there, depending on what you can afford (check out sedona.com for options.) If it doesn't appeal to you, then keep looking for other alternatives to drugs if you would rather avoid them.

If you are suffering from serious depression or other major psychological disorders, then get professional help, especially if you have already been trying to deal with such issues on your own. My suggestions are probably going to appeal mostly to people whose lives are basically OK but would just like to improve them. If you are under a doctor's care and taking drugs, don't just stop taking them and then go to one of these seminars as a way of trying to deal with your problems.

Free Therapy
What about people who can't afford any kind of therapy and don't like to read books. Are there any other options available to such people who are mildly or moderately depressed? Yes, they need to get up and move their bodies. Exercise works as well for many people in getting rid of and preventing depression as antidepressants and psychotherapy. And it doesn't have to cost any money. People with mild or moderate depression don't need to join a gym or expensive yoga club, but they do need to exercise.

I wrote a lot about exercise in my first book *FutureLife* and one of the endorsements I received came from a world champion triathlete who said that it was one of the best books he had ever read on exercise (although that subject was only a small part of it). I work out almost every day doing vigorous aerobic workouts, weight lifting, and yoga-type exercises. Other than the electricity for my treadmill, it costs me nothing. If you can afford to join a gym and get a personal trainer, then do it. Most people need to be pushed to exercise, especially people who are depressed.

Multiple studies have shown that exercise alone can often be as effective as drugs or psychotherapy for many people with depression. If you can do both CBT in some form or another and exercise as well, that would be the safest bet. Some of the studies have shown that it doesn't make that much difference what kind of exercise you are doing. In other words, you don't have to pretend like you're training for a marathon. Just walk everyday as much as you can and do whatever other exercise you can fit in. Something is better than nothing.

I will not make any specific recommendations because I don't know any of you readers or anything about your health status. Here is the necessary warning. Before you start on any exercise program, have your physician do a complete evaluation and then tell you what he or she thinks would be a safe program for you. Don't just decide to start running five miles a day when you may have undiagnosed serious coronary disease and then try to blame me because I suggested that exercise might help your depression and somehow caused you to have a heart attack after running a quarter of a mile.

That reminds of a story related by a preventive medicine doctor named Kenneth Cooper who has been extolling the benefits of exercise for thirty years. A man who had a heart attack was found on evaluation to have inoperable coronary artery disease. He became quite despondent about his diagnosis and decided there was no point in living any more. He didn't want to traumatize his family by committing suicide, so he decided he would start running around his neighborhood every day. He was sure that he would just drop dead if he did that and cause no embarrassment to his family. After a few runs, nothing happened, much to his amazement. He continued running, started feeling better, and realized that his life was still worth living after all.

When told they need to exercise, people sometimes answer honestly and say, "Yeah, I know, but I don't have the time." Others claim that they do exercise and believe it. They walk from the couch to the refrigerator to get food or they walk to the car to drive to the nearest fast-food restaurant. Thirty percent of American children and more than 60% of adults are overweight. Despite all the gyms and exercise equipment stores in the U.S., the fact is that only about 15% of Americans exercise regularly in any serious way (Playing nine holes of golf using a golf cart and having a cocktail before you start each hole doesn't count). Probably less than 10% of Americans follow my kind of routine, and I'm not in training to do anything. I just like staying healthy, feeling good, and definitely not being depressed.

Our bodies were made to be in motion much of the time, but our modern sedentary lifestyle has changed all of that. The old yellow pages add "let your fingers do the walking" has been carried to absurd extremes. Now we can do our grocery shopping online, have gourmet dinners delivered to our homes, and order just about anything we need off of the Internet. The only thing you have to do is walk to the door to get the delivery. Then you can go right back to watching TV or web surfing.

I'm not saying that I don't have mainly a sedentary lifestyle sitting in front of my computer all day when I am focussed on writing. But that is exactly why I place a top priority on exercising every morning. I do more than I probably need to for 45–90 minutes depending on what I feel like. I realize that it's difficult for most people to find that much time for exercise and it really isn't necessary, especially for people who are depressed.

I know what it's like to not have enough time to do things you would like to. When I was a surgery resident, I often worked more than a hundred hours a week. I not only didn't get to sleep very much, but sometimes was only able to eat one complete meal a day supplemented with junk food from machines in the hospital because the cafeteria was often closed when I got out of surgery.

When I was a junior resident on cardiac surgery, the chief resident was a petite female who demanded that we all eat breakfast together at 6:30 after making rounds and before starting surgery. Was this some quirky ritual? No. She knew that on many days, that would be the only meal we would get. All the surgery residents working under her were males, and she realized that we wouldn't eat anything healthy some days unless she made us. She probably also wanted to insure that we didn't pass out in the operating room from hypoglycemia while she was replacing somebody's aortic valve. None of the male residents I worked under ever cared whether I ate, slept, or did anything else other than my assigned duties. (You can read more about her in *Boy to Man*.)

During that brutal residency training, there was no way that I could have found time to formally exercise, although I did run up and down the hospital stairs a lot. But how many of you are honestly working that hard? Not many, I would guess. The reason most people don't exercise is that they don't make it a priority. Or as one guy in a Sedona Method seminar said when the speaker asked if anyone wanted to discuss a particular problem, "I've been thinking about exercising for the last 30 years, but I just don't seem to be able to do it." Everyone laughed including the instructor who then explained that he used to have the same problem. When he first got married, his wife wanted him to go to the gym with her. While she took a one-hour aerobics class, what did he do? He got a massage. He later realized how important exercise was and had been doing it religiously every day for years.

Studies in the late 1980s showed that the risk of developing depression in baby boomers like myself increased by ten or even twenty times that of people born in the first half of the 20th century in the U.S. Less westernized cultures did not show such trends. In "primitive" people like the Bushmen in Africa who have been hunter gatherers for thousands of years and were studied extensively in the 1960s, depression and suicide were almost unheard of. Now that they have become more westernized, like much of the world, all bets are off. What is it that differentiates these groups from most modern people? The development of a sedentary lifestyle.

If you look at the Amish people in the U.S. who have retained their mid nineteenth century lifestyle rejecting electricity, cars, and the many laborsaving machines used by everyone else, what can you learn? With physical activity as a central part of their lives, they have one-fifth to one-tenth of the incidence of major depression (non-bipolar) seen in the rest of the U.S.

Is exercise the only factor playing a major role in decreasing depression rates in people who live off the land without all the modern conveniences available to most of us? No, there is undoubtedly more to it than that, such as the way they think. But exercise plays a major role in my opinion. Maybe the American Psychiatric Association doesn't officially recognize exercise as a valid treatment for depression, but I do, and so do a lot of psychiatrists and psychologists. So get with the program and start exercising, especially if you are just mildly depressed. Make sure your exercise program is approved by your medical doctor and if you are already getting treatment of any kind, then work on a path forward with your own doctor, therapist, or other health-care provider.

If you begin exercising regularly as a part of your therapy for depression, you will not only speed up your recovery in many cases, but might possibly prevent future episodes by continuing to do it for the rest of your life. There will also be many other potential beneficial effects. First of all, your body will be healthier overall. Depending on the kind of exercise you do and how much you do it, you may decrease your risk of heart disease, stroke, and developing certain cancers (the three main causes of death, at least in most first-world countries). A mile a day keeps the doctor away. Get moving and good luck.

15

Kids on Drugs

One of the most haunting patients I treated as a jail doctor was an 18-year-old white male named Nick. My first encounter with him followed what the deputies had described as a suicide attempt. As I sewed up what was a superficial wrist laceration, I asked him, "Were you trying to kill yourself?"

"No," he said. "I was just mad at one of the deputies." I was quite perplexed by this response.

Noticing other scars on his arms, I asked, "Where did these come from?"

"Those were other times I cut myself," he said calmly. "I do that whenever I get really upset."

I had seen patients during my surgery residency and private practice who engaged in one form of self-mutilation or another, but no one like this. Those people were doing things subconsciously for what psychiatrists call secondary gain. I'll give you an example of this phenomenon. Without consciously being aware of it, a patient may reach under a dressing and contaminate a fresh surgical wound, thereby causing the wound to get infected.

One of my most difficult patients in private practice did this repeatedly. She found that being hospitalized elicited great sympathy from her husband and children, who generally were neglectful of her (at least from her point of view). It was extremely hard to prove that this was the cause of repeated strange infections, but we did. When the psychiatrists got involved, they were never able to get her to acknowledge that she had done this.

As far as mutilation in suicide attempts goes, I had previously treated a lot of people in ERs following attempted suicide, but most of them did not have life-threatening injuries. Many people who hurt themselves don't really want to die; this is just their way of trying to let people know that they need help. But Nick was not hurting himself to get attention or help; it was simply his way of coping with stress. Our psychiatrists had diagnosed him as having some sort of nonspecific personality disorder and had put him on antidepressants.

Because I was somewhat confused by his story, I spent a few minutes talking to him after sewing up his laceration. Although he was polite, cooperative, and able to communicate fairly well, the most unusual thing about him was his striking appearance, somewhat similar to Tom Cruise at the same age. You don't see a lot of people who have movie-star looks in jail. All other things being equal, people who are very attractive often have a distinct advantage over others in life. But he wasn't exactly the valedictorian of his high school class. He probably never finished middle school.

"Do you use drugs?" I asked.

"Yeah, all of them," he said.

I had seen a lot of drug abusers with a variety of problems, but no one quite like this. "How long have you been using drugs?"

"Since I was nine," he said, matter-of-factly.

Although I considered myself to be pretty hardened from my many years of medical training and practice, I was really flabbergasted. "Where were your parents?" I asked.

"Oh, they gave them to me." He was using cocaine by the time he got to fourth grade. I was amazed that this kid was still alive after hearing this. Not many people's good looks or even intelligence could pull them out of a past like this one.

The next time I saw Nick two months later, he had a self-inflicted five-inch laceration that went all the way through the fat layer to the abdominal wall muscles. He was angry with one of the deputies who wouldn't let him go into the day room and watch a TV program he wanted to see. During the half-hour it took to sew him up, I thought I might be developing some rapport with him. I asked him to promise me that he would not do anything like this again. He said he would try to look for other ways to relieve his anger.

I felt good that I might be having a positive influence on his self-destructive behavior. He was very pleasant and cooperative when I took the sutures out the next week. However, my naïve delusion of having gotten through to him was shattered a few weeks later when he was brought up with multiple wrist lacerations. I don't know how to categorize his self-destructive behavior, but he was one of the most frustrating and depressing patients I encountered in my jailhouse experience.

Warning

Before you start to read any more of this chapter, I have to give you a warning. It deals with an extremely controversial issue (at least in the U.S.). If you believe that millions of children suffer from ADD and other psychiatric illnesses, then you better stop and think about moving on to the next chapter instead of reading this one. Or perhaps you are a teacher or parent and have seen many cases of children whose lives have been transformed by psychiatric drugs.

On the other hand, if you are not sure whether psychiatric drugs are good for children and would like to know more, then keep on reading. True believers in giving children mind-altering drugs to help them learn and behave better should stop right here. Please skip this chapter. I will guarantee you that some of you will get angry, and the last thing I want to do is get people upset. Make them think, yes, but not stress them out.

Accelerated Learning

A big craze back in the 1970s and 80s was accelerated learning. The Russians and other eastern bloc countries under their control supposedly developed a number of secret techniques that were then marketed in the U.S. to help people read and study more efficiently, learn languages much more quickly, and so on. But then we Americans found a much easier solution to learning problems. Instead of listening to baroque music while you read a textbook or listen to language tapes, you could just take some speed.

The collusion of the psychiatric profession with the pharmaceutical industry can be well demonstrated with so-called attention deficit disorder or ADHD where the H stands for hyperactivity. From my perspective, this is merely one of many attempts by psychiatrists as a group to pathologize normal and natural but often unwanted or undesireable human behavior. If you carefully read all of the criteria for ADD in the DSM-IV, it is nothing more than a list of behaviors that annoy teachers (and many parents). I've got news for you: Children are supposed to be annoying, disobedient, uncooperative, and difficult to deal with at times—just like puppies (not to mention many adults).

Even the staunch advocates of ADD stimulant drugs will admit that many children out grow this "disease." It's funny how that tends to happen when their home and school environment improves. Also many parents freely admit that the problem often seems to go away during summer vacation when many kids on these drugs can get along just fine without them. These and many other observations do not support the position claimed by many psychiatrists and especially the pharmaceutical companies that ADHD is caused by some kind of biochemical problem in the brain.

Long before this psychiatric condition had ever become a widespread epidemic in the U.S., I had some brief experience teaching children. After I graduated a semester early from college, I worked as a substitute teacher in the Montgomery County schools in Maryland, which I had attended myself throughout my childhood. As is true of most kids, my teachers ranged from lousy to average to occasionally excellent.

In the latter category was Mrs. Hadari, my 10th grade teacher in science who had a PhD in biology and got me interested in becoming a doctor. I would also include Miss Casey (my 10th grade English teacher), Mrs. Jenkins (my 11th grade Spanish teacher), and Mr. Woolford (my 12th grade teacher in calculus) in this group. As many of my fellow baby boomers can probably relate to, the day I remember most vividly in high school was when another teacher rushed into Mrs. Jenkins class in a panic and announced that President Kennedy had been shot.

Even though I would only be teaching for a semester before I started medical school, I wanted to be as good as they had been. I would like to point out that most of my fellow students hated Miss Casey and Mr. Woolford because they were very formal and strict. Although some of my classmates may have been suffering from ADD in those classes (unable to stay focused on Shakespeare or calculus equations), I definitely was not. I thought they were fantastic teachers.

After my first several weeks of substitute teaching, I had little trouble with the high school students but quickly decided that I would never be able to control seventh graders. Although I wanted to teach them something in the one or two days I would be with them when their regular teacher was ill, it seemed hopeless. My reaction was not anger when they acted like children. Quite the opposite, I could not help but laugh out loud at some of their antics to get attention. Once that happened, they knew that they had the rule of the house.

When I taught language courses in French and Spanish, I quickly found a way to get cooperation from older children. After my second year in college, I took a summer course in French literature at the University of Paris. While there and when later traveling in Spain, I discovered that many rock and roll hits in English had been remade in their languages. The records that I brought back quickly allowed me to get complete cooperation in language classes. I simply told the students that I would play one song at the beginning of class and one at the end if they let me teach them the material I had for that day (or several days). I enticed them with the idea that they would eventually be able to understand and sing the lyrics themselves in French or Spanish if they studied hard.

I then tried this on the younger kids in non-language classes and they loved it. They thought it was really cool to hear rock and roll songs in a foreign language and started paying attention to whatever I had to teach them. Needless to say, none of their other teachers had done anything like this. Because most of the students liked me and I made the class interesting, they usually did what I asked them to.

Since those days in the late 60s, ADD has evolved into an epidemic in the U.S. Although I am far from an expert on this subject, what psychiatrist Peter Breggin says about it in *The Ritalin Fact Book* and *Reclaiming Our Children* makes a lot of sense to me. His mission seems to be to get as many people as possible (and especially children) off of psychiatric drugs. Although I have never raised any children, he has raised four of his own and treated thousands of patients over his long career. His approach has always been talk therapy, and he has never started anyone on psychiatric drugs. The only drug prescriptions he writes are to help people already on drugs to slowly withdraw from them. Many of his patients are addicted to various psychiatric drugs and have been unable to get off of them by themselves or with the help of other physicians.

Attention Deficit—It's Real

Now let me ask you this. Isn't it true that many children are suffering from an attention deficit? The answer is an unqualified yes. They are not getting enough attention from their parents, teachers, and other adults in their lives. Because they crave attention in the form of love, caring, understanding, and respect, they act out when they don't get it. Once they reach adulthood, I think it is possible to get many people out of those patterns, but children are in an entirely different situation; they are totally dependent on the adults taking care of them. They don't have any other choice. They need love, kindness, and compassion. However, what most of them do not need are drugs to make up for the lack of attention they get.

What they do need are good parents and teachers. But since that requires too much time and effort for many adults in our society, they have fallen for the promise of the pharmaceutical companies that drugs will correct behavior problems and thereby make kids more compliant. This ideal of control is nothing new; it has been with us for centuries. Ever heard this: Women and children should be seen and not heard. Many men in patriarchal societies would like to return to the good old days when women and children did as they were told and only spoke when they were spoken to.

For those of you who thought we had moved beyond all that with the women's movement, you are wrong. Now that they have achieved some degree of equality and freedom, many women and mothers are only too eager to have their children or students drugged so that they behave properly in school and at home. Large consumer advocate groups want to support expanded diagnosis and treatment of ADHD. I understand their motivation. They are tired of hearing that deficient parenting and teaching are to blame. This diagnosis helps relieve them of much of the guilt they may have been experiencing. Because of this, they often buy into the popular belief that their children have a disease which can be treated with drugs that will dramatically improve behavior and compliance both at home and in the classroom.

I'm not saying that being a parent or teacher is easy. I know that many parents have to deal with serious marital problems, divorce, or the absence of a spouse. They may have to work several jobs, have inadequate income to maintain the kind of home they want, and deal with countless other issues that make it difficult to give their children the kind of caring and attention they would like to.

Since most single parents raising children are female, they are missing the help they would be getting from a husband. The absence of a father (or at least some male figure present in their lives) in itself can cause problems, especially for boys. A study in Canada compared two groups of families followed over a seven-year period. In the families undergoing divorce, compared to the stable ones with two parents, the incidence of ADHD diagnosis and drug treatment was doubled. This led some to dub the problem as DADD where the first D stands for dad (attention deficit disorder caused by a father who is either absent or playing a minimal role in the children's lives.)

Teachers also face many obstacles that impair their ability to provide the kind of attention children need. They are usually burdened with classes that are too large and sometimes have to follow teaching programs that are not interesting or stimulating to many of their students. Often they are not given freedom to alter the curriculum in ways that would be more appealing to their students. Unfortunately there are also some teachers who are inadequately trained, poorly motivated, and seem to care much less about what the students are learning than the fact that they behave and are not disruptive in any way.

If you are a parent or teacher who is primarily concerned with the fact that your children or students behave all the time, then start working on that problem (which is yours not theirs) instead of trying to figure out which methamphetamine-like drug will work best at keeping your kids compliant at home and in the classroom. I know that advice sounds ridiculous to some of you who are taking care of children who have been chronically neglected throughout their childhood. Some kids who have had lousy teachers and parents may become teenagers completely out of control. I have no easy answers for you once they get to that point, but I do know this—drugging them will not solve their problems.

That is the solution many of them end up seeking on their own with the use of alcohol or some of the illegal drugs I am talking about in this book. For many children, prescribed psychoactive drugs may turn out to be almost as bad for them as street drugs. Although the prescription drugs may be the same or quite similar, the quality control will be a big advantage. Is that all you want—good quality control for your child's psychoactive drugs? Ritalin, cocaine, amphetamines, and methamphetamines are all doing the same things to your children's brains. (You will hear much more about what these drugs actually do to the brain in chapter 17.)

What about those of you who think you've been good parents but still find your children unmanageable. I guess it's too late for you to hear this, but at least you can honestly pass on your experience to friends who are thinking about having kids. Maybe raising children is a wonderful experience for some, but not many (at least not according to most of the thousands of people I have known and patients I've had). For most people, it's about as much fun as going through a surgical residency or Navy Seal training. In other words, expect massive stress and disappointment interspersed by magical moments when your children are being little angels.

Don't have children unless you are willing to accept the huge long-term responsibility that comes with child rearing. I have had pets that I loved but eventually had to give away because I could not honestly provide the attention they needed and still do other things that were important to me. Don't have children unless you are ready and willing to give up a lot for them. You can't just give them away if caring for them proves too much for you. Sex is fun; raising children is not. Don't get the two things confused.

Little Jesus
I like to read religious literature. One of my favorites is the *Infancy Gospel* of Jesus probably written in the early 2nd century. It was excluded with many other Christian texts from the actual New Testament created in the mid 300s after Emperor Constantine made Christianity the official religion of the Roman Empire. He asked the Catholic Bishops to pick the books in circulation for the last two hundred and some years that should constitute the official religious cannon.

According to the text of the *Infancy Gospel*, Jesus was quite a mischievous little boy, to say the least. For example, he reportedly sometimes caused children who annoyed him to die. When parents complained to his non-biological father, Joseph, that he had killed their child, Jesus caused them to go blind. He also engaged in kinder acts and sometimes brought dead children back to life. He was quite insolent to his father as well as other adults occasionally, but at other times a wonderful boy. If you just look at this bit of scripture that many early Christians accepted as gospel, you can't help but conclude that even the son of God can turn out to be a serious problem child.

To repeat my earlier statement, don't take the decision to have children as anything but one of the most serious you will ever make. If you approach the issue casually, as many people do, instead of ending up with a boy who is a perfect angel, you may get little Damien instead, who will turn your life upside down. I wonder how a lot of modern psychiatrists would have dealt with the little Jesus described in the *Infancy Gospel* (lots of drugs would be a good bet).

Donny—the Little Angel
Compared to the little Jesus I just described, I really was almost an angel.
I always did well in school, was liked by my classmates and teachers, and
behaved well around relatives as well as adults I didn't know. But there
was a dark side—my relationship with my brother. Starting when I was
around eight, we developed a volatile relationship. I'm not talking about
ordinary sibling rivalry here. We destroyed things trying to hurt each other.
One time my brother threw a fork at me that stuck in my arm just before
dinner. Another time I threw a wood carving at him. He ducked and it
smashed through a window and landed about 50 feet away from our house.

This fighting continued for years. My mother desperately tried to stop
us but couldn't. My father wasn't there much because he was dedicated
to his job at the CIA and often worked seven days a week. When he was
home and my brother and I started fighting, my mother would plead with
him to make us stop. He usually just walked away after saying, "They're
just boys." The only time he would intervene was when we violently threw
each other against some piece of furniture and broke a chair or table. Our
fighting suddenly stopped when I started high school and he went to college. After that we never had any serious problems. By the time the battle
ended, we had destroyed most of the Asian artwork my parents had bought
when we lived in the Philippines for two years starting when I was four.

Why did my brother and I have this violent relationship? I have no
idea. He was also an excellent student and well behaved outside our home
during the whole time. My father's hands-off, placid approach to our conflict may have ultimately been good for me and my brother given that we
turned out to be successful adults by most standards. However it obviously
put my mother through holy hell. But as they say, what goes around comes
around. When she got older, she became a master manipulator and sometimes drove me and my brother nuts. We didn't know how to deal with her.

For you psychiatrists and psychologists out there, what's your diagnosis? Did my whole family suffer from multiple disorders? Were they
the results of biochemical imbalances in our brains? (I didn't mention my
younger sister because she was always well behaved.) No, we were suffering from life problems. Maybe counseling of some type would have been
helpful, and my father should probably have done a better job of disciplin-
ing me and my brother at home.

However, I'm glad that my parents never took me to a psychiatrist.

Talking might have been OK but no drugs, thank you. I don't know whether my mother ever wanted to do that, but my father would not have allowed it. As was true of much of the general U.S. population in the 1950s,
he had a low opinion of the profession. As I have already said, turning
around that tarnished image was a big part of the motivation for creating
a new, improved, and much more respectable field of biopsychiatry over
the next 20 or 30 years.

Edmund, the Big Bad Boy

During my time as a jail doctor, some of my patients were murderers. In an
attempt to make you feel better about your own children and whatever undesirable behavior they may be engaging in, I would like to tell you about
an unusual little boy named Edmund. He grew up to be a serial killer. One
reason I'm writing about him, besides trying to make you feel better, is
that I think he has been neglected. I could write about several serial killers
that I actually took care of, but their stories are not very interesting. Only
one book was written about him, long out of print. Ted Bundy, Henry Lee
Lucas, and many other serial killers have had books, movies, and docu-
mentaries made about their exploits. Yet we have little insight, based on
their own testimony, into what drove them to their depravity. Ted Bundy,
probably the most famous serial killer in the U.S., maintained his inno-
cence up until shortly before his execution. Knowing that all appeals had
been exhausted and that he would die, he finally admitted to killing almost
30 women. Not so with Edmund Kemper.

   Before I go on, let me provide a note of caution for readers who might
be offended by the next few pages. If you read the book or saw the movie
Silence of the Lambs, did you stop reading or get up and leave the theater
when some of Hannibal Lecter's crimes were described or visually portrayed? In case you've forgotten, he bit off and ate the tongue of a nurse
who was doing an EKG on him. He also killed a census taker who apparently annoyed him by knocking on his door. He then carved him up and ate
his liver for dinner, along with some fava beans and Chianti. In addition,
he killed two cops and mutilated one of them. If you could handle that,
then you can deal with Edmund's gruesome exploits. Otherwise, skip the
next few pages.

   If you had to describe the childhood of Edmund Kemper III in one word, it would be "short." His parents were at each other's throats from his early childhood and finally separated when he was nine. His mother and sisters constantly made fun of him and banished him to the basement, where he was often locked in. He frequently sneaked out of the house at night and stared at women, as he fantasized that they might love him. But having been constantly berated by his mother for his poor social skills, he decided that relationships with women would be impossible for him—unless he killed them first.

Eventually his mother tired of him and sent him to live with his father. Edmund was very attached to his father and had brooded about being separated from him for several years. However, his dad didn't want to deal with the boy either. At the age of 13, against his will, Edmund was sent to live with his paternal grandparents.

As a child, he had been prone to torture and kill animals, including a family cat he had buried alive and then decapitated. His grandfather gave him a rifle to help him take out his aggression in a more acceptable way—shooting rabbits and gophers on their ranch. At the age of 14, when his grandfather left the house to buy groceries, Edmund told his grandmother that he was going out to shoot rabbits. He took the rifle out on the porch and then looked back to see his grandmother sitting with her back to him. She was editing her latest children's book. Without thinking consciously, he suddenly raised the rifle and fired a bullet into her head. He then shot her in the back twice and stabbed her multiple times. When grandpa came home, Edmund shot him in the head as he was unloading the car because he was afraid that he would have a heart attack if he saw his dead wife.

When the police later questioned the boy, they told him that they understood why he shot his grandfather but wanted to know why he shot his grandmother. His reply was: "I just wondered how it would feel to shoot Grandma."

He was sent to the Atascadero State Mental Hospital. Most 16-year-old boys are studying math and English, but Edmund was studying serial rapists and listening carefully to their stories. He concluded that they had been caught because they attacked women they knew, did it in too public a place, didn't cover their tracks, and left behind witnesses. This knowledge would come in handy later.

During the first year, he was diagnosed as a sociopath. Because such people are usually quite uncooperative, the doctors were surprised that

Edmund was eagerly and cheerfully helping them administer psychological tests. As he secretly worked hard to learn the psychological language of treatment and recovery, he became a model patient who kept his violent fantasies to himself. He even claimed a religious conversion and often quoted from the *Bible*.

After five years at Atascadero, the psychiatrists and psychologists proclaimed him rehabilitated and ready to be reintegrated into society. Although his doctors warned the officials at the California Youth Authority not to send him back to the care of his mother, they did just that. His mother had always made fun of his large size as a boy; now her 6'9", almost 300-pound baby was back home again at the age of 21.

Edmund had a strong desire to become a cop. He was a clean-cut man with short hair in the 1969 Bay-Area world of hippies. There was a problem though. You might think it would be the prior murder of his grandparents. However, he had been declared not guilty by reason of insanity and subsequently rehabilitated. In other words, he was not a convicted felon. Whether the police would actually consider hiring him with his prior history became a moot point. He couldn't qualify anyway because the police department had a height restriction. Not only could you not be too short, but you couldn't be too tall.

He was very disappointed by this but spent many nights hanging out a local bar frequented by the Santa Cruz police. He was respectful of them and enjoyed hours of talking about the merits of various guns and ammunition. They liked him and gave him a nickname—big Ed.

Although he couldn't be a cop, he got a motorcycle because it made him feel like a cop. He crashed it twice and broke his arm the second time. The money from an insurance settlement allowed him to buy a car that looked like an unmarked police cruiser. This was when he began to pick up girls who were hitchhiking. He carefully studied how they reacted to him and what he needed to do to gain their confidence. He did this for a year, as he fantasized killing them.

In preparation for his first victim, he jimmied the lock on the passenger door so that it couldn't be opened from the inside and placed blankets, plastic bags, and knives in the trunk. His killing spree started in May of 1972 when he picked up two Fresno State College roommates and drove them to a remote location. After putting one of them in the trunk, he handcuffed the other girl, placed a plastic bag over her head and then attempted to strangle her with a rope. She bit a hole in the bag and the rope broke. Frustrated that this wasn't working, he repeatedly stabbed her and then proceeded to do the same to the other victim.

Now living in an apartment, he took them back there and started a ritual that would become his trademark. He cut off their heads and hands and dumped them in separate remote locations so that the bodies could not be identified if they were ever found. (Remember that this was long before the days of DNA testing.) He was able to disguise the burial sites using techniques he had learned as a Boy Scout.

In later interviews, he said that the first girl had pleaded with him not to kill them. He was "quite struck by her personality and her looks, and there was almost a reverence there." Having thrown her head into a ravine, he later went back several times to visit her and be near her because he "loved her and wanted her."

For the next four months, he was happy to simply enjoy the Polaroids he had taken of the two girls' bodies. In September he picked up his third victim. She was a 15-year-old girl on her way to a dance class who had tired of waiting for a bus and started to hitch hike. As she panicked when she saw his gun, he tried to calm her by saying that he had been planning to kill himself. Because they were in a city area where she could have gotten attention, he had to convince her that he wouldn't hurt her. He drove to a secluded area where he suffocated and then raped her. He stopped at a bar on the way home for a few beers because he was "hot, tired, and thirsty."

The following day, Edmund attended his final parole hearing and in later interviews related his thoughts: "They kept asking me a lot of questions, but all I could think about was what I was going to do with that girl's head in the trunk of my car." The two psychiatrists agreed after the meeting that he was now "safe" and recommended that his record be sealed so that he could live a normal life. Edmund then drove over to a friend's house and buried the girl's head in his back yard as a kind of joke.

Over the next four months, victims of two other serial killers in the Santa Cruz area were found, but Edmund was not drawing anyone's suspicion. He bought a .22 Ruger pistol and apparently had no trouble getting it. He killed his next victim by placing her in the trunk and shooting her in the head. Having moved back in with his mother, he took the body to his room at her house.

When his mother left for work the next morning, he had sex with the corpse and dissected her body in the bathtub. He took care to remove the bullet and meticulously cleaned up afterward. That day he threw most of the body parts off a cliff. Although they were discovered the next day, Edmund wasn't worried because he knew that the police wouldn't be able to identify her. Several days later, he took the head out of his closet and buried it in his mother's back yard.

Because he had picked up the last girl in his own town, he grew more confident about his skills. A month later, he picked up two girls who were hitchhiking on the campus where his mother worked as a university administrator. He managed to kill them without even stopping the car. After he shot the girl in the front seat in the head, he turned and fired bullets at the girl in the back seat as he continued driving. The girl in the back was lying on the seat gurgling as he drove past the campus guard station. A few minutes later, he slowed down and finished her off. He decapitated them in the trunk that evening in his mother's driveway and the next morning took them in the house. He had sex with one of the headless bodies and then carved them up.

The following month, he had a flash of insight. He was killing these women as a way of symbolically getting back at his mother. She was the one he hated and had really always wanted to kill. He stayed up one night as she slept, thinking at one point, as he later recounted, "I certainly wanted for my mother a nice, quiet, easy death like I guess everyone wants."

He went into her bedroom with a hammer at 5:15 am. After one blow to the head, he slashed her throat, decapitated her, and removed her larynx. He found some dark irony in the fact that when he put her larynx in the garbage disposal, it spit it right back out. During the day, he worried that although he had covered his tracks well in the prior murders, the cops would soon be on to him. He came up with an idea that might throw them off. He invited one of his mother's friends to come over for a surprise dinner for her.

When she arrived after an exhausting day at work, she walked in and said, "Let's sit down. I'm dead." Edmund later recounted, "And I kind of took her at her word there," and proceeded to strangle her. Later that evening, he decided that there was no way to hide his guilt and left a note for the police regarding his mother: "No need for her to suffer any more at the hands of this murderous Butcher. It was quick—asleep—the way I wanted it."

The next morning he drove to Reno and then on to Colorado. He was stopped for speeding when he first got into Colorado and was disappointed that the policeman seemed to know nothing about him. After all, it would be hard to miss a 6'9" giant if an APB had been put out for him.

He finally decided to call the Santa Cruz Police Department from a payphone in Pueblo. At first, one of his drinking buddies thought it was a prank, but he finally managed to convince him. Then Edmund spilled his guts out. He could have easily confessed to this crime alone, but he had a lot to get off his chest. He described the grizzly details of all the murders during his police escort back to Santa Cruz.

Once there, he continued what seemed to be an endless confession and took the police to all the dumpsites. This left his court-appointed defense attorney with no option but an insanity defense. Doctors who had treated him at Atascadero said that he was insane, but the jury didn't buy it. He was convicted of eight counts of first-degree murder and sentenced to life in prison (in the period when the U.S. Supreme Court had temporarily suspended the death sentence in the entire country).

In his later interviews and writing, he proved himself to be an articulate and intelligent man who gave the forensic psychiatrists and psychologists more insight into the mind of the serial killer than probably any offender of his kind. He currently continues to enjoy his celebrity status in prison as the "genius" serial killer.

Don't Shoot Me

I want to assure all readers that I am not in any way trying to demean or belittle the problems you may be having with your children or those you care for or are concerned about. But just remember that things could always be a lot worse. Psychiatric care is not the answer for many children. Edmund had plenty of it. Whether he was treated with drugs or not, I don't know. But what I do know is that psychoactive drugs are not the solution to many kids' problems. For some there may not appear to be any good answers, but drugging them should be an absolute last resort, not the latest fashion.

After the Columbine shooting rampage, there was a great hue and cry among many politicians for making sure that our children are getting plenty of psychiatric care and screened for their potential violent personalities. Well guess what? Although I never read about it in the media, it turned out that Eric Harris, the mastermind of the massacre, was taking a popular prescription antidepressant. His partner was on prescription stimulants presumably for ADD. Is it possible that if Eric had not received these drugs that the massacre would never have occurred? Maybe it wasn't too many viewings of the Matrix that inspired Eric but the fact that he was under the spellbinding effect of Luvox.

A school shooting several years later in 2001 got my attention because it happened at a high school close to my home, Granite Hills. The shooter was an 18-year-old senior named Jason Hoffman who was under the care of a psychiatrist for depression being treated with two antidepressant drugs. His attorney tried to suggest that the drugs might have triggered this violent episode, but Jason's psychiatrist said that they were both safe and couldn't have caused such an act. Local university psychiatrists agreed. The boy was convicted and sent to prison where he hung himself a year and a half after the shooting.

There have been more than 50 school shootings in Europe and the U.S. since 1996 (more than 90% in America). The fact that some of these kids were under psychiatric care was downplayed or even covered up, especially those taking antidepressants. I would like to see a comprehensive study of all such incidents by independent investigators to see how many of these children who suddenly turned into mass murderers were not only under psychiatric care but also taking antidepressants when they committed the act. If you want to know more about the details of Columbine and other school shootings, read Peter Breggin's book *Reclaiming Our Children*. (Check out my web site donaldchapin.com for other related books about the use of psychiatric drugs in children.)

Angry Alan
In the same book, Dr. Breggin tells the story of a ten year old boy who was taken to a psychologist because he was so angry all the time. His parents were separated and constantly fighting, and his father was dating a young girl only about twice Alan's age. After witnessing the boy's anger on display in his office, the psychologist talked to the parents alone as they ripped each other apart. He did not seem to think that their marital discord was a serious problem and told them that they had nothing to do with what was wrong with their son.

After completing a few psychological tests, he announced that Alan had ADHD and ODD. Oppositional defiant disorder is a list of eight behaviors you would find in someone who is angry. You only needed four to qualify for that diagnosis, and Alan had all eight. The psychologist reassured the parents that medication would be the best treatment and referred him to a psychiatrist that he worked with closely.

The psychiatrist started him on lithium for his ODD (despite the fact that the FDA does not approve it for that use). After several weeks, his parents were quite concerned. Alan was much better behaved but very subdued and had a zombie-like appearance to them. The psychiatrist told them that this was normal and that it could be managed by adding stimulant medications. When they weren't happy with that explanation, he just laid down the law and told them that their son had a serious biochemical imbalance and would probably have to be on medication for the rest of his life. That's when his parents started looking elsewhere for help and got referred to Dr. Breggin.

After his evaluation of the three of them, he concluded that Alan was having a natural reaction to his parents' constant bickering, back biting, and impending divorce. He told them that Alan needed no medication or counseling but that they did need help. He spent several months with them trying to see if there was a way to reconcile their marriage. They decided to get back together after their relationship had been transformed by the therapy. A few months later, Alan's ADHD and ODD disappeared. He was back to being just a normal boy.

Poor Paul

Paul, a ten-year-old boy I first met at a friend's birthday party eight years ago, is now in his last year of high school. I have had no contact with him or his family but received a phone call recently from my friend who has kept in touch with them. Because he knew I had been working on this book for some time and considered me to be an expert on psychoactive drugs, he related the following story. Paul started taking Acutane for acne about two years ago and a year later started having problems that his family doctor believed were the result of depression. He was initially started on Prozac but didn't seem to get much better over the next two months. The doctor added Remeron, another antidepressant, to his drug regimen. Shortly after that, Paul started having anxiety problems that seemed to be new, so he was started on the benzodiazepine Klonipin. Not seeming to get better after four months on the three drugs, the doctor decided to add Wellbutrin.

The family called my friend for help hoping that he knew someone who was knowledgeable in this area. Although Paul's parents felt he was actually much worse than he had been previously, they were primarily concerned that their doctor was moving his practice to another city and weren't sure who would take over his care. I told my friend that I didn't have any really hopeful advice to give his parents. First of all, they probably wouldn't be ready to hear the truth about the predicament their son was in. Also they may have simply been hoping to get a referral to another doctor who could continue to write his prescriptions.

Before you read this book, you may not have seen the big problem here, but I hope you know better now. Although many of you may not be aware of it, Acutane is well known to cause depression as a side effect of the drug for unknown reasons. What should have been done initially was to stop that drug and see what happened over the next month or two to Paul's depressive symptoms. Instead he has now been taking three antidepressants and a benzodiazepine for at least six months and one of them for a year. He may be addicted to one, two, three, or maybe all of them.

He will need to see a good psychiatrist who is willing to help him withdraw from all of these drugs. This could prove to be a difficult task and take a long time. He would have to get off one drug at a time and each one could take a few months depending on his withdrawal symptoms and other problems. Because discontinuing each antidepressant might be associated with increased anxiety problems, the Klonipin would probably have to be dealt with last. Some people addicted to benzos can take a year or more to get off of them. To find a psychiatrist willing and able to do this in the small city Paul lived in could be quite difficult or maybe impossible.

Thousands of people have been put in this kind of position as a result of our cavalier attitude in many modern societies about taking psychiatric drugs, especially benzos and antidepressants. Some people have taken many months or even a year or more to get off one antidepressant. This kid getting ready to start college next year faces a potential nightmare which for some could end in suicide. The most serious error in his care was not stopping the Accutane as a first step. But even if he had simply gone to the doctor with symptoms of depression initially, the care was still inappropriate. The more teenagers and parents I can get to read this book, the less likely those people will be to fall into this type of potential quagmire. Helping prevent such problems was one of my main goals in writing this book. Sadly I can't do anything to help Paul at this point other than to refer him to doctors like Peter Breggin who could help him get off these drugs as he has over many years for hundreds of others in the same situation.

Defective Kids

Many kids are being taught that they are defective when often there is nothing wrong with them. The problem can occur with good parents and teachers who idealize what their behavior should be like and expect way too much of them. And of course many parents who have poor parenting skills and serious problems of their own don't want to accept their responsibility for their child's behavior problems. To accommodate them, psychiatry has pathologized childhood with its many disorders, and the pharmaceutical companies are more than happy to supply drugs to the parents that will supposedly correct their children's behavioral problems. Is this a somewhat simplistic and overreaching analysis of our current predicament with the use of psychiatric drugs in children? Yes. But does it have a lot of truth in it? You bet.

For most children, mind-altering drugs are not the solution to their behavioral problems. If you would be horrified to find out that your kids are using cocaine or amphetamines like meth, then don't be so quick to give them stimulants like Ritalin. If your kid decided to start smoking marijuana because he was depressed, how would you react? You should have the same concern about having him take an antidepressant. Be very reluctant to follow casual suggestions by physicians or therapists to put children on mind-altering drugs, especially antidepressants.

16

When You Label Me

In contrast to my patient Nick (who I talked about at the beginning of the last chapter), David, another teenage patient of mine in jail, was quite obviously seriously mentally disturbed at first glance. When I evaluated him for a bruise on his arm one evening at the downtown jail, he was moderately agitated and rapidly jumping from one unrelated sentence to another (free association, in psychiatric terms).

A deputy told me something strange before David came in the room—that he had been giving CPR to a dog at the time of his arrest. Although he was rambling and spewing out many strange statements, several got my attention. He said he had been arrested forty times for indecent exposure at a bar near his home. I knew that couldn't be true. David also claimed to have been arrested many times for drug use (usually methamphetamines).

The day of this arrest, he threatened to stab his parents with a large kitchen knife when they refused to give him $20. As they called the police, he ran up to his room, stabbed his dog, and then threw it out of the window. Suddenly distraught at what he had done, he ran downstairs and out to the yard where he began giving CPR to the dog.

Drug tests done after his arrest were negative. This indicated to me that his illicit drug use was probably not causing but possibly exacerbating an underlying severe mental disorder, most likely schizophrenia. I followed his trial later, in which he was prosecuted for animal cruelty and making terrorist threats against his family. The fact that he was clearly seriously mentally ill didn't seem to factor into the situation, and he was sent to prison for four years. Not getting a label before his trial turned out to be a bad deal for him.

Mental Illness in Jail

An extensive discussion of mental illness is incredibly complex and beyond the scope of this book. Also I am hardly the best qualified person to give you that. However, before getting into the main subject of this chapter, I will try to give you a brief summary of the kinds of mental problems that often result in incarceration. I will not talk about organic mental disorders that develop as the result of dementia from aging, strokes, or chronic substance abuse. I have already talked about mental problems that can sometimes result from substance use and abuse. What I will primarily address is schizophrenia.

But before I do that, let me briefly touch on the personality disorders that land many people in jail. Without getting into specific psychiatric diagnoses, let's just look at the general concept of antisocial behavior. When this gets extreme, a person may become a sociopath or a psychopath. Some people use those words synonymously, but I see them as being quite different.

To me, a sociopath is someone who engages in antisocial activity but knows that what he is doing is clearly wrong. He has some insight into what he's doing but continues the behavior because of some compulsion to do so. If he assaults or kills someone, he is capable of feeling some empathy for the victim and often has some remorse for the crime he committed. Edmund Kemper and Jeffrey Dahmer would be good examples of sociopaths.

A psychopath engages in antisocial behavior, knows that it's wrong, but doesn't give a damn. He can brutally kill people and have no remorse for his action or any empathy for his victims. Richard Ramirez, the Night Stalker, who raped, tortured, and killed many people in Los Angeles in the 1980s, was a prototypic psychopath in my opinion. He laughed mockingly at his trial when shown crime-scene photos of people he had mutilated and murdered, including two women in their eighties. But don't get confused by the word psycho. From my point of view, he clearly had a disturbed mind but was not crazy or insane (in the same sense as a documented paranoid schizophrenic.) His lethal injection a few years ago was long overdue and well deserved. (Although I am basically opposed to the death penalty, I have to make an exception for him.)

Although I have no sympathy for adult sociopaths and psychopaths who commit horrible crimes, I do have empathy for the child they once were, often growing up in an environment of psychological and physical abuse. That's how a lot of them ended up developing their antisocial personality. It certainly isn't always true but often is. For example, Dahmer appears to have had good parents while Kemper did not. Not surprisingly, bad parents can create bad adults.

Psychosis and Schizophrenia
Let's briefly consider what constitutes serious mental illness starting with
a basic rule of thumb that I learned in medical school, but don't take it too
seriously. If you've been carefully listening to someone for a while and
have absolutely no idea what he's talking about, then there are generally
two possibilities—either he is crazy or you are. If you are pretty sure that
you're not, then he probably is.

Now let's consider a little more scientific approach. Psychiatrists
characterize schizophrenia, one of the extremes and well-known forms of
mental illness, by what they refer to as a disturbance in thought content
and form. Abnormal thought content can be summarized for the average
layperson by the word delusions. They are simply ideas that have no possible basis in fact (e.g., "The government is trying to assassinate me.")

The usual manifestation of a disorder in thought form is loose association. A person may shift from one idea to another, with no connection
between them, without realizing that these thoughts are unrelated. If the
disconnection between thoughts is severe, the person may be completely
incoherent.

The third major characteristic of schizophrenia, in addition to delusions and loose association, is a disturbance in perception, manifested
most often as auditory hallucinations. The person may hear one or more
voices which might be insulting, commenting on his behavior, or perhaps
commanding him to do something.

The fourth major component is that of inappropriate affect (expression
of emotion). Someone who has been severely physically abused, beaten,
or tortured, for example, may relate the experience with no expression (flat
affect). Or he may laugh as he describes horrific events that happened to
him (inappropriate affect). Other features may be manifested as well, but
these are the primary ones.

The active phase of psychosis from any cause, such as drug intoxication, organic syndromes, and schizophrenia, is manifested by delusions,
hallucinations, loose association, and illogical thinking. Psychosis can occur acutely as a result of drug use or stressful life events and then subside
spontaneously. At the other end of the spectrum, it may develop slowly
and evolve into a chronic mental disorder, like schizophrenia.

Other mental disorders that do not manifest as psychosis may cause
people to engage in criminal acts such as paranoid disorders, anxiety

disorders, and affective disorders (various forms of depression). Insanity is a legal term that is no longer used in the medical literature. When most doctors think of someone as being insane, this is usually in the context of acute or chronic psychosis.

Now that I have given you a brief synopsis of the most severe kinds of psychiatric disorders, let's get back to those with much less serious problems such as anxiety or mild to moderate depression. Those are the people I am trying to reach with this book, not people with the kinds of problems I just discussed or the patients I described at the beginning of the last two chapters. I am more than happy to leave their care to psychiatrists and psychologists because I really don't know how to help them.

Soren Kierkegaard, a Danish theologian and great philosopher of the 19th century, said this: When you label me, you negate me. That, my friends, is one of the most profound statements ever made in the history of the human race. Because some of you may not understand why I say this, I'll try to explain what I mean in this chapter.

Although some of you may think that I have been somewhat unkind or perhaps even unfair to psychiatrists at some points in this book, you'll be happy to know that I bring many of my criticisms about them to other parts of the medical profession as well. However, let me start with psychiatrists. They are super specialists in putting labels on people. This has become especially useful over the last 50 years now that we have developed so many new psychoactive drugs. Once they are able to come up with a label that describes you and your problems, then they can give you a designer drug for that. It really makes the job pretty straightforward. You've got depression and you need an antidepressant.

The problem is that a lot of people who get such labels don't have depression and shouldn't be started on an antidepressant. Are psychiatrists alone or unique in giving people labels (also known as a diagnosis)? Of course not. Psychologists are pretty good at it too, just as are most medical doctors. This has a lot to do with insurance reimbursement as I will explain soon.

The DSM Bible

Regardless of the kind of therapy used, most psychotherapists fall lower on the totem pole than psychiatrists in the minds of many people because they don't have MDs. Although that may actually make many of them better at helping people with psychological problems (especially those doing CBT), they still have to follow a lot of the rules that psychiatrists make up. They are all well versed in what is often called the bible of psychiatry— The DSM (The Diagnostic and Statistical Manual of Mental Disorders).

Now that I've brought up the word bible, let's take a look at the Bible most people know about. I know that many people believe that it was a direct transcription from God, without any revision or editing on the part of people. If that's what you think, that's fine. But even if you believe that, there were certainly some issues that needed to be resolved regarding doctrine for the Christian church once it became the official religion of the Roman Empire after Emperor Constantine decreed it to be such.

From his point of view, there was a major question that had been debated for two hundred years but never resolved. Was Christ the son of God or was he actually God? Constantine summoned Bishops from around the Roman Empire in 325 to meet and resolve this issue at the Council of Nicea. Of the three hundred and three Bishops in attendance, only three felt that God and Christ were one and the same. But when the final vote was taken, the other 300 voted for the doctrine of the holy trinity—Father, Son, and Holy Spirit, which remains the doctrine to this day. (Don't ask me to explain it. Ask a priest or minister if you have any questions.)

So what does this have to do with the bible of psychiatry? To the casual observer, it might seem as though the various disorders and diagnostic categories are arrived at in much the same way. The Bishops of Psychiatry get together and decide what kind of behavior constitutes a psychiatric disorder. Let's look at a pretty controversial one, just for the fun of it—homosexuality. That was an official disorder (often referred to in the media and books in the 1950s and 60s as a disease) in the DSM I and II. After Stonewall and the start of the gay liberation movement in the late 60s, psychiatrists were under a lot of political pressure to change their position. (Did this have anything to do with the fact that gay members of their own organization were creating a scene with the media? I wonder.) The American Psychiatric Association took a vote in 1974 that eliminated homosexuality as a disorder when 58% of the membership voted to remove it (in accordance with the suggestion of the elite group of elders within that organization who proposed that it be done the year before).

Gay people and others rejoiced at the decision, but I say this. Why did the psychiatrists really take it out of the DSM? Did they ever admit that it should never have been in there in the first place? After all, Father Freud had said at least 70 years before that homosexuality was just a normal variant of human sexuality. Am I being somewhat disrespectful here? Yes, I am. The powers that be in psychiatry (still mostly men, but some women too) just get together and make stuff up every fifteen years or so (at least some of it). If there is a hard scientific basis for any of their disorders, I haven't been able to figure out what they are—and I'm not all that stupid.

Maybe after this book becomes popular, they will ask me to participate in the final preparation of the DSM-V (actually they decided to drop the Roman Numerals and make it DSM-5). I don't think so, but if they did, I would probably discover that many if not most of the psychiatrists working on it were very intelligent, nice people. I don't have a problem with any of them as individuals, just their way of approaching psychological problems and their treatment. I have the same problems with many internists and surgeons.

Although I facetiously described myself as a somewhat angelic child in the last chapter (excluding the relationship with my brother), I am no angel. Although I may say unkind things about psychiatrists and other physicians, I do not stand in judgment of any of them as individuals. I seriously considered going into psychiatry in medical school. If I had, I might well have ended up doing many of the things I criticize in this book.

Trying to help people with their psychological problems is stressful work. I have been frustrated many times in my attempts to do this with friends, relatives, and patients. I know that trying to help people with depression can be very depressing because I have sometimes become depressed when trying to do it. I seriously doubt that I would have spent my life fighting the system the way Peter Breggin has if I had become a psychiatrist. As I said, he never starts people on psychiatric drugs who aren't already on them. Others like David Burns use them discretely and with great caution. I might well have become one of the biopsychiatrists who give drugs to most patients and buddy up with the pharmaceutical industry.

Now let me try to put you, the reader, in the position faced by many psychiatrists. Imagine that you spent eight years of your life going through medical school and psychiatric residency and are now doing well in practice making $150,000 a year or more. You spend most of your day seeing patients briefly and writing prescriptions for most of them. You can make a good living if you see four patients an hour. You don't do psychotherapy because you were never really trained to. (Many psychiatrists will admit this, at least privately.) Suddenly you become disillusioned and begin to doubt that many of these drugs are really helping a lot of people. How likely would it be that you would decide to get some training in psychotherapy and start doing that with most of your patients when it meant that you would have to take a 50% cut in your salary or more? Now you can only see one or maybe two patients an hour and insurance reimbursement would drop considerably. How many of you would make that change? That's the dilemma many psychiatrists face, even if they agree with much of what I say in this book. It's not an easy choice.

I have made plenty of mistakes and screwed up a lot of things in my life but fortunately not by getting involved with mind-altering drugs. I'm just trying to help as many people as possible avoid that potential path of troubles or even disaster. Surgery is a stressful field of medicine but not so bad once the training is over. After you become skilled at complex operations, it's not so difficult any more. However dealing with a hostile, angry, depressed patient who is yelling at you and threatening to commit suicide is always stressful. God bless all the therapists of whatever kind who are honestly trying to do their best to help people with their life problems. That said, let me get back to my role as critic of the many problems with diagnosis of diseases and psychological disorders. I'm not trying to hurt psychiatrists in this book. I'm just trying to help people understand the potential problems with and dangers of psychoactive drugs.

Question Your Medical Diagnosis
Just so that I can be an equal opportunity offender, let's start with internists. Although they don't have quite as much freedom to invent diseases as the psychiatrists, they still do a pretty good job. Before I get started, let me explain something to you. I would estimate that at least 75% of the patients who present to family doctors or internists with a new medical problem have a psychosomatic condition that will resolve on its own. I'm

not talking about people who are being referred with a physical condition or disease documented by other doctors who have already conducted a battery of tests after doing a history and physical exam. These are people coming in to be evaluated for new aches and pains or other symptoms that are often non-specific.

And what exactly is that patient wanting and expecting the doctor to do? What do you want doctors to do for you? You want them to come up with a diagnosis and give you something to get rid of the problem. If you are like most people, you definitely don't want the doctor to perform a history and physical exam, run a lot of tests, and then tell you that he doesn't know what's causing your symptoms and has absolutely no idea what to do about them.

Doctors are well aware of what most people want and try to give their patients what they are coming to them for—a specific diagnosis and treatment. Unfortunately that can't be done in many cases. In order to get around that problem, many doctors just make up stuff. It looks like you've got such and such, so I recommend that you take this treatment. If what the physician recommends is that you take 500 mg of vitamin C every day for the next week for your psychosomatic problem, that will probably be pretty harmless and may even have some placebo effect.

But most patients would react to such a recommendation with disappointment at the least and many would get angry, especially if they had to pay money out of their pocket. What do you mean you don't know what's causing my pain? I just paid money to have you examine me and run tests and all you can say is that you're not sure what's wrong. It's not just professional or wealthy people who have such reactions, it's most people, including those who are poor and not paying anything for their care.

When I first started working in the jails, I was doing sick call in a room adjoining another one next to it. Because we had an open doorway between us, I could hear everything in the other room where another doctor was seeing patients. An inmate who was displeased after his quick evaluation by the other doctor, said on his way out of the room, "Where did you get your medical training—at Coleman College" (a local vocational school for computer science)? Many inmates were quite assertive about what they wanted from the doctors and nurses and didn't hesitate to express their displeasure.

Actually I encourage such behavior. Although most doctors don't like demanding patients, my advice to friends and relatives has always been to be exactly that. I don't mean that you should be aggressive or obnoxious, but you should definitely not be passive. I have seen many patients harmed seriously because of this kind of passivity. One of my relatives even ended up dying because he passively accepted the advice of several doctors without ever seriously questioning the diagnosis and treatment being recommended, despite my strong insistence that he do so.

Although you shouldn't passively accept a diagnosis or medical treatment that might have serious consequences, neither should you automatically get upset or angry if a doctor doesn't find anything wrong and can't give you a specific diagnosis for whatever symptoms you may be having. Most problems go away with a little time. The body is very good at getting rid of many aches and pains without any medical intervention. In most cases, if there is an underlying serious problem, it won't just go away. That's when you can reasonably start pressing your doctor for more tests and a specific diagnosis.

Psychiatric Diagnosis

Although that is good advice for anyone receiving medical treatment, I'll stick with the subject of this part of the book—legal mind-altering drugs and the diagnosis that usually precedes their prescription. (Obviously some people just buy them off the street or get them from friends.) I will talk more later about casually accepting prescriptions for psychoactive drugs from doctors, but for now I want to focus on what comes before that—the diagnosis.

As I have said elsewhere in this book, when it comes to getting a diagnosis by a psychiatrist or psychologist, you are only getting an opinion. The same is true for a medical diagnosis based on simply taking a history, before a physical exam or any lab tests or other diagnostic procedures are done. The difference with diagnosing mental problems is that there are no physical exam findings or lab tests that can support the diagnosis. It just remains an opinion and various people evaluating the same person may come to quite different conclusions.

Consider a typical case that might be presented to a medical or surgical group at a hospital. A 40-year-old woman found a lump in her breast. Her physician wasn't sure what it was. A mammogram showed some calcification in the lesion and the radiologist said it was suspicious for malignancy. A needle biopsy of the tumor was read by the pathologist as an adenocarcinoma. This woman has breast cancer. Although the doctors listening to the presentation may disagree about the best way to treat her, no one is going to say that the diagnosis is wrong.

Now let's look at the patient I described at the beginning of this chapter. While he was in jail and before going to trial, the psychiatrists were not able to agree on what his mental problem was. Although he was clearly psychotic to me when I first saw him (and given his age, I would have thought he was schizophrenic), they could never establish a clear diagnosis that his lawyers could use in his defense. Treated as a relatively normal kid who just suddenly went into a rage, he got his prison sentence.

But why didn't his doctors just run blood tests, order MRIs, and get brain scans to figure out what his problem was. As I said previously, no psychiatric disorder in the DSM-IV can be documented based on any such test. Psychiatrists often say that people with such and such a problem often have brain scans showing this or that. This is what psychiatrist Peter Breggin has called "the brain scan scam." No psychiatric disorder can be diagnosed based on any medical test. Neurological diseases, yes. Not psychiatric problems.

If you are like the woman I described with a definitive diagnosis of breast cancer, then it's pretty hard to get away from that label initially. You can certainly choose among a variety of treatment options depending on tumor size and other factors. Although you can't defy the diagnosis, you can certainly do that with the prognosis, which is often nothing more than a wild guess.

On the other hand, you can defy both when someone tries to give you a psychological or psychiatric label (diagnosis). You have depression. It's caused by a biochemical imbalance in your brain, and you will need to take antidepressants for the rest of your life. The diagnosis is serious and the prognosis is bad. If someone ever said that to me, my response would be this: Go fuck yourself. I would of course say it politely and then leave.

Accepting labels that other people want to give you is usually not very helpful and sometimes can be destructive. Yet most people are more than happy to accept them and often with great resignation. As I see it, this is not good for most people most of the time. If you want to move beyond the limitations that the world will always try to place on you, then you need to stop blindly accepting the labels those in authority try to pin on you. (I will explore this issue more extensively in an upcoming book.)

Escaping Responsibility

One of the reasons that many people love labels is that this helps them to escape responsibility for their behavior and actions. Let's look at an extreme case. After a dentist's secret behavior was exposed, he lost his license to practice because he had fondled the genitals of many female patients under sedation or light anesthesia. A psychiatrist said in his defense that he was suffering from "frotteurism." This is supposedly a compulsive disorder that makes you touch women's genitals. The dentist used that argument to sue his disability insurance company for $5000 a month compensation under his policy. According to him, he was disabled and unable to practice dentistry because he suffered from a disorder over which he had no control.

This is kind of like Edmund Kemper's attorneys claiming that he was a victim of CDD (compulsive decapitation disorder). No, he just killed a few women and decapitated some of them. That's about all you can say as far as I can see. Why he did it, I don't know. As far as the dentist goes, maybe he should join Edmund in prison and find out what it's like to have people play with your genitals without your permission.

Let me be clear here. If your goal is to develop a legal defense for some crime you have been charged with, then you should absolutely gather up every label any doctors will assign you. That will give you the best possible shot at avoiding having to take responsibility for your action. Or if you want to scam a government agency into giving you disability compensation for problems that you don't actually have, then you must get as many good and impressive labels applied to you as possible.

Similarly if you want to be a victim and have all your friends and family members feel sorry for you, then you should do exactly the same thing. This is also the best strategy if you just want to scam doctors for as many drugs as possible. If you like taking drugs, then get all the labels you can.

On the other hand, if you are not trying to scam the world and avoid responsibility for your stupid choices and bad behavior, then you want to get on a different path and start taking responsibility for your behavior and actions. Beyond that, if you really want to be as healthy and happy as possible, you should avoid labels like the plague. (Is it OK if I use trite metaphors occasionally?)

A lot of cognitive therapy aims at helping you dispute labels that others have given you or that you have adopted for yourself such as these: I'm stupid; I'm clumsy; I'm not athletic; I'm a procrastinator; I'm just a drug addict, and so on, endlessly. The problem with many therapists, and especially psychiatrists, is that they will help you break down those images of yourself, but then replace them with an official diagnosis. You do have a lot of problems but it's mainly because you have adult ADD (or OCD or depression, or a combination of multiple labels), and we can treat that. You may still think you're a loser, but at least now you know why. And thank God, there's a pill, or maybe multiple drugs, that will magically turn your life around. If you buy into that BS, get ready for the Pain Train. It's coming soon. All aboard!

Science Labels Everything

Now that I've told you not to easily and without question accept labels that doctors try to put on you, here is the big problem that makes that so difficult. Everything in medicine and science in general is all about describing and differentiating things and putting labels on them. If a geologist finds a rock and isn't sure what it is, he wants to do whatever studies are required to give it a name. When you go to a zoo, you want to read all the signs so that you can know exactly what the animal you are looking at is called. At a flower show, it's not enough for most people to just look at an orchid and say, "Isn't that beautiful." It has to have a name.

This is what we are taught to do as young children—give everything a name. Then we are trained in school to compare and contrast all of these things that we have learned the names of. Systematic classification of everything around us in the material world works fine in most areas of science. However, when you get into the realm of emotions, behavior, and the human mind, it doesn't always work out so well.

Medical students are taught to follow this same method of carefully classifying human diseases. The history and physical evaluation is usually described in terms of what is called a SOAP note. What are the subjective symptoms the patient is experiencing? What are the objective findings from the physical exam, lab tests, X-rays, and so on? Based on those, what is your assessment or diagnosis? And finally what is you plan to treat the problem?

This works fine for a lot of straightforward problems such as this one that I saw frequently in jails and ERs. A man complains of coughing up yellow sputum for several days and his physical exam is normal. My assessment would be acute bronchitis and my treatment oral antibiotics. (If he had other complaints and medical problems, he might require some tests.) He would be seen again in a few days if not substantially improving.

But what if someone complains of having vague abdominal discomfort off and on for a few days without other complaints or medical problems? If his exam was normal, I would just tell him to come back in a few days if his pain continued or immediately if it suddenly got much worse. (Other tests might be required in some people depending on the symptoms.) My diagnosis would be abdominal pain of unknown etiology and my plan would be re-evaluation if the pain persists.

That would be the most honest way of dealing with such a patient. But many doctors wouldn't do that. They would make up a tentative diagnosis and recommend some kind of treatment such as OTC pills and antacids. Knowing that the pain would probably just disappear in a few days, the doctor would have satisfied the patient's desire for some kind of diagnosis and treatment. Another reason to do this would be to make it more likely to get reimbursed by the insurance company for the visit.

Now we have hit on the second problem most doctors have to face everyday besides the fact that many patients want a specific diagnosis and treatment plan. So do the insurance companies. And if you don't give them exactly what they require in their often complex rule book, you won't get paid. This is true across all fields of medicine. I get information all the time about upcoming conferences for surgeons on how to properly code patients' illnesses in a way that will be most likely to assure proper reimbursement from insurance companies.

This is not only a big problem in medicine and surgery but psychiatry and psychology as well. Let's pretend that I'm a clinical psychologist and you come to me because you are not happy with the way your life is going. After talking to you for a little while, I decide that I can help you with psychotherapy. But assuming that I work on a fee for service basis (not for a government agency that pays me a salary), then I have to discuss the money issue with you. How am I going to get paid?

Because it can be difficult to get proper reimbursement from many insurance companies for psychotherapy, some therapists require the patient to pay them directly and then help him or her try to get money back from the insurance company. If they are willing to take what the insurance pays them, then they need to be very careful about what they use for a diagnosis.

Because I am both honest and want to get paid, I would tell you exactly what the problem is. For example, I might say that you are mildly depressed and that I can help you. However, I would also explain that there are a few different diagnostic categories I could put you in. The most benign might be some kind of adjustment disorder. This diagnosis is important because it is going to go on your insurance record and could possibly follow you for the rest of your life.

You might want me to use a non-specific diagnosis for just that reason. Then I would explain that the insurance company isn't required to pay for the treatment of that problem. If you want me to accept their payments, then I will have to put you in some sort of depressive disorder that state law will require them to cover. If you pay me directly and are willing to take your chances on getting reimbursed, then I'll use the most benign diagnosis I can.

You may think it strange that I could just pick and choose among diagnostic labels, but that is not so hard to do when dealing with mental disorders (and sometimes medical ones). Back in the 1950s and 60s when psychiatrists (as well as psychologists) worked with the DSM 1 and 2, studies showed that there was agreement on the same diagnosis in the same person evaluated by multiple examiners sometimes only 20% of the time. It was not unusual to still see rates around 40% after the DSM 3 first came out. This is why psychiatrists made so many changes during the 1980s deleting some categories and adding many others in trying to come up with the DSM 4 in 1994.

Now the concordance is pretty good. In fact it is so good that some psychiatrists and psychologists have complained that a clerk could come up with the correct diagnostic category the way the DSM is now structured. This probably makes it easier to work with the insurance companies and get paid, but I bet a lot of the people using it are not so happy about being forced to pigeonhole their patients this way. Also I must point out that just because multiple psychiatrists may agree on the category a particular patient falls in does not make it correct. Agreement on a specific diagnosis does not mean that it is accurate. Reliability is not validity. Remember that the whole DSM-IV was designed with the goal of making it easy to slot people into certain categories.

So now you have the bad news, which you probably had already noticed. The entire system of medical and mental health care requires its providers to put labels on everyone in the system. And like the numbers tattooed on people in Nazi concentration camps, they may serve a temporary purpose but be very hard to ever get rid of. For people who have severe diabetes, their labels may not be a problem.

However when it comes to getting a label like depression, that's an entirely different situation, especially if it's put on you erroneously and treated with drugs that end up causing adverse mental and physical problems for you. To repeat what I said earlier, I would recommend that you always question and certainly not blindly accept any diagnosis a doctor gives you. Get as much information as you can first.

This advice is doubly true when a psychiatric label is put on you. Just ask a lot of questions, do some research, and get other professional opinions if necessary. And after you have done that, still be very careful about starting psychoactive medicines unless you understand the risks, know what side effects to watch for, and have a game plan to get off of them. The entire system is designed to work against people who don't like to be labeled, and I am certainly one of them.

I have been able to stay away from doctors as a patient for many years. But I have an advantage that most of you don't. I do a lot of things to keep myself healthy and can treat my health problems when they occasionally develop. I also realize that I'm lucky that I haven't had any major health issues. I will have to face that problem eventually, but until then, nobody has been able to pin any medical or psychiatric labels on me.

Core Identity

Although it's hard to avoid getting labels when you are dealing with medical doctors, psychiatrists, and psychologists, that doesn't mean that you have to accept them as a part of your core identity. Thoughts and feelings come and go, but when you start to identify with them, that's when you sometimes get into trouble. When someone is treated rudely by a salesclerk and then meets a friend for lunch, she doesn't say that she feels angry. She says, "I am angry." That makes the emotion linger much longer for most people. When you identify with a psychological diagnosis, the negative effect is magnified perhaps thousands of times. Believing that you have a biochemical imbalance over which you have no control is not only disempowering but may disable you for the rest of your life.

Since I have compared depression to diabetes elsewhere in this book (as the companies selling psychotropic drugs often do), let's compare those two problems in this context. Even believing that a real disease like diabetes is a biochemical disorder over which you have no control is ultimately disempowering. Many doctors have been able to get insulin dependent diabetics from high doses of insulin down to relatively low doses by showing them how to carefully control sugar intake, exercise, and make other changes. Those starting on low doses of insulin can sometimes make a transition to oral medications.

The same is true of people with serious coronary artery disease. With major lifestyle changes, the disease can be reversed in some people. Even with cancer, identifying with the disease often means on a deep level that you consider yourself to be helpless in dealing with it. You may say that you can beat it to put on a good face to other people, but if you have identified with the disease as being at the core of your being, your body mind will often make sure it does you in. When your mind is sending messages like "I have cancer and I'm going to die," your body is always intently listening and may be more than willing to do whatever it needs to carry out what it thinks you want.

Now that I have warned you not to allow yourself to willingly and unquestioningly be pinned with a psychiatric diagnosis and adopt it as a core part of your individual identity, let me give you more reasons to seriously question the theories of psychopharmacology.

17

Psychopharmacology 101

If I really wanted to impress you, I could provide a detailed explanation of what exactly psychotropic drugs do from a pharmacological point of view right down to the cellular level. I could describe the lock and key mechanism explaining how opiates attach to highly specific receptors in the brain and thereby work their magic. I could talk a lot more than I already have about the mesolimbic dopaminergic reward pathway going from the ventral tegmental area through the nucleus accumbens to the frontal cortex. I could say a lot of other things as well because I know something about biology and have read many scientific articles and books on the subject. But I would rather tell you the truth. Despite my experience, my understanding of psychopharmacology leaves me with many questions. I don't really understand how psychoactive drugs work in the brain, other than a few minor details that actually make sense to me.

For example, if you look at what happens at the synapse between two neurons, some known facts sound logical. Let's take dopamine being released by one neuron and taken up by another on the receiving side of the synapse between them. An excitatory effect occurs. In order to control the response and prevent overstimulation, the dopamine is quickly taken up by transport proteins and moved back to the cell that released them.

Cocaine and methamphetamine both block those transporters, which leaves the dopamine in the synapse to continue stimulating the receiving cell. Methamphetamine also has a direct excitatory effect on the neuron releasing the dopamine as well. So does that explain the rush that you get by snorting cocaine or shooting up meth? No, because it's way more complicated than that.

If you look at what opiates do on a cellular level, it gets more difficult to understand. When heroin is consumed, it is not capable of producing any effect because it is a pro drug. It is called diacetyl morphine for a good reason—it has two acetic acid molecules attached to it that prevent it from having any effect. Enzymes in the brain and elsewhere remove those acetic acid molecules leaving morphine, which can then fit into a highly specific receptor site on certain cells. However, this creates exactly the opposite situation described with stimulants like cocaine. When the morphine attaches to the receptor, it actually inhibits the neuron from releasing its chemicals.

But we know that it causes something to happen in the brain, so how do we explain that? The simplistic explanation is that if it attaches to a brain cell that releases dopamine, you get an inhibitory (depressant) effect. On the other hand, when it attaches to a cell releasing an inhibitory molecule like GABA, a relative excitatory response results. You put all those little synaptic reactions together and bam—you get a heroin rush, which is quite different from cocaine or meth. Now you clearly understand how narcotics work on the brain, don't you?

I don't think so, and neither do I. Now if you want to get really confused, try reading a few sophisticated articles explaining alcohol's mechanism of action in the brain. Some of the addiction experts have their pet theories but most of them won't admit what I will. I do not have a clue what alcohol does in the brain. The only thing I know is that it gives me a pleasant buzz if I keep the dosage reasonable.

The one thing I do know for sure about the brain, just like the rest of the body, is that it likes to maintain a state of equilibrium or balance. When you use psychoactive drugs, they disrupt this state and the brain fights back. It can recover quickly from a cocaine high, but it may have to struggle when you are bombarding it every day for months on end with antidepressants, benzodiazepines, and other such drugs. When the drug is suddenly stopped, there is nothing to counteract the changes the brain has made as a reaction to the drug. With the brain's adaptation to the drug now unchallenged, withdrawal reactions can occur or a new and often unanticipated psychiatric disorder may be precipitated. While these drugs are in the body, the brain is in a constant battle to counteract their effects. The longer they are there, the more serious the potential problems of this conflict. If it is unable to restore equilibrium, you suffer adverse consequences, sometimes severe or possibly even fatal.

Brain or Mind?

I have described effects of various drugs on the brain and explained what tolerance to, dependence on, and withdrawal from addictive drugs are like earlier in this book. But don't ask me to explain how and why those phenomena occur from a cellular or neuropharmacological perspective. The good news is this—that's not the critical issue. What you really need to understand is the mind, not the brain—if you stay away from psychoactive drugs.

Although a lot of neuroscientists see them as the same, I don't. A pathologist would tell you that the brain is a collection of mostly proteins, fats, electrolytes, cells, and water located in a three-pound mass of tissue inside the skull. But here is what a world renowned neuroscientist might say: There are a hundred billion neurons in the average human brain. Given that a neuron can have somewhere between a thousand to ten thousand synaptic connections, there could be as many as 150 trillion synapses. This might well be more than the total number of stars in the entire universe—in one human brain. Even if the person telling me this was not only a brilliant neuroscientist but a highly respected astrophysicist, my response would be this: So what? Does that help me in any way understand why my life has been filled with so much psychological pain and suffering.

I don't deny that the brain is incredibly complex and can do some wonderful things, but the mind is something far greater (and non-local as well). Many doctors and other scientists seem to think that psychology is just a result of biochemistry and pharmacology. If you have the right balance of serotonin, GABA, and dopamine, you feel normal. If you are depressed, you just need a pill that can block the reuptake of serotonin at synapses, such as Prozac and Paxil.

Freud was way ahead of his time when he treated depression with cocaine more than a hundred years ago. (Actually Hippocrates was really the first great doctor to do this. Supposedly he treated melancholia with mandrake. If you forget what that was, go back to the chapter on hallucinogens.) However, as Freud discovered, psychopharmacology has some drawbacks. Not only does it not work for many people, but it also often carries unpleasant and sometimes dangerous side effects. Although it may have its place in some cases, many people would do better to simply try to understand how their mind works. Whether the problem is addiction of some kind or one of many psychological problems, that will be a safer and better solution for many. (I will deal with my approach to this issue at much greater length in an upcoming book.)

Lone Voice ?

A major problem that puzzles many neuroscientists is that most addictive psychoactive drugs seem to increase the level of dopamine in the nucleus accumbens in the mesolimbic reward pathway. These drugs include caffeine, nicotine, cocaine, opiates, cannabis, and alcohol. But these drugs are drastically different from each other in many ways including the kinds of psychoactive effects they have on people. But if they were all working through a similar mechanism, namely the dopamine reward pathway as postulated, then they should be interchangeable. But they are not—in any way, shape, or form. A heroin addict can't just switch to caffeine, nicotine, alcohol, or cocaine to get the same effects. That's why I think that this theory is vastly too simplistic.

Am I a lone voice crying out in the wilderness? I readily admit that I am not a neuroscientist of any kind nor am I a chemist or a pharmacologist. But I do keep good company in terms of the books I read voraciously. One of these published by the American Chemical Society called *The Chemistry of Mind-Altering Drugs* goes into extensive detail in presenting what is known about the molecular biology and chemistry of psychoactive drugs. Although highly knowledgeable, the author is also honest. In the first chapter entitled *Mind and Molecule*, he says the following regarding his discussion of receptors and neurotransmitters in the brain: "With all that is understood about receptors and neurotransmission, one might expect that much light could be shed on the human phenomenon of drug use and abuse. But the darkness is still extensive." Beautifully said, sir. Earlier in the same chapter, the author quotes one of the pharmacologists who developed Prozac as saying this: "If the human brain were simple enough for us to understand, we would be too simple to understand it."

When Einstein published his general theory of relativity in 1915, he believed that the universe was static. It was not until 15 years later that the scientist and Catholic Priest Lemaitre and astronomer Edwin Hubble were able to convince him that the universe was in fact expanding. And Einstein was a pretty smart guy. I want to give all the neuroscientists at all the universities in the world as much credit and recognition as they deserve. But I would also like to see some of them stand up and say what I am saying. Neuroscience is still in its infancy, just as astronomy was after Tyco, Kepler, and Galileo put in their two cents on the subject. Even though they made massive contributions to our knowledge, little did they know that their observations and laws may only govern four percent of the universe. At this stage of the game, we still don't know much about how the brain works. And when it comes to the mind, forget it.

Psychoactive Drug Behavior Modification

I may have sounded a little bit negative about the widespread practice of using stimulant drugs in kids for behavioral problems in Chapter 15. Here's why. I already discussed what illegal stimulants like cocaine and methamphetamine do previously. Most people don't think those are good drugs for adults to take so why should we believe that drugs that are almost the same (or in some cases are exactly the same) should be good for children. Here is the answer commonly given about how they work. They calm down hyperactive kids through a paradoxical effect, doing exactly the opposite of what you would expect for reasons we don't understand. But of course this is only true for kids who actually have the "disease" commonly known as ADHD. Sorry to be unkind, but this is just more BS from the pharmaceutical companies and some of the biopsychiatrists.

We do actually know a lot about what stimulant drugs do based on extensive animal experimentation as well as studies on humans, including children. First of all, these drugs do not have a paradoxical effect at all on many kids. Many of them become more anxious, nervous, and agitated than they already were. This makes their ADD behavior seem to even get worse often leading to a dosage increase or addition of other drugs rather than stopping the stimulant drug.

Although many kids react as you would expect from a stimulant, some do seem to calm down and become more easily manageable. Is that the paradoxical effect? No, it's exactly what you see in experimental animals given stimulants. What happens when you give chimps the same drugs children are taking such as Ritalin or Adderall in equivalent clinical doses? They go from being spontaneous, inquisitive, and active to being compulsive, dull animals who are no longer interested in socialization or play. And guess what else? They stop trying to escape. The drug has succeeded in turning an annoying animal into one that is now compliant and "happy" living in his cage.

Animal researchers view these behavioral changes as being quite negative. But advocates of ADD drugs in kids see the same behavior in children as a significant improvement. They don't talk out of turn, mess around with the children around them, or disrupt the classroom in any way. Many of them are now willing to sit quietly and listen to whatever is being taught no matter how boring it may seem to them. They will also be happy to sit and copy line after line off the chalk board monotonously for as long as the teacher asks them to. In other words, they have become ideal students.

Just as is true of animals on stimulants, many kids become more compliant from the teacher's point of view, but what is the trade for this more manageable and obedient child? It may be the suppression of imagination, spontaneity, creativity, and enthusiasm in many of them. Preserving those characteristics seems far more important to me than what they learn in school if that is the tradeoff. Much of what I learned in grade school, middle school, high school, and even college has been of little value to me in my life in the grand scheme of things. I was always fortunate to be what my teachers considered a good student and am glad I didn't have to take drugs to try to become a better one.

Now let's look at another issue—side effects of stimulant drugs in children. Clinical trials have shown that 39% of children can become depressed as a result of taking amphetamines like Dexedrine and Adderall. A little less than 9% have that problem with Ritalin. But guess what many doctors do when this occurs? Yes, some of you are starting to get the picture. Instead of removing the offending stimulant drug, they just add an antidepressant to the regimen.

If you were given an antibiotic by your doctor for a bacterial infection and then developed a generalized rash several days later, what should she do? Give you a tube of cortisone cream to rub all over your body? No. Stop the drug that you're allergic to. But when it comes to psychiatric drugs and their side effects, the response is often to just pile on more drugs to counteract the adverse effect of the first one. Before you know it, you're on two or three drugs which may be doing you no good whatsoever and possibly all causing side effects at the same time.

Are side effects besides depression rare with stimulants? The National Institute of Mental Health (NIMH) published a study in 1990 saying that half of children treated with stimulant drugs develop an obsessive-compulsive disorder. For example, a child may pursue a boring, repetitive task for hours without ever stopping to ask if it is necessary or needs to be continued. And once again, a drug side effect may not be recognized as such. With a new diagnosis, possibly more drugs may be added.

Sometimes the drug effects are more subtle and may only be noticed by the child's parents. The zombie effect that Alan's parents complained about in my story near the end of chapter 15 is not uncommon. Many parents notice that the child's personality seems to have changed in ways not apparent to others but disturbing to them. In Peter Breggin's *The Ritalin Fact Book*, he relates a response he has seen many times in dealing with parents of children on these drugs. They say things like this: My child just doesn't seem like himself anymore. I hardly know him. Another example he gives: Sure he was easier to be around, but it often made me sad, because I'd lost him in the process.

Wonderful Zombies

In the late 1990s, clinical trials were carried out using stimulants in children 4–6 years of age. They found that the majority of children experienced undesirable adverse side effects. 69% became more unhappy or sad on these drugs. Many of them became uninterested in others and spent less time talking to other children or adults. Despite that negative experience, the NIMH agreed to conduct further studies in children as young as two. Let me ask you this. Are certain branches of our government (such as the FDA and NIMH) looking out for and beholden to the American people or the pharmaceutical industry? I would ask the same question of many politicians who allow these agencies to function the way they do.

I would also like to point out that various governmental agencies seem to be fighting with each other. The DEA has taken a strong position on keeping all stimulant drugs currently used for ADHD in Schedule II. Just as a reminder, those are drugs deemed to have very limited medical use, be highly addictive and prone to abuse. Some consumer groups fanatically supporting these drugs in children tried to get Ritalin taken out of Schedule II so that it would be easier for doctors to prescribe and have less stigma attached to it. Fortunately in this case (as opposed to the marijuana one I discussed in the chapter on that subject), the DEA stuck to its guns and said no. The fact is that the mechanism of action on the brain is almost the same for cocaine, amphetamines, Ritalin, and methamphetamines.

About ten years ago, while the DEA was warning Americans how dangerous stimulant drugs are, the NIMH was willing to seriously consider helping the drug companies test them on kids who are still learning to walk and talk. (Whether they carried through and actually did it or not, I don't know.) Would the goal of such studies be to help children? Not in my opinion. We know that amphetamines can cause brain damage and massive death of brain cells in animals, so why exactly would we conduct studies using these drugs on very young children? Two reasons—to expand the potential market for the drug companies and find ways to make kids more compliant. You've all heard of the phrase "the terrible twos" to describe the difficulties most parents face when their children reach that age. Thanks to stimulant drugs, maybe parents will soon have a much more pleasant way to refer to that stage of early life—the wonderful zombies.

Alcohol Deficiency Syndrome

If I ever become enough of a celebrity, I think I'll start my own line of alcohol-related products. Here's how I will pitch the whole idea to the public. The human race was born with a biochemical deficiency and the only thing that can correct it is the ingestion of ethyl alcohol. Adam and Eve may have been the first people to discover this. I suspect that the fruit on the forbidden tree was over ripe and infested with yeast. They couldn't resist eating them because the yeast had been breaking down the sugars into alcohol which they probably knew intuitively would correct their metabolic deficiency. (By the way, a lot of inmates use the same technique to correct their alcohol deficiency problems—by letting their fruit start to rot before eating it.)

Obviously in addition to making people aware of a serious biochemical deficiency that they never realized they had, I would of course assure them that my alcohol-containing products would be superior to the many already on the market. For the millions who think that alcohol is just alcohol, I would correct that misimpression through massive advertising.

This theory of mine may sound crazy to some of you, but it is grounded in biology and chemistry more than all of those biochemical imbalance theories. Although I didn't find this out until many years after I finished all of my medical and surgical training, here's a big secret. Many of the body's cells preferentially metabolize alcohol over anything else as a source of energy. The body's primary source of energy is glucose and the backup is fat. However when you drink alcohol and it is in your bloodstream, many cells will take that molecule up and use it for energy instead of sugar. It only seems logical that if alcohol is a primary energy substrate for the body, it should be as important to us as the major three food groups (carbohydrates, proteins, and fats).

Once I am able to convince people of what they are missing biochemically, marketing my products to them will be much easier. I think you can see what my point is here. Nobody drinks alcohol because they are suffering from a biochemical deficiency or imbalance. They drink it to get high or relax or for social or religious reasons. Nor do they take any of the recreational drugs I talk about in this book because they believe that the drug will help correct a biochemical imbalance. Those who are intelligent probably realize that many of these drugs may in fact create an imbalance that accounts for the pleasant effects as well as the often unpleasant after effects. However because of the intense marketing and programming campaign over the last 50 years by the pharmaceutical companies assisted by many cooperative psychiatrists and government authorities, the theory of the biochemical imbalance theory is widely accepted as fact.

Unfortunately psychiatric medications are psychoactive (or psychotropic) drugs just like all of the recreational drugs. As I have mentioned earlier in this book, many of the now illegal drugs were at one time widely used and recommended by psychiatrists. I'm not saying that no one should ever take or use psychoactive drugs. As Solomon said in *Ecclesiastes*: Eat, drink, and be merry. (In my opinion, he was definitely depressed. That's why it is one of my favorite Bible books. My kind of guy.) Drink alcohol, smoke marijuana, or take psychiatric drugs if that's what you want to do or believe you should do. But don't do it because you think that your drug or drugs of choice are correcting any imbalance in your brain. They are not. Also don't use these drugs if you might end up endangering other people (for example if you are going to drive after taking them.) And never forget that if you get caught using illegal drugs, the government may unbalance your life for a long time (or even terminate it in some countries).

Calm Down with Alcohol
Now that I have raised the issue of alcohol, let's look at how we deal with that drug in children. In the U.S., it is illegal for anyone under 21 to use it and the rules are strictly enforced. In many other countries, children are allowed to drink wine at meals with their families because it is socially accepted. Imagine American parents who found the best way to calm down their seven-year-old boy was with some wine. Neighbors who became

aware of this might report them to the police. They could be charged with child abuse and possibly even lose custody of him. However it is perfectly legal and socially acceptable for parents to give a boy that age methamphetamine prescribed by a doctor for months or years to keep him calmed down. Maybe that makes sense to some of you, but it doesn't to me.

The Four Humors

The biochemical imbalance theory is nothing new. Hippocrates had a biological explanation for depression and many other problems—an imbalance of the four humors. He explained melancholia as resulting from an excess of black bile. The other three humors were yellow bile, phlegm, and blood. They were all in balance in a healthy body. This theory was widely believed until some started questioning it in the 18th century.

Let's say that I have adapted his theory to my own. I believe that depression is not caused by black bile but just ordinary greenish bile coming from the liver. Because it is stored in the gallbladder, I decide to start treating people who are depressed with cholecystectomy. As someone who has taken out quite a few gallbladders, I can assure you that you can get along just fine without one. The liver keeps pouring out the bile into the common duct that takes it to the duodenum where it helps breakdown fats coming from the stomach.

If I was allowed to conduct a study based on my theory, I bet that a lot of my patients would be improved by my operation if I had a chance to properly indoctrinate them first. If they really believed my theory, they would have the best chance of recovery from depression. To enhance the placebo effect, I would insist that I had to do the operation through a large incision under their right rib cage (not using laparoscopy, which wouldn't produce much pain postoperatively). Also the large scar would always be a reminder to them that I had cured their depression.

Don't like my plan for treating depression? Let's look at one that isn't much more scientific. Instead of the Hippocratic theory, we now have a similar one for psychiatric disorders. Most of them are caused by an imbalance of the four key monoamines (neurotransmitters) in the brain—dopamine, noradrenalin, serotonin, and GABA. Scientists a hundred years from now (perhaps a lot sooner) may look back on this theory with the same disregard as we now have for the humoral theory of 2500 years ago.

Rajas and Tamas

Since the mind and not the brain is the real source of most psychological problems, maybe we should be looking at something besides biochemistry for the answer. If you read the teachings of some of the great spiritual leaders of the 20th century, such as Ramana Maharshi or Sri Nisargardata Maharaj, you would also get a story about imbalance, but in the mind. They would explain that there are three great tendencies, qualities, or gunas of the mind (called tamas, rajas, and satva). Tamas can be described as passivity or inertia. If that dominates, you have apathy and depression. Rajas can be characterized by motion, activity, energy, restlessness. If that dominates, you experience fear, anxiety, anger, or in the extreme psychosis. If you learn to control and balance those two, then you achieve a state of harmony (satva).

Although you can't test that theory on chimps, it still makes more sense to me than the biochemical imbalance theory, which has never been scientifically corroborated in any convincing way. If depression really was just the result of a biochemical imbalance that could effectively be treated with drugs, then I would be all in favor of using them, if the side effects didn't outweigh the benefits. But that isn't the case at all. Antidepressants are not antibiotics.

Another look at Tolerance

Although I don't really understand drug tolerance very well, I'll tell you how the experts explain it. First of all, there is a metabolic tolerance, which makes sense to me. The body has a variety of enzymes that break down most psychoactive drugs. As you consume more drug, the enzymes that break it down increase (remember, the body doesn't like to be thrown out of equilibrium). For example, alcohol is broken down by alcohol dehydrogenase in the liver. A chronic drinker will have much more of that enzyme than the average person and therefore need to consume more alcohol to keep the levels up.

But here's the problem. He should be able to keep the alcohol level up by just drinking more and stay high that way. The question is this: Why did he feel really high with a blood alcohol concentration of .06 a few months ago but barely get a buzz with that level now. The neuroscientists' usual answer is that cellular tolerance develops in the neurons themselves. They supposedly adapt to the drug and get less sensitive to its effects over time.

It takes more drug to get the same result.

Although it sounds like a good theory on the surface, there are some serious problems with it. Why do people develop massive levels of tolerance for opiates but not nearly as much for benzodiazepines, alcohol, cocaine, and sometimes little or none for many psychiatric prescription drugs that have major effects on the brain? Relating to what I said earlier, tolerance may be sometimes just be the result of the brain's attempt to fight back the effects of the drug being used. The reaction may occur very quickly making it necessary to increase the drug dose to get a desired effect. In other words, you need more of the drug to counteract the brain's reaction to it. That makes sense to me.

However, when looking at the big picture, I still don't really understand the basis for tolerance and the wide variation that occurs in people. Regardless of why, it does happen. Some would say that's all you really need to know. (This statement has a parallel with a somewhat similar cynical attitude expressed by some doctors and pharmacologists—as long as a drug works, who cares why? Believe me, the mechanism of action for many prescription drugs on the market is poorly understood or not known at all.)

A lot of people, and especially college kids, commonly quote Friedrich Nietzsche's statement that whatever doesn't kill you will make you stronger. I think he was trying to say that adversity in your life frequently ends up making you a stronger person in the long run, which is often true. (By the way, he was a brilliant philosopher who ended up in an insane asylum for the last years of his life.) However, when it comes to drugs (legal or illegal), there is a different rule—they can make you sick or sometimes chronically disable you, even if they do not kill you. Keep that in mind whenever a doctor hands you a prescription, a friend offers you a pill, or a drug dealer tries to sell you a bag of whatever.

Drug Relapse

Although a lot of neurobiologists seem pretty confident that they know how addictive drugs work, the one thing most acknowledge they can't explain is why people who have used these drugs often relapse after they have stopped using for months or even years. That one I can explain—not from a pharmacologic point of view—but in terms of creamed onions.

When I was a kid, we spent every Thanksgiving and Christmas at my grandmother's house. She made fantastic creamed onions that I couldn't resist. Although I ate turkey, dressing, and the rest in moderation, I could not stop eating the creamed onions. The family never knew exactly what was going to happen on those holidays except for one thing—Donny was going to eat creamed onions until he got sick. Every time, I spent several hours lying on my grandmother's bed after the meal while everyone else talked in the living room.

Was I ever addicted in any way? That would be highly unlikely given that I only had access to them twice a year. (My mother couldn't make creamed onions, at least not that I liked.) Perhaps you could attribute my stupid behavior to my immaturity. Fast forward to my mid thirties when I was a successful plastic surgeon. On the holidays, we always had potlucks at the hospital the day before everyone was off on vacation for a few days (not me or many other doctors—we were usually on call).

No one prepared creamed onions, but a couple of nurses made incredible brownies and deviled eggs. Although I rarely ate either of these, at the first event I consumed about eight brownies and fifteen deviled eggs, in addition to a few other things. Needless to say, when I went home after the party, I was sick for many hours. No nausea or vomiting—I just felt horrible.

So what do you think happened the next year? I promised myself the day of the potluck that I would have only one brownie and two or three deviled eggs. You know exactly what happened. I repeated my experience from the previous year and continued to do so for the next several years. Many of you have probably had similar experiences. So do we really need a biochemical explanation of why people go back to drugs that gave them pleasure followed by pain either once or perhaps many times in the past?

When a friend, counselor, or therapist asks how you could possibly have relapsed with drugs, alcohol, or something else after some period of time, you have my permission to explain your mistake in two words— creamed onions. We have all been there. Don't make it into a big crime (although the authorities may). Just decide after your slip up whether you really want to get back into a prior pattern if it previously caused a lot of problems in your life. Now let's look at what I think are the minor and major reasons motivating people to use psychoactive drugs.

18

Why People Really Use Drugs

Aside from the standard reasons given by most people treating addiction (seeking pleasure, stimulating the pleasure center in the brain, and so on) that I mentioned at the beginning of this book, there are certainly other things motivating people to use drugs. One of my favorites is boredom, which some people find almost intolerable. This one I can't relate to since I haven't felt bored in many years. At any given time, I have a hundred or sometimes more books checked out of the library. I can't find the time to read many of them I would like to in addition to getting all of the other things done related to my books, music, exercise, and so on. There really aren't enough hours in the day for me to be able to get bored. The problem many people have is that they are not really interested in learning new things. Rather they just want to be entertained when they aren't forced to work at jobs they often don't like much. When some of them run out of movies or other entertainment, they take drugs.

Of course people also take drugs to facilitate social interaction. Let's get a cup of coffee or go have a drink. Those can be pretty harmless, but when you decide to take meth, super K, or ecstasy at a party to fit in, then you move into a different level of potential harm and risk. Sometimes people are just afraid to refuse a drug because the person offering it will be hurt or offended. These are not good reasons to use mind-altering drugs.

Some people take drugs to enhance what would otherwise be an ordinary experience. A common example would be to have wine with a meal. Others might prefer to occasionally smoke a joint or cigar before or after eating. Although those choices can be relatively harmless for a lot of people in moderation, taking hallucinogens to enhance your experience at a rave or other party may get you into a lot of trouble.

Another reason some people take psychoactive drugs is to enhance athletic performance. Although drug testing in professional athletes has made this more difficult, plenty of amateur athletes still do it. I won't get into the issue of steroids (even though these are widely abused) since they don't really fall into the same kind of category as the other drugs in this book. Milder stimulants like nicotine are still allowed, even in professional athletes. Some baseball players still chew tobacco during games.

So I guess that means that the world's most addictive drug is still OK in many situations.

Many artists use psychoactive drugs because they believe that they help enhance their creativity. Alcohol, opiates, cocaine, marijuana, hallucinogens, and amphetamines have been extolled by a variety of great writers and artists over the last few centuries. Although I consider myself to be somewhat creative, I certainly can't attribute that to any psychoactive drugs since the only one I use is alcohol. It not only does not enhance creativity for me but in fact stifles it in anything more than small doses. I can't personally comment on the others, not having used most of them at all and certainly never in that context.

Another big motivation for people to use drugs, especially those that are illegal, goes back to Adam and Eve—the forbidden fruit. This is especially true of many young people who see rebellion as a necessary rite of passage to get through adolescence. Drug prohibition often psychologically acts to increase drug use. Many people, and especially young people, start using drugs simply because they are the "forbidden fruit." Just as children protest and try to reject the authority of their parents during their years of teenage rebellion, they often do the same with government authorities. If the government says, "Just say no to drugs," they answer with, "Fuck you. You can't tell me what to do." As an example of this phenomenon, 20 years after the Dutch legalized (or technically just decriminalized) marijuana, the percentage of their high school students using that drug was one tenth that of those in the U.S. in which many states had serious penalties (like long prison sentences) for simple possession.

This rule doesn't only apply to kids and teenagers. Many adults during Prohibition who had no prior compulsion to drink alcohol began to do it as a protestation of what they considered to be a ridiculous, hypocritical, and unenforceable law. Unfortunately, some of them ended up blinded or killed by something called "bathtub gin." This was a concoction containing some methanol that was substituted for the much less toxic, but more expensive form of alcohol, ethanol, to increase profits. Yes, some previous non-drinking adults actually died while protesting what they believed to be an absurd law. Similarly, some teenagers and adults today who want to thumb their nose at the authorities are injured or die from drugs that have been laced with toxic impurities to cheapen production costs and increase profits.

As I mentioned in chapter eight, the current war on drugs really started out as a war on dissent when then President Nixon decided to go after the Vietnam War protesters on drug charges. Can I interject a little practical advice here? Do not try to protest drug laws that you feel are unfair by taking drugs that may be harmful for you just to make a statement. Do whatever you can to get such laws changed first. Then maybe you can use the drugs legally if you really want to. In fact, always try to resist the temptation to try the forbidden fruit in any form (drugs, sex, whatever) just to say fuck you to the people in authority. Most of the time, if your action hurts anyone, it will only be you.

Beyond these motivations, to me there are much more profound reasons that prompt people to take mind-altering drugs. The first of these is that many of them often help to stop or at least slow down the incessant chatter of the mind, much of which is quite unpleasant and usually completely useless from any practical point of view. Do you know how to turn off the mind chatter? That is a rhetorical question because unless you are a cat or dog reading this book, then you don't. I say that as someone who has had a great deal of experience with self-hypnosis and meditation for more than 30 years. (I first started using hypnosis as a plastic surgeon to calm down children with lacerations I had to repair in ERs.)

For those of you reading this book who happen to be monks living in a Zen Monastery in Japan with special powers, let me say this. If you can sit in a very cold room in the middle of winter naked and have someone place cold wet towels on you without freezing to death, then good for you. But if you are one of those rare people who can sit there in a state of profound meditation and get your body temperature up so high that the cold towels on you start to steam, then I say this: I don't want to hear about it because most of the rest of us can't do that. If we want to get our body temperature up high enough to make steam, we need to get into a hot sauna.

Given the fact that most people are not experts in controlling the body-mind such as those I just mentioned, many turn to drugs to alter their mental state. The truth is that if it were not for the rampant drug and alcohol use in many societies, the violence and mayhem on this planet would probably be much higher than it already is. The problem with drugs is that they only provide temporary relief from the interminable onslaught of the thinking mind. Alcohol (and perhaps narcotics) might be an exception since you can you can stay high much of your waking time if you control your intake. Russian vodka may have played a major role in keeping that country from exploding into uncontrolled chaos during the painful transition from communism to some form of democracy.

Self-proclaimed experts in drug addiction have their elaborate scientific explanations of why people use drugs. It is just a complex biochemical process related to stimulation of the pleasure center in the brain. I don't think so. Whether they are aware of it or not, many people use drugs because it is the easiest and quickest way to have a spiritual-like experience or perhaps momentarily get closer to God.

Now is that some kind of profound insight on my part? Maybe or maybe not. As I mentioned earlier, drugs in ancient India, China, and elsewhere were used sometimes as a way of getting in contact with the gods or experiencing heaven. Psychoactive plants have been used all over the world for centuries to get in touch with the spirit world. Alcohol has played a big role in religious rites in major religions like Judaism and Christianity for centuries. The question I have is this: Do psychoactive drugs actually get you closer to understanding God or spirituality in any lasting or meaningful way?

Let me ask you this: How does God manifest in this world? Much scripture says that God is love, so that is obviously important. The Bible describes a peace that passeth all understanding. Certainly most people would associate joy with God. So what do mind-altering drugs do? Depending on the drug, they give you one, two, or sometimes all of those experiences at the same time.

Heroin will certainly give someone a profound sense of peace as it temporarily shuts down the incessant mind chatter that causes so much discomfort for all of us. Cocaine and methamphetamine will have a quite different effect but certainly make you feel joyful and happy (heroin may do this as well but without the high energy.) Now if you want to experience love and joy at the same time, then ecstasy would be the right drug to take. If you would prefer to see the profound beauty in and feel at one with everything, then LSD might do the trick for you. You can sit in state of rapture looking at an ordinary flower for a few hours.

So what is wrong with all this? Well, really nothing—except that you might get a heart attack or arrhythmia while you're coked up or high on meth. Or you might get robbed or raped while you're stoned on heroin. Or you might be at a really cool party where everyone's high on Ecstasy and feel a sense of love and attraction for everyone. Then you may have sex with many people you hardly know and end up pregnant or maybe getting hepatitis or AIDS.

Now what if using drugs did create some kind of actual spiritual transformation? Would the risks be worth taking then? Probably so, if we are talking about an experience that truly changes your life. However, I suspect that such a transformation following drug use is incredibly rare. Look at two icons of the 1960s drug revolution, Bernard Alpert (later known as Ram Dass) and Timothy Leary, both professors of psychology at Harvard back then. They helped to popularize the phrase "tune in, turn on, and drop out."

I heard Ram Dass speak publicly several times in the 1990s, and it seemed to me that he had yet to experience a spiritual transformation. He knew the lingo (I am a Buddha looking away from myself), but still appeared to be stuck in his intellect. He later basically admitted this in a book after he had a bad stroke that left him quite disabled for a while. Although never totally recovered physically, he has continued to do much great humanitarian work through the Seva foundation. I am not trying to put him down and have nothing but admiration for the work he has done over many years.

Leary believed that computers and the Internet were the coolest things around in the last years of his life before he died of prostate cancer. He thought it would be really cool if his death could be viewed live on computers around the world. If drugs didn't lead to their spiritual awakening (and they took most of them), then they are not likely to work for you either. So if that is your motivation, then don't bother.

Of course, this is not the professed goal of very many people who use drugs, especially those who are young. Likewise, people in their 40s and 50s who are suddenly concerned with their own mortality because of an illness or death of a loved one are not likely to turn to hard drugs for a spiritual experience. However, if you are on a spiritual search, I would not suggest using drugs as your pathway to a positive life transformation.

In reality, drug use will lead to a decidedly negative life change most of the time such as medical problems, money problems, possibly jail time, and so on. But if you're not concerned about getting gangbanged, contracting an incurable sexually-transmitted disease, or maybe dying of an overdose, then perhaps drugs might be a way to try to have a spiritual experience or get closer to God (at least briefly).

As we come closer to the end of this book, it may seem to have been too brief to some. Would a 600-page volume filled with lots of citations and complex scientific language have been more helpful to you? I don't think so, at least not for most of you (although some excellent books I recommend on my web site do fall into that category). I have read hundreds of books on this subject and they're all out there for you to read if you are interested. However I would like to be clear about my intention with this book. It is not a medical text or reference book. That's why I have no footnotes, reference list, or even an index. I'm not trying to explain everything that is known about all psychoactive drugs. I only want to convince people to use caution before they decide to take them.

I found as a surgery resident when I had to prepare presentations to several hundred people ranging from medical students to professors that I seemed to have a skill for taking complicated subjects and making them simpler and more understandable to the least experienced people and yet still interesting for those with the most experience and knowledge. At least, that's what many people often told me. If I haven't succeeded in doing that for you, I'm sorry. That was my goal.

Despite my extensive experience taking care of thousands of people with drug problems, I still had to do a great deal of research because I have never personally used any of them myself except marijuana a few times. My drug of choice has always been the legal one—alcohol. But I seem to have left out the world's favorite psychoactive drug. No, that subject deserves to get another book all to itself. Now you can read about the ultimate high before this journey officially ends.

19

The Ultimate High
Jumping Out of an Airplane on Cocaine

After my second year of surgery residency at UCSD, I did a year of research. I chose to do it in cardiac surgery because I was considering becoming a heart surgeon at the time. Also I had developed a good relationship with the chief of cardiac surgery when I rotated on his service as a resident for two months.

Once I started doing research for him, our relationship quickly became much less formal than that of student and professor. He asked me if I wanted to go flying with him the week after I started. I knew he was a private pilot, but not much more than that. I met him at Montgomery Field, a small private airport just south of the Miramar Naval Air Station in San Diego. It turned out that we would be flying in an open cockpit biplane that he owned. It was a Pitts Special, an aerobatic plane commonly used in national competitions. I was excited but a little nervous at the same time. I had never even been in a small plane before, much less an open-cockpit biplane.

When he handed me a parachute, I thought it was a joke. He told me to put it on and then said if I fell out of the plane or he said to jump, to pull on the D ring. "What the hell have I gotten myself into," I thought as I was trying to figure out how to pull the D ring.

Then he said, "Now make sure you don't pull on it until you're completely free of the airplane."

"Holy shit," I thought.

He could tell I was getting concerned. He checked to make sure the parachute was on properly and then said, "Let's get in the plane. Oh, by the way. If for some reason the chute doesn't open, don't worry. The name of the guy who packed it is inside." I thought he was serious and now I was scared shitless.

I climbed into the rear seat and he helped me put on the seat belt and shoulder harness. I pulled those belts so tight I couldn't move a millimeter. We both wore headsets so we could talk to each other. When he got clearance to take off, he put on full power and started weaving back and forth down the runway. I couldn't figure out what he was doing. Then the plane lifted off and we started to climb.

Once we were several thousand feet up, he explained that the plane was designed in such a way that you couldn't see straight ahead on either takeoff or landing so you had to weave back and forth to make sure you stayed on the runway. That didn't make a lot of sense to me but I was just enjoying the scenery from the plane. We climbed up a few thousand feet and then headed north over the Miramar air base to the fields east of Del Mar. It was really exciting and not frightening at all. I decided maybe I had overreacted at the airport.

All of a sudden, he said, "Let's do a roll." He then slowly rolled the plane over and came back to an upright position. "How was that?" he asked.

"Fine," I said. Then he did a loop which I thought was kind of fun. It was like the rides in amusement parks.

"Any problems?" he asked.

"No," I said. "That was great."

"Good," he said. "Then I'll go ahead and do a few stunts."

"OK."

I was completely unprepared for what occurred next. I would only come to understand what had happened months later. He started off with a figure of eight followed by an eight-point roll. That was fun, but then he did a hammerhead where you fly straight up until the plane almost stalls, then roll it over and head straight down for the ground. Then you bring the plane up and pull three Gs to get level. That wasn't bad until he turned the plane over and was flying upside down.

He asked if I was OK and I said "yes" although I wasn't exactly sure. Then he pushed up and did an outside loop, recovered upright, then went into a hammerhead with an inverted recovery, followed by six more maneuvers. When he came out of the last one, he said, "How are you doing?" I couldn't answer at first. He repeated, "You OK?"

"Yeah," I said, "but I think maybe I blacked out for a few seconds on that last one."

"Yup," he said, "so did I." I wasn't sure whether I should be scared to death or having fun.

When we got back to the hangar, he said, "Well, what did you think?"

"I thought it was great."

He started laughing and said, "I gave you a hell of a ride for the first time. You know I took Gary up last week" (a cardiologist who he didn't like that much because he was so arrogant), "and he started puking after the first roll, so we had to come back. He was pretty sick and I had to clean up the damn plane afterward. You want to fly again next weekend?"

"Yeah," I said. "Definitely." I suddenly had another goal that year now that I had a lot more time than I would during the rest of the grueling residency, working only 40 hours a week instead of 90 to 120. I was going to learn to be an aerobatic pilot so I could scare the shit out of my friends. And I did, but the rest of the story is in my book *Boy to Man*.

What does this story have to do with a book about psychoactive drugs? If you don't see the analogy, there are ways to experience pleasure that don't involve taking drugs. We can achieve a different kind of high by engaging in various physical activities. This could be popular sports like weight lifting, running, tennis, skiing, snowboarding, and scuba diving, all of which I did quite a bit at various points in my life. Then there are more exotic sports such as mountain climbing, race car driving, and skydiving.

I personally have no interest in doing any of these latter three, not to mention many others. Why? Because they sound dangerous to me. Someone like parachuting expert and prolific author, Dan Poynter, who has jumped out of planes hundreds of times may think I'm really missing out on a great thrill, but I don't. Although I didn't see flying small planes as being too dangerous, I did discover that certain issues made me quite nervous. The first time I ran into unexpected turbulence in a small plane, I was with an instructor who was able to correct the problem of the plane bouncing all over the place. However I was still concerned that I might not be able to do the same thing if I were alone. That's why I decided to spend a lot of time learning aerobatics so that I would know how to properly handle a plane that was suddenly going out of control because of unexpected turbulence.

Becoming a good pilot is in many ways like becoming a good surgeon. You can't just be prepared to deal with the average challenges that may come your way in the operating room, but the horrendous and sometimes totally unpredictable things that may happen. So again, what does this have to do with using drugs? Well, the answer is this. There is no training program you can take to fully prepare you for all the strange things that may happen to you and your body when you take psychoactive drugs. You will always be at their mercy and never fully able to control them or their effects. Not only that, but you may have to deal with long-term or sometimes permanent side effects, even after you have stopped using them (as I have emphasized repeatedly in this book).

To Use or Not to Use

As far as deciding whether or not to use drugs, let me give you some examples of what I am talking about. If you are invited to the house of a friend who lives a block away from you for dinner, he might ask you if you would like a beer when you get there. If you drink and like beer, then this is not a complex issue for you. You know what beer does to you and you don't have to worry about some bizarre event that might occur. But instead of offering a beer, what if he asks you if you want to snort some cocaine? Should you worry about offending him and say, "Sure, sounds good."

If you would do that, then you may be in for some trouble, my friend. What would I do? I would just say, "No thanks, man. Do you have any beer?" Not only would I not take him up on his offer just to please him, but I would also be reluctant to go back under similar circumstances. I have been to parties where I was offered cocaine (sometimes at the homes of distinguished physicians) and always said the same thing. "No thanks." Responding as I did does not mean that you're some kind of wimp afraid to party and have a good time. It means that you're too intelligent to take recreational psychoactive drugs that other people offer you, no matter how reliable you may think they are.

Many of you might agree that you would do exactly the same thing. So what's my point? How about a different situation. You are in a family doctor's office for a minor problem or maybe an annual physical (if you have good insurance) and tell him that things aren't going the way you want in your life. His immediate reaction, without asking you any questions about what you mean, is that you are depressed and he starts writing a prescription for an antidepressant. Some of you who might have walked out on the previous situation, or just politely refused, will willingly take the prescription and get it filled.

That casual and reflex reaction on your part could possibly take you down a road that could lead to serious problems for months or possibly years, and, for some people, turn out to be vastly worse than doing a line of cocaine. Just as I did not trust my former professor, for whom I had great respect as a surgeon, when he offered me cocaine at a party, neither should you blindly trust your high school or college buddy who does something like that to you. The same principle should carry into the doctor's office. Be very careful before you start taking any psychoactive drug, legal or illegal.

Why would so many doctors casually recommend that you start taking antidepressants for depression or benzodiazepines for anxiety without getting a full and complete history of what's really going on in your life? The answer is simple: they don't have time. Often they are family doctors (formerly called general practitioners) or internists. Many of them are working for HMOs or other similar medical organizations that carefully regulate what they do. A lot of them are terribly frustrated by being forced to get the patients in and out of the office as quickly as possible. There may be some who are cynical and just don't care anymore, but most do. They simply don't know how to deal with patients who come in with lots of life problems rather than straight forward medical problems that they can confidently and competently treat.

Although many of them might love to spend an hour talking to you about your life problems and try to give you advice, they don't have time. And in most cases, they won't be paid to do it. If they do it very much, the medical organization they work for may sanction or even fire them. In addition, patients put tremendous pressure on doctors for a quick fix to their problems and many are angry if they don't leave with a prescription of some kind. Now we have the makings of a perfect dysfunctional couple—the patient who wants and even demands drugs and the doctor who is only too willing to write the prescription because he doesn't have time to do anything else, including taking time to explain why this isn't the best course of action.

What should you do if you think you're depressed? Should you ask your doctor for a referral to a psychiatrist? First of all, if your doctor is a gatekeeper in your HMO or similar medical organization, he probably won't approve it. After all, he can write any prescription that a psychiatrist can, so why waste the time. Secondly, many psychiatrists are in the same bind as the other doctors—they need to get the patients in and out, no matter how much they might want to spend time talking to them. Thirdly, many psychiatrists consider themselves to be brain doctors whose job is just to make a diagnosis and then write whatever they consider to be the appropriate drug prescription. Many residency training programs seem to have adopted the strict medical model that has become so pervasive over the last 30 years and didn't even bother to train their psychiatric residents how to do psychotherapy anymore. That has changed over the last eight years after a medical accreditation board demanded that psychiatric residency programs provide at least some training in cognitive-behavioral therapy for their residents. How much they get is probably highly variable and still no guarantee that they will actually use it in their practices.

Got the Blues?

What can you do if you have the blues? The first thing I would recommend is to not even mention it to you doctor unless that is the main reason you are seeing him, especially if he is a family doctor or internist. Try to deal with it in other ways first unless it persists and seems to become more serious. If you have a great relationship with a caring doctor who does have time to talk to you, then by all means talk to him. But if he quickly recommends a psychoactive drug for your problem, then beware. You can be polite and take his prescription with you but don't fill it and certainly don't start taking any drugs until you have gotten a lot more information.

Although I mentioned my concern about the professional reliance on the Hamilton Depression Scale in Chapter 13, there is a self-test for depression developed by psychiatrist David Burns, a protégé of Aaron Beck, that appears to be reasonably accurate and has proven helpful to many people. You can find it in his popular book first published in 1980 and updated in 1999 (*Feeling Good*). He will give you a good idea of how cognitive therapy can help you. If you're not severely depressed, it might be of great help to you. You can also find the test online by doing a seach for Burn's Depression Checklist. You take the test by yourself, so you don't need to share it with anyone or lie about how you really feel. The scale goes from zero to one hundred. If you score 15, you are mildly depressed. If you're over 50, then you are severely depressed and need to get professional help right away. Definitely check it out if you think you may be depressed.

If you simply talk to your doctor about your life problems and she quickly suggests a psychoactive drug, then I would recommend that you respond with something like this: "Are there any other options besides drugs." She may actually be happy to hear you ask that and suggest that you talk to a counselor of some kind. This might be a social worker or psychologist. If she wants to give you a referral, then ask what it might cost. If you can't afford it, then inquire about free clinics or other options.

I'll briefly repeat what I said previously. If you can't afford a professional therapist of some kind, you can still talk to friends, family members, clergy, or try to find people in similar circumstances through the many social networks on the Internet. Another way to get help from experts without paying any money is to go to your local library. That's what I do when I need help with something or specific information. I wrote this book hoping that I could help people dealing with the issue of psychoactive drug use or abuse. Lots of other authors have done the same thing and many of their books are just sitting on the shelf in your local library waiting for someone with the problem they are addressing to check it out and read it. Look through the many books I recommend on my web site DonaldChapin.com and see which of them might be most helpful to you.

In addition to helping adults considering taking psychiatric drugs, I would especially like to get my message to kids, teenagers, or other young people who are exposed to illegal psychoactive drugs in many ways and are thinking about using them. Some of them perceive much of the information they get from authorities to be nothing more than antidrug propaganda. For example, many teens don't think meth is dangerous because they have been told the same thing about marijuana as I mentioned earlier. If that's their belief, perhaps I can change it for some of them. I hope many younger people will see my information and advice as being unbiased and based on truth rather than what they perceive to be simply an antidrug agenda.

Life Problems and Drugs
I don't think that any of the drugs I am talking about in this book are a good way to deal with life's problems, but at least I can be objective about the relative dangers that they pose based on much experience treating patients and the extensive research I have done over many years. I don't have an axe to grind or an infallible belief system that I want to promote. I would just like to give people the most honest and accurate information

I can to help them make the best decisions about whether they should or should not be using various psychoactive drugs in their lives.

Besides younger people who are by far the highest risk group for getting involved with and possibly addicted to illegal drugs, I am hoping to reach the parents of those children so that they have accurate information and know how to deal with their children's questions. I would also like to let those parents know that if they are taking psychoactive drugs prescribed by doctors that some of these could be doing them more harm than good. Also their children may not find their warnings about some illegal drugs to be credible or perhaps even perceive them to be hypocritical if their parents are regularly taking prescription drugs to make them feel better or relieve anxiety.

Others I would like to reach are adults who are thinking about taking prescription psychoactive drugs. I have tried in this book to make such people aware of the risks they may be facing and get them to understand that much of what they have read and even been told by their doctors is to a great extent just propaganda from the pharmaceutical industry. They spend millions to indoctrinate doctors of all kinds (including psychologists who can't prescribe drugs but can make referrals) as well as the general public. Information that seems to be unbiased may be actually be coming directly or indirectly from people on their payroll. Or it may be someone who thinks he's independent but doesn't realize that he's just been caught up in their propaganda.

Don't Jump

Let's get back to the title of this chapter. If you get an invitation from a friend who happens to be a former parachute expert for the U.S. military to go skydiving after snorting some cocaine, what should you do? He seems like a reasonable person and says it's really a blast. I hope you would just say no thanks. I would give you the same advice if a dealer on the street offers you some drugs, or a friend tries to give you a line or pill at a party, or a physician casually hands you a prescription for a psychoactive drug without knowing much about you. Don't ever take psychoactive drugs casually without seriously considering what you may be getting into.

Maybe if you have already had bad problems with psychoactive drugs, this advice may seem simple. "Yeah, I know that," some might say. But how did you find out that you should be very careful before you decide to start taking psychoactive drugs. Did you become addicted and tolerant, lose money, wreck a marriage, or mess up your children before you learned the lesson? That is precisely what I am trying to prevent with this book. If you already know what I am saying is true, then tell your friends who may be about to make the same mistakes you did to read it. Believe me, many of them may not listen to you, but they might listen to me. I don't want to try to figure out the best way to get people off of drugs. I'll leave that up to psychiatrists and others who do that day in and day out. My goal is to keep as many people as possible from getting on them in the first place. As the old Ben Franklin saying goes, "An ounce of prevention is worth a pound of cure."

I want to emphasize what I have said elsewhere in this book. If you are already on prescription drugs and possibly addicted to them, do not try to wean yourself off or stop cold turkey. I can't provide you any help in that area. I can point you in the right direction by recommending books written on that subject by true experts at treating addiction and helping people get off all kinds of psychoactive drugs. But that is not my area of expertise, so don't look for that information in this book. If you are having problems with prescription drugs, try to get help from your doctor or other health-care provider first. If that doesn't help or satisfy you, then try reading some of the books I have previously mentioned in other chapters and recommend on my web site and go from there.

Fear and Desire
One of the most important principles of psychology I have learned explains that much human intrapsychic conflict comes from the two motivating emotions, fear and desire, working in opposition to each other. More specifically conflict arises when fear and desire are centered on the same object. I'll give you some simple examples. A guy in college just got dumped by his girlfriend. He gets a crush on another girl (desire) but is afraid that she may do the same thing to him as his previous girlfriend (fear). If the fear is much stronger than his desire, he may not even ask her out on a date.

How about a simple example using psychoactive drugs and specifically the only one I use—alcohol. If I am invited to a neighbor's house for dinner and he offers a drink before and wine during the meal, I will partake if I'm in the mood and the alcohol he's offering is something I like (desire without fear). But what if I drive ten miles and face the same situation? The desire might be the same, but fear will kick in and create conflict. What is the basis of the fear? I have a phobia for car accidents, emergency surgery (on myself), dui arrest, and spending time in jail. The end result of the conflict is that I won't have anything to drink (even though I have never actually experienced any of those problems except for a car accident).

Now let's look at someone else faced with the decision of whether to take psychoactive drugs. Kathy, a senior in high school, is invited to a party at a friend's house whose parents are out of town for the weekend. Someone has brought some drugs with him that he got from a friend who stopped taking them without telling his parents or doctor. He was on Desoxyn for ADHD. Kathy says when asked if she wants to try a pill, "Sure my brother was on Ritalin and then Adderall starting when he was eight for ADD." Now why is she so willing to take this drug? It is because she has no fear of it and her friend says it will make her feel really good.

Do you know what Desoxyn is? It is methamphetamine used to treat ADHD. (It is also approved by the FDA for the treatment of obesity and depression.) And logically why should Kathy be afraid of it? Her brother's doctor gave similar drugs to her brother for many years with the approval of her parents (and maybe even at their request). If there was anything wrong with those drugs, doctors wouldn't be prescribing them. This is the big message we as a society are giving to our children. First of all, if you have life problems, you don't need to figure out how to deal with them— you just take drugs. Secondly since their use is widespread and condoned by the people in power (doctors, teachers, parents, and politicians), they must be safe. I said in the chapter on amphetamines that many high school students in the U.S. don't even consider methamphetamines to be drugs. Now you know why.

Good Luck

Because most human beings crave pleasure, it is easy to market psychoactive drugs to them that promise to make them feel better. Drugs have a big advantage because many things that people find pleasurable take time, training, planning, and often a lot of money (like traveling, skiing, scuba diving, or whatever else turns you on). If someone offers you a drug, it can be cheap or free with the promise of giving you the feeling you want right now. When you have the desire to get high, relax, or feel better, then you will use drugs almost automatically if you have no fear of the consequences.

My goal in writing this book has been simple. I just wanted to give you enough information to instill fear in you when someone offers you a psychoactive drug, whether it's a friend, a doctor, or anyone else. My intention has not been to make you paranoid as some of the antidrug crusaders and drug warriors often try to do with their propaganda about illegal drugs. On the other hand, I don't want you to blindly accept much of what is really pharmaceutical company propaganda telling you that their drugs are safe magic pills that will make you feel better without any significant risks or consequences. I'm just trying to convince you to think seriously before taking psychoactive drugs for any reason—recreational or medical. In other words, when the desire to feel better by taking drugs comes up, I hope I have been able to instill in you an automatic fear response that will prevent you from doing it reflexively or casually. On the other hand, if you like pain and suffering, then pay no attention to me. Good luck in this adventure called life.

About the Author

Donald Chapin started practicing medicine in 1973. Many of his patients over the years have had serious problems with a variety of legal and illegal psychoactive drugs. He received his board certification by both the American Board of Surgery and the American Board of Plastic Surgery and has been a longtime fellow of the American College of Surgeons and the American Society of Plastic Surgeons.

His varied career has spanned many areas of medicine including general, thoracic, and cardiovascular surgery, trauma surgery, plastic surgery, and emergency medicine. He was a former staff surgeon at the Scripps Clinic and Research Foundation in La Jolla and an assistant clinical professor of surgery at UCSD Medical Center in San Diego. He worked for a few years as a jail doctor where his skills across all areas of medicine were tested. It was during that time that he gained his greatest insight into the use and abuse of mind-altering drugs, motivating him to subsequently intensively investigate that field for a number of years.

You should be warned about one thing. He is very sensitive to criticism, so don't be mean to him. If you have something negative to say, then please convey that to his agent or publicist if he can find one willing to work for him. If what you say seriously upsets him, his reaction may be shocking. Try to be nice even if you don't like this book.

Just kidding. You can be mean if you want to. He can take the pain. He's used to it.

CPSIA information can be obtained at www.ICGtesting.com
226650LV00004B/39/P